Ibsen on Theatre

...On Theatre Series

*What the world's greatest dramatists
had to say about theatre, in their own words*

Chekhov on Theatre
compiled by Jutta Hercher and Peter Urban
translated by Stephen Mulrine

Ibsen on Theatre
edited by Frode Helland and Julie Holledge
translated by May-Brit Akerholt

Shakespeare on Theatre
edited by Nick de Somogyi

Ibsen
on Theatre

edited by
Frode Helland and **Julie Holledge**

with new translations of Henrik Ibsen's writings by
May-Brit Akerholt

foreword by
Richard Eyre

NICK HERN BOOKS
London
www.nickhernbooks.co.uk

A NICK HERN BOOK

Ibsen on Theatre
first published in Great Britain in 2018
by Nick Hern Books Limited, The Glasshouse,
49a Goldhawk Road, London W12 8QP

Copyright © 2018 Frode Helland and Julie Holledge
Foreword copyright © 2018 Richard Eyre

Frode Helland, Julie Holledge and May-Brit Akerholt
have asserted their right to be identified respectively
as the authors and translator of this work

Designed and typeset by Nick Hern Books, London
Printed and bound in Great Britain by
Ashford Colour Press, Gosport, Hampshire

A CIP catalogue record for this book
is available from the British Library

ISBN 978 1 84842 312 1

FSC
www.fsc.org

MIX
Paper from
responsible sources
FSC® C011748

Contents

Appendices

Foreword

I've often felt that I'd like to apologise to Ibsen. With the scant evidence of seeing a very poor production of *The Wild Duck* and a worse one of *Rosmersholm* and directing a misconceived production of *The Master Builder* in the late sixties, I used to share Chekhov's intemperate view of him: that he wasn't a playwright. He said that to Stanislavsky; to another friend he said 'Ibsen's an idiot.' He recoiled—as I did—from Ibsen's apparent neatness, his use of symbols, of dialectic, of discussion. I was drawn to Chekhov because of his mordant wit and his worldliness: his dispassionate doctor's eye. I favoured his talent for transforming experience of life and love into art. His characters seemed to exist entirely independently of their creator, whereas in my eyes Ibsen's characters were inanimate tools of their maker. Forty years later I still retain a passion for Chekhov's writing—the stories as much as the plays—but now I regard Ibsen as very much his equal.

My view of Ibsen started to change when I directed *John Gabriel Borkman* with Paul Scofield, Vanessa Redgrave and Eileen Atkins at the National Theatre in the nineties. I discovered that you scalded your hand when you touched this icy play—a sensation sustained during the whole two hours of its action. I thought it was like pouring liquid nitrogen. 'There is no point in painting winter after Ibsen has done that in *John Gabriel Borkman*,' said Munch. But more surprising to me than its fierce chilliness, and its blistering vision of the future of capitalism, was that it ached with the need for love.

A few years later I directed *Hedda Gabler* and was capsized by the daring and the wit of it, the unexpected lack of solemnity, the defiance of an audience's expectations and the reluctance to conform to reductive theory. Is there any other dramatic heroine with such a confection of characteristics as Hedda—feisty, droll and intelligent, yet fatally ignorant of the world and herself? Snobbish, mean-spirited, small-minded, conservative, cold, bored, vicious; sexually attractive but terrified of sex, ambitious to be bohemian but frightened of scandal, a desperate romantic fantasist but unable to sustain any loving relationship with anyone, including herself. And yet, in spite of all this, I was mesmerised by her; I was drawn to her; I pitied her.

Far from creating characters that appeared to exist solely in order to illustrate the playwright's ideas, Ibsen seemed to me to be doing much the same thing as Chekhov:

> I realised quite late that to write means essentially to see, but, specifically, to see in such a way that what is seen is received just as the writer saw it. But only what is really lived through can be seen and received in this way. And the secret of the new literature of our time lies precisely in this relation to experience, the lived through. I have spiritually lived through everything I have written in the last ten years (see pp. 9–10).

Ghosts was the next of Ibsen's plays that I directed. When he was working on the play he wrote this to a friend:

> To me, each new piece of work has served the purpose of a spiritual liberation and cleansing process; for you are never without responsibility for, and are always complicit with, the society to which you belong. Therefore I once wrote the following lines as a dedication at the front of a copy of one of my books:
>
> To *live* is to war with trolls
> in the vault of the heart and the brain
> To *write*—*that* is to hold
> doomsday over oneself (see p. 49).

To hold doomsday over oneself means sitting in judgement on oneself, which is to say mediating one's ideas, emotions and anxieties through one's characters, who in their turn have to absorb the subject matter into their bloodstream—in the case of *Ghosts*: patriarchy, class, sex, hypocrisy, heredity, incest and euthanasia. In that sense Helene Alving, the protagonist of *Ghosts*, is as much an autobiographical portrait as Hedda: yearning for sexual freedom but too timid to achieve it, fearing the wrong moral choice, longing for love.

At the heart of all of Ibsen's works there is a war between the conflicting parts of his personality, almost transparently visible in the next of his plays that I directed: *Little Eyolf*. The play was written by a sixty-six-year-old man whose thirty-six-year-old marriage had been a source of quiet unhappiness to him and almost certainly more so to his partner. He'd returned from twenty-seven years in self-imposed exile in Italy and Germany to discover that he was revered at home. He began to audit his life in his plays: the conflict between love and work, between selflessness and selfishness, between comradeship and isolation, between the brightness of passion and the bleakness of unrealised emotions. In *Little Eyolf* he asks how can a marriage survive without sex, without mutual respect, without children.

To direct any play you have to try to understand the author's intentions. The best way of doing that is to write it yourself, but if somebody else has done the heavy lifting, then even copying out the text in longhand will help. If the play is written in another language you have, somehow, to climb inside it, to wear its skin: you're forced at every moment to ask what the author intended. I adapted the last three plays of Ibsen that I directed, working from literal versions with the original (Dano-Norwegian) texts by my side, always curious about the length and sound of the original lines even if their sense was only accessible with a dictionary. I tried to make the English of my adaptations live in a way that felt true to what I understood to be the author's intentions, but even literal translations make choices and the choices we make are made according to taste, to the times we live in and how we view the world.

All choices are choices of intention, and in order to get nearer to Ibsen's intentions I rifled biographies and Google entries for any of his statements about any of his plays. This book, *Ibsen on Theatre*, not only does that work for you, it also contains material previously unavailable in English. For anyone interested in Ibsen's plays—actors, directors, students, audiences—it's a marvellously accessible compendium of the thoughts of a man I now unhesitatingly describe as a very great playwright.

Richard Eyre

Acknowledgements

Editing any collection of Ibsen's writings involves drawing on a wonderfully rich history of scholarship, but we are particularly indebted to the teams of scholars, editors, technical staff, and data-entry personnel behind the digital publication of *Henrik Ibsens skrifter* HIS (www.ibsen.uio.no) and IbsenStage (ibsenstage.hf.uio.no). These online resources have made it possible for us to collaborate while living in different cities and on different continents. Special thanks go to Narve Fulsås, the HIS editor of Ibsen's letters, and to Ståle Dingstad and Jens-Morten Hanssen for their advice about our selection of Ibsen's writings. We would also like to thank those people who have helped us with the fine tuning of this book: William Dunstone for his invaluable contribution in advising us on nineteenth-century English syntax; Michael Morley for translating the few letters written by Ibsen in German and French; and Torhild Aas for her excellent copy-editing skills. Finally, we would like to thank Nick Hern for inviting us to contribute to his *…On Theatre* series, and for his infinite patience in waiting for the delivery of the manuscript.

Note on Text

A […] within the text indicates there is a part of a paragraph missing. A […] on its own line indicates that there is at least a paragraph missing between two extracts from the same original document.

Introduction

…As long as a nation considers it more important to build chapels than theatres, as long as it is more ready and willing to support the Zulu Mission than the Art Museum, the arts cannot expect to thrive in good health; yes, they will not even be considered a day-to-day necessity. I do not think it helps a lot to plead for the arts with arguments based on its own nature, which is still hardly understood at home, or rather, is thoroughly misunderstood. What we must do first of all, is to attack and scrupulously eradicate the dark, medieval monkishness which blinkers perception and makes people stupid. My meaning is: for the moment, we cannot use our weapons to fight *for* the arts, but *against* hostility to the arts. Wipe that out first, and then we can start building.

Letter to Lorentz Dietrichson,19 January 1882

Three new productions of plays by Ibsen open somewhere in the world every week. As a playwright so firmly associated with the rise of modern drama in the late nineteenth century and the spread of spoken word theatre across the globe during the early twentieth century, readers might have suspected that Henrik Ibsen's importance is dwindling in this century. Yet the 20,440 records in IbsenStage, the database of international Ibsen performances, show the opposite: the frequency of global productions has steadily increased over the past thirty years. While Ibsen's plays have been associated historically with theatres of modernity, today they are adapted into multiple genres: Chinese and Western Opera forms, Japanese Noh theatre, puppet plays, musicals, dance performances, tourist spectacles, promenade performances, applied theatre, community events, and every possible screen technology. In addition to the plethora of global adaptations of his plays recorded in IbsenStage—performed in 8,592 venues by 80,178 artists in 244 countries, and translated into sixty-seven languages—Ibsen's dramas are included in educational curricula on five continents.[1]

When Nick Hern invited us to edit an Ibsen volume for the …On Theatre series, we were confronted with a problem. Ibsen wrote twenty-six plays, but the more successful he became as a playwright the more reluctant he was to make public statements about the practice of theatre, even regarding his own works. There are no polemical writings by Ibsen, other than the articles he wrote as a young man advocating a Norwegian national theatre. Ibsen's thoughts on the art form must be gleaned from prefaces to the reprints of early plays, approximately 2,400 letters, and the speeches he gave at functions held in his honour. All of these documents contain fascinating reflections by Ibsen on theatre and are available online through *Henrik Ibsens skrifter* HIS (www.ibsen.uio.no), but they are fragments within texts devoted to other subjects—and are only available in Norwegian. We have gathered these fragments together, translated them into English, and created a volume dedicated to Ibsen's views on theatre production, casting, translation, the business of theatre, and most importantly his own plays.[2]

Translations of Ibsen's letters, speeches, articles, and prefaces into English have appeared periodically throughout the twentieth century. Approximately a quarter of the Ibsen letters held in HIS are available in three edited collections published in English in 1908, 1910 and 1965.[3] The plays have also been translated in numerous editions, most of which have introductions with references to critical literature, dramatic sources, important contemporary productions, and significant quotations from Ibsen. The eight volumes of *The Oxford Ibsen* edited by James MacFarlane (1960–77) still provide the most extensive of these commentaries, but recent editions featuring new translations and scholarly introductions are currently being published in the *New Penguin Ibsen* series edited by Tore Rem

(2014, 2016). There are major biographies written or translated into English by Robert Ferguson (1996), Michael Meyer (1967–71), Hans Heiberg (1967), Halvdan Koht (1928–29), Edmund Gosse (1907) and Henrik Jæger (1888). These biographies contain important anecdotal information on Ibsen's views on theatre as well as extracts from his letters, reported speech, and early critical writings. Just as Ibsen's comments on theatre exist as fragments in his own writing on other subjects, they also exist as fragments within these biographical studies. The originality of *Ibsen on Theatre* lies in its arrangement of these writings into a narrative that delivers background research to readers embarking on a production, an adaptation, or a scholarly project.

After a short introduction to Ibsen, written by Ibsen and his contemporaries, the following four chapters are devoted to Ibsen's writings on his plays. They contain his views on the creative process, reflections on characters, suggestions for staging and production advice. The extracts are organised by play title following the chronology of composition, in accord with the letter Ibsen addressed to the readers of his collected works published in 1898:

March 1898 to the Readers

When my publisher kindly suggested publishing a chronological edition of my collected literary works, I immediately realised the great advantages this would offer for a better understanding of the texts.

A younger generation of readers has grown up during the course of my writing career, and I have often noticed with regret that their knowledge of my more recent works is considerably more comprehensive than that of my earlier ones. Consequently, these readers fail to be aware of the internal connections between the works, and I conclude that this oversight plays a not insignificant part in the strange, inadequate and misleading interpretations my later works have been subjected to from so many quarters.

Only by comprehending and grasping my entire production as a continuous and coherent whole will one be able to form an appropriate intended impression of its individual parts.

My friendly appeal to the reader is therefore, in so many words, that he will not put any play aside for the moment or skip anything, but that he absorbs the works—by perusing them and experiencing them intimately—in the order in which I wrote them.

The two chapters that follow Ibsen's writings on his plays address his involvement in the business world of nineteenth-century European theatre. The first of these chapters concerns the strategies he used to supervise the translation of his plays into multiple languages, and to circumvent the lack of international copyright available to nineteenth-century writers working in little-known languages. To maximise his earnings, Ibsen insisted that his plays should be published before they were performed, which explains why he refers to his 'books' rather than his 'plays' in so much of his correspondence. A detailed analysis of Ibsen's accounts from 1870 to 1900 has shown that 44 per cent of his income from writing came from performances and 56 per cent came from publication.[4] By contrast, successful playwrights today earn several times more from performances than publication. The business theme is further developed in the last chapter, which focuses on Ibsen's negotiations with theatre managements, particularly at the Christiania Theater in Norway. It reveals a fascinating narrative of a shifting power relationship between a playwright and his national theatre.[5]

Appendix 1 is dedicated to Ibsen's early critical writings. These extracts come from the articles and reviews written by Ibsen in the early years of his theatre life while studying and working in Kristiania and Bergen. It focuses on his contribution to the debates on the creation of an authentic Norwegian theatre and uncovers a polemical aspect to his thinking as well as an intellectual generosity. As most of this material has not appeared previously in English translation, it provides a new perspective on Ibsen's involvement in the history of a Norwegian national theatre, as well as revealing his views on the integration of traditional source material within an emergent national dramaturgy.

Appendix 2 contains biographical notes on the recipients of Ibsen's letters and other authors quoted in this book; brief introductions are also included when these individuals are mentioned for the first time in the text. Finally, a Select Bibliography is attached, together with links to digital resources. The links to records in the IbsenStage database on the performances mentioned in the book can be found in the endnotes to each chapter.

1. These figures represent the total IbsenStage records as of 1 March 2017.
2. Sources for extracts originally published in English can be found in the bibliography. Michael Morley provided new translations for the letters in this collection that were written by Ibsen in German and French.
3. *Speeches and new letters* [*of*] *Henrik Ibsen* (1910), translated by Arne Kildal; *Letters of Henrik Ibsen* (1905), translated by John Nilsen Laurvik and Mary Morison; *Ibsen. Letters and Speeches* (1965), edited by Evert Sprinchorn.
4. See Narve Fulsås and Tore Rem (2017, 201–5) for this analysis of Ibsen's separate income from publication and performance.
5. The capital of Norway assumed the name of Oslo in 1924. For three hundred years, it was known as Christiania, though the official spelling reform changed the 'Ch' to 'K' in 1877. Many of the older institutions, including the theatre, continued to use the original city spelling in their titles.

1

Ibsen on Ibsen

Ibsen has proved a popular subject for biographers; he even appears in A.S.Byatt's novel, *The Biographer's Tale* (2000). But he wrote very few autobiographical fragments. We begin with Ibsen's own brief account of his childhood, written in 1881 and later revised in 1887 for inclusion in the Henrik Jæger biography published in 1888. It deals with Ibsen's early life prior to his father's bankruptcy, which resulted in the family moving from Skien, an important southern coastal town, to a farmhouse in the surrounding countryside. The bankruptcy transformed the young Henrik's life, and at the age of fifteen he was apprenticed to an apothecary in Grimstad, a small town south of Skien. The preface to the second edition of his first play *Catiline* provides a glimpse of Ibsen's life in Grimstad and his first efforts as a poet and playwright. He depicts himself as a young man living on the periphery of major European upheavals caused by the wave of revolutions in 1848. Norway and Sweden were largely unaffected, but Denmark was embroiled in war with the German states over the sovereignty of Schleswig. With some irony, Ibsen describes the militancy of his youth as expressed in poems demanding that the Swedish King support Denmark, and in praise of the Magyars, who were struggling for Hungarian independence from the Habsburg Empire.

These autobiographical extracts, written for publication when Ibsen was in his fifties, contain the reflections of a successful writer hinting at themes and metaphors that occur in his later writings. There are no equivalent reflections from Ibsen about his adult life and the only glimpses we have of his practice as an established writer come from his contemporaries. Their descriptions echo the image of the respectable bourgeois immortalised in his photographic portraits. They also reflect his daily routine in Gossensass, as described to his wife Suzannah (who was on holiday in Norway) in a letter dated 4 July 1884:

> So far I have risen at six thirty, had my breakfast sent up half an hour later, and after that gone out while the room is being serviced, then been writing from nine to one. Then eaten dinner with a ravenous appetite. I have also been able to write something, or do some underlining in the print manuscript of *The Wild Duck*, in the afternoon. The second act will be finished in five to six days. I do not drink beer; and thus I feel very well. Instead, I drink milk and some white wine, but not much, with water added; supper at seven thirty. So far, I have been in my bed before ten o'clock and slept well.

Yet the image of the abstemious artist is only part of the Ibsen story: it belies the numerous anecdotes about his erratic and sometimes drunken behaviour while living in Italy between 1864 and 1868. As these anecdotes have no reference to Ibsen's views on theatre, they are not included in this collection, but can be found in the biographies by Michael Meyer and Robert Ferguson.

From Ibsen's 'Childhood Memories'

When the streets of my native town of Skien were named—or perhaps only re-named—some years ago, I enjoyed the honour of having a street named after me. At least, so I learnt from the newspapers, and I have heard it since then from reliable travellers. By their description, this street leads from the town square down to the harbour.

But if this information is correct, I do not understand why the street has come to bear my name, for I was neither born there, nor did I ever live there.

On the contrary, I was born in a house on the town square; Stockmann's Building, as it was then called. It stood exactly opposite the front of the church, with its high flight of steps and conspicuous tower. To the right of the church stood the town pillory, and to the left the town hall, with the prison and the lock-up for the insane. The fourth side of the town square was occupied by the Latin school and the common school. The church stood apart in the middle.

This vista, then, was the first image of the world that presented itself to my eyes. All architecture—nothing green, no open country landscape. But the air in this quadrangle of stone and wood was filled all day with the distant roar of two cascading waterfalls, the Langefos and the Klosterfos, and of the many other waters; and from dawn to dusk, above the constant rumble of all these cataracts, came something that sounded like sharp, sometimes piercing, sometimes moaning, women's screams. This was the sound of hundreds of saw blades at work out by the falls. Later on, when I read about the guillotine, I could not help thinking of these blades. The church was naturally the grandest building in town. When Skien was burnt down one Christmas Eve towards the end of the last century, owing to the carelessness of a maidservant, the old church was destroyed as well. The girl was, reasonably enough, executed. But the town, which was rebuilt with straight wide streets down the hollows and up the slopes to which they clung, gained a new church in the process. The inhabitants claimed with a certain pride that it was built of yellow Dutch brick, designed by an architect from Copenhagen, and that it was exactly like the church at Kongsberg. I did not appreciate this distinction at the time, but what powerfully attracted my attention was a huge, burly white angel, which, on weekdays, floated in the air under the arched roof with a bowl in its hand, but on Sundays, when a child was to be christened, softly descended earthwards.

Even more perhaps than the white angel in the church, the black poodle residing in the upper tower engaged my fancy. At night, the watchman used to proclaim the hour from this tower. The poodle had fiery red eyes, but he was rarely visible. Indeed, as far as I know, he only ever appeared once. It was one New Year's morning, at the very moment when the watchman shouted 'One' through the tower window. The black poodle came up the turret-stair behind him, stood still, and looked at him with his fiery eyes, nothing more; but the watchman leapt head first out of the tower window down into the town square, where the devout, who had gone to usher in the New Year's morning by listening to a sermon, saw him lying dead. From that night, the watchman never calls 'One' from the tower window in Skien's church.

This incident of the watchman and the poodle happened long before my time, and I have since heard of similar events supposed to have taken place in several other Norwegian churches in the old days. But that particular tower window was significant to me while I was still a child, because it was from there I received the first conscious and permanent impression on my mind. My nurse carried me up the tower one day and allowed me to sit in the open window, holding me firmly from behind, of course, with her faithful arms. I recollect perfectly how amazed I was to look down on the tops of the hats of the people below. I looked into our own rooms, seeing the window-frames and curtains, and my mother standing at one of the windows; indeed, I could see over the roof into the yard, where our brown horse stood hitched up to the stable-door, whisking his tail. A bright tin pail was hanging against the door. Then suddenly there was a great hustle and bustle and signalling from our house, and the nurse hastily snatched me in and hurried down with me. I remember nothing more; but I was often told afterwards that my mother had caught sight of me up in the tower window, and with a loud shriek had fainted away, as people used to do in those days; and that when I was presently returned to her, she cried, and kissed and fondled me. As a boy, I never went across the market-square without looking up at the tower window. I always felt as though that window and the church-poodle were some special concern of mine.

[…]

We did not live for long in the house on the town square. My father bought a larger house, into which we moved when I was about four years old. This new home was a corner house, a little higher up the town, at the foot of the Hundervad Hill, so named after an old doctor who spoke German; his dignified wife used to drive in a 'glass coach', which in winter was transformed into a sleigh. There were many large rooms in our house, lower and upper rooms, and here my parents led a busy social life. But we boys did not spend a lot of time indoors. The market-square, where the two biggest schools were, was the natural meeting-place and battlefield for all the lads of the town. The Latin school was then under the direction of Rector Örn, a very distinguished and amiable old man; the headmaster of the common school was probably Iver Flasrud, the beadle, a fine old man too, who was at the same time in great demand as barber. The boys from these two schools fought many a fierce battle under the walls of the church; but I, belonging to neither, was generally a looker-on. Besides, I was not eager to fight in my childhood.

[...]

Skien, in my young days, was an exceedingly lively and sociable town, quite unlike what it subsequently became. Several highly cultivated and wealthy families of consequence lived in the town itself, or on their estates in the neighbourhood. Most of these families were more or less closely related, and dances, dinners, and music-parties followed each other in almost unbroken succession in both winter and summer. Many travellers also passed through the town, and as there were as yet no real hotels, they lodged with friends or relatives. We almost always had guests in our large roomy house, especially at Christmas and Fair time, when the house was full and we kept an open table from morning till night. The Fair at Skien was held in February, and it was a very happy time for us boys; we began to save up our money six months beforehand, to be able to see the jugglers, and rope-dancers, and horse-riders, and to buy ginger-bread down in the booths. Whether this Fair was an important one from a commercial point of view I do not know; it survives in my memory only as a great, popular holiday that lasted for about a week.

The 17th of May was not kept with any special festivities at Skien at that time.[1] [...] But St. John's Eve [Midsummer's Eve] made up for it. There were no public observances, but the boys and young men assembled in five or six or more parties, each with the task of collecting fuel for its own bonfire. So as early as Whitsuntide we would begin to haunt the shipyards and stores to beg tar-barrels. This peculiar custom had existed from time immemorial. Anything we could not get by fair means we stole, without either the owner or the police ever thinking of proceeding against the crime. Thus, by degrees, each group collected a whole heap of empty tar-barrels. We enjoyed the same customary right over old stranded boat-hulks. If we were lucky enough to succeed in dragging one away and hiding our booty, we won the right of possession, or at any rate no one disputed it. Then on St. John's Eve the hulk was carried in triumph through the streets to the place where our bonfire was stacked. A fiddler was perched in it. I have often seen such a procession, and once took part in one. (HIS, vol. 16, 496–501.)

21 September 1882 to Georg Brandes
(Danish critic and author.)

My father was a merchant with varied and extensive business activities, who affected a reckless hospitality in his home. He faced bankruptcy in 1836, and all that was left to us was a property close to the town. We moved there, and that was how we lost touch with the circles we used to belong to.

Preface to the Second Edition (1875) of Catiline

The drama *Catiline*, with which I entered upon my literary career, was written during the winter of 1848–49, that is, in my twenty-first year.

At the time, I was in Grimstad under the necessity of earning with my own hands the wherewithal for daily life and the means for instruction, preparatory to my taking the entrance examinations to university. The age was one of great anxiety and perturbation. The February revolution, the uprisings in

Hungary and elsewhere, the Schleswig war—all this had a great effect upon and hastened my development, however immature it may have remained for quite some time afterwards. I wrote resounding poems of encouragement to the Magyars, urging them to hold out for the sake of liberty and humanity in their righteous struggle against the 'tyrants'; I wrote a long series of sonnets to King Oscar, including in particular, as far as I can remember, an appeal to set aside all petty considerations and to march forthwith at the head of his army to the aid of our brothers on the outermost borders of Schleswig. In as much as I now doubt, contrary to those times, that my winged appeals would have helped the cause of the Magyars or the Scandinavians to any significant degree, I consider it fortunate that they remained within the more private sphere of the manuscript. However, on more agitated occasions I could not keep from expressing myself in the impassioned spirit of my poetic effusions, which meanwhile brought me nothing but a questionable reward—from friends or non-friends; the former greeted me as peculiarly gifted for the unintentionally droll, and the latter thought it in the highest degree strange that a young person in my subordinate position could undertake to enquire into affairs concerning matters about which not even they themselves dared to entertain an opinion. I must be truthful and add that my conduct at various times did not justify any great hope that society might have had of an increase in my sense of civic virtue, in as much as, with epigrams and caricatures, I also fell out with many who deserved better from me, and whose friendship in reality I prized. Altogether, while a great struggle raged in the outside world, I found myself on a war footing with the small society in which I lived, cramped by the conditions and circumstances of life.

[…]

My drama [*Catiline*] was written during the hours of the night. I practically had to steal the spare time for my study from my employer, a good and respectable man, occupied heart and soul, however, with his business; and from those stolen hours of study I had to steal further moments to write my verses. Thus I had only the night to resort to. I believe this is the unconscious reason that almost the entire action of the piece takes place at night. Naturally, something as incompatible with my surroundings as the fact that I was busying myself with the writing of plays had to be kept secret; but a twenty-year-old poet can hardly continue like this without anybody being privy to it, and therefore I confided in two friends of my own age about what I was secretly engaged in.

The three of us pinned great expectations on *Catiline* once it had been completed. First and foremost it was now to be copied for submission under an assumed name to the theatre in Christiania, and furthermore it was to be published, of course. One of my faithful and trusting friends undertook to prepare a handsome and legible copy of my uncorrected draft, a task which he performed with such a degree of conscientiousness that he did not omit even a single one of the innumerable dashes which, in the heat of composition, I had liberally interspersed throughout, wherever the exact phrase did not occur to me at the moment. The second of my friends, Ole C. Schulerud, who was at that time a student and later a lawyer, and whose name I here mention since he is no longer among the living, went to Christiania with the transcript. I still remember one of his letters in which he informed me that *Catiline* had now been submitted to the theatre; that it would soon be given a performance—about that there could naturally be no doubt, as the management consisted of very discriminating men; and that there could be as little doubt that the booksellers of the town would, one and all, gladly pay a handsome fee for the first edition, the main point being, he thought, to discover the shop that would offer the highest bid.

After a long and tense period of waiting, a few difficulties began to appear. The management returned the piece to my friend with a polite but equally decisive rejection. He now touted the manuscript from one bookseller to another; to a man, they expressed themselves in terms similar to those of the theatrical management. The highest bidder demanded such and such to publish the piece without any fee to me.

All this, however, was far from lessening my friend's belief in victory. He wrote to the contrary, that it was probably for the best; I should become the publisher of my drama myself; he would advance me the necessary funds; we should divide the profits, keeping in mind that he would undertake the business end of the deal, except for the proof-reading, which he regarded as superfluous in view of the handsome and legible manuscript the printers had to follow. In a later letter he declared that, considering these promising prospects, he contemplated abandoning his own studies in order to devote himself completely to the publishing of my works; he thought I should easily be able to write two or three plays a year, and according to a calculation of probabilities he had made, our surplus would enable us in a not too distant future to undertake the journey through Europe and the Orient we had so often discussed and agreed upon.

For the time being, my travels were limited to Christiania. I appeared there in the beginning of the spring of 1850, and *Catiline* had appeared in the bookstalls just previous to my arrival. The drama created a stir and considerable interest among the students, but the critics dwelt largely on the faulty verses and thought the book immature in other respects. A more appreciative judgement was voiced from one particular quarter; it came from a man whose appreciation has always meant a great deal to me, and whom I herewith offer my renewed gratitude.[2] Not many copies of the limited edition were sold; my friend had a good share of them in his care, and I remember one evening, when our housekeeping expenses seemed insurmountable, that this pile of printed matter was fortunately disposed of as waste paper to a huckster. During the days immediately following we lacked none of the necessities of life. (HIS, vol. 1, 129–32.)

10 September 1874 Speech at the Norwegian Students' March

I realised quite late that to write means essentially to *see*, but, specifically, to see in such a way that what is seen is received just as the writer saw it. But only what is really *lived through* can be seen and received in this way. And the secret of the new literature of our time lies precisely in this relation to experience, the lived through. I have spiritually lived through everything I have written in the last ten years. But no writer experiences something in isolation. What he experiences, his contemporaries experience with him. For if that were not the case, what would build the bridge of understanding between the creator and the recipients?

And what is it, then, that I have lived through and based my writing on? The range has been broad. In part, I have based my writing only on what has stirred vividly, in glimpses and in my best hours, as something great and beautiful inside me. I have created from what I would say has stood higher and loftier than my everyday self; and I have created out of it, so as to fasten it, give it permanence, both within and for my own self.

But I have also based my writing on the opposite, on what appears on inward reflection to be the dregs and sediments of one's own nature. In this case, then, to write or create has been to me like a bath from which I arise cleaner, healthier and freer. Yes, gentlemen, no one can write creatively about what has not, to some degree and at least at certain times, served as a model of himself. And where is the man among us who has not on occasion felt and acknowledged within himself a contradiction between word and action, between will and task, between life and learning? Or where is he among us who has not, at least at certain times, been egoistically sufficient unto himself and has, half in suspicion, half in good faith, glossed over this condition both to others and to himself? (HIS, vol. 16, 476 ff.)

Ibsen at his Writing Desk

Recollection from Henrik Jæger
(Norwegian literary historian, man of letters, and first biographer of Ibsen.)

He thinks carefully through the material for a long time in his head before putting pen to paper. Much of this thinking is done out in the fresh air, on his walks, and during the long time he takes to dress in the morning.

[…] He always makes sure that when he ends the day he has several lines ready in his head with which to start the next day; he feels that this helps him to get going. But should it still happen that he gets stuck, he stays put until he has got the thing moving again.

He considers the first manuscript as only a preliminary draft; when it is completed he feels that he is getting close to his characters and is confident that he knows both their temperaments and how they express themselves.

Then comes the working through of a second draft, and finally the third, which is the fair copy. […]

When he starts a work, he feels that it weighs heavily upon him; when it is finished, he feels as if he has been relieved from a burden; but when he is close to completion, new plans always start to pop up. […]

He must constantly walk while he is writing; when working on his books, he needs to move between three or four rooms.

Henrik Ibsen's daily life follows an extraordinarily regular pattern. He rises at seven in the summer, a little later in the winter; he dresses slowly and carefully, spends an hour on his toilette then eats a light breakfast. At nine he sits at his desk, where he stays until one. Then he takes a walk before dinner, which in Munich he eats at three. […] In the afternoon, he reads; he takes his evening meal early, around seven. At nine he drinks a glass of toddy and goes to bed early. He eats with a hearty appetite and sleeps well. During the winter, he is busy thinking through his plans, during summer he executes them; the summer is his best working time; almost all his works have been written in summer; of those he has published since he left Norway in 1864, only two, *The League of Youth* and *Emperor and Galilean*, have been written during winter. When he begins to write a play, he cannot eat or drink more than the barest minimum; it inhibits him in his work; a small piece of bread and half a cup of black coffee are all he takes before sitting down to his desk. He smokes a little while working, otherwise not at all. He cannot understand how people can benefit from stimulants while working; the only thing he can imagine that might have the intended effect upon him is a couple of drops of naphtha on a lump of sugar. In this respect, he is like the caterpillar that ceases to take nourishment when it has to spin its cocoon.

In general, he is regular to the point of pedantry; his day is divided according to the clock. These three days I've been living in his immediate proximity, dwelt next door to him and eaten at his side, we have lived by the clock from morning to night to a degree I could never tolerate in the long term. [...]

He needs good air in quantity; lofty, airy rooms with high ceilings are an absolute necessity to him; he told me this yesterday when we were discussing where he might lease an apartment in Munich for the winter. He praises the air up here in northern Jutland because it is so clean and fresh owing to the unceasing wind. It must be for this reason that he has so often spent his summers in the Gulf of Naples or at Gossensass in the Tyrol. To my question why he wants to settle in such a cold and harsh a climate as Munich, he replied that the Munich climate suited his temperament excellently [...]. Although it is already September here, and it has been so very windy these past few days that we've had to put double fasteners on the open windows, he has kept two windows open all the time, one in each bay, though his desk is placed right next to one of them.

Each morning and evening he takes a cold rub-down. (Qtd. in Midbøe 1960, 156–8.)

Recollection from William Archer
(Scottish theatre critic, writer, and the major translator of Ibsen into English.)

It seems that the *idea* of a piece generally presents itself before the characters and incidents, though, when I put this to him flatly, he denied it. It seems to follow, however, from his saying that there is a certain stage in the incubation of a play when it might as easily turn into an essay as into a drama. He has to incarnate the ideas, as it were, in character and incident, before the actual work of creation can be said to have fairly begun. Different plans and ideas, he admits, often flow together, and the play he ultimately produces is sometimes very unlike the intention with which he set out. He writes and rewrites, scribbles and destroys, an enormous amount, before he makes the exquisite fair copy he sends to Copenhagen.

As for symbolism, he says that life is full of it, and that, consequently, his plays are full of it, though critics insist on discovering all sorts of esoteric meanings in his works of which he is entirely innocent. (HU, vol. 19, 171.)

Recollection from P.A. Rosenberg
(Danish writer and theatre director.)

He once remarked that if possible, he liked to plan his day's work in the morning when he awoke, because then he felt his imagination to be at its liveliest; whereas his critical sense was at its least sharp then, in the half-dreaming hour of dawn. This did not fully awaken until he was seated at his desk, when it often rejected all the ideas he had hit upon when lying in bed. He also kept small gutta-percha devils with red tongues on his desk. 'There must be trolls in what I write,' he said, and in a tone midway between jest and earnest, he spoke of his 'super-devil'. 'He only comes out last, when things are really difficult. Then I lock my door and bring him out. No other human eye has seen him, not even my wife.' (HU, vol. 19, 217–18.)

Recollection from Gerhard Gran
(Norwegian literary historian, editor, and essayist.)

As a rule, I make three drafts of my plays, which differ greatly from each other—in characterisation, not in plot. When I approach the first working-out of my material, it is as if I knew my characters from a railway journey; we have made a preliminary acquaintance, we have chattered about this and that. At the next draft I already see everything much more clearly, and I know the people roughly as one would after a month spent with them at a spa; I have discovered the fundamentals of their characters and their little peculiarities; but I may still be wrong about certain essentials. Finally, in the last draft, I've reached the limit of my knowledge; I know my characters from long and close acquaintance—they are my intimate friends, who will no longer disappoint me; as I see them now, I shall always see them. (1918, 166.)

Recollection from Rosa Fitinghoff
(Swedish author and daughter of prize-winning novelist Laura Fitinghoff.)

He told us that he had small pieces of paper with the names of the characters he was writing about on a string in front of his desk. When one of them 'died' during the writing process, he pulled down the character's piece of paper and tore it up. 'You do not want too many pieces of paper in front of you,' he explained.

There was a mixture of the happy larrikin and the gloomy brooder in Ibsen's laughter, and in his eyes, when we were together in his home.

'Sometimes all these imaginary people exhaust me,' he said. 'They fight with each other, grieve and love and hate, and then I become really tired, then I pull out my desk drawer and look down into this little box.' He showed her a small box with a few letters from her, as she was looking into the drawer. 'And then I sit and talk with you, and then, after a while, I can continue with the other people I am writing about, and I can thank you for this.'

Ibsen was very keen to start a great new play he wanted to write. He had the outline all ready. 'If only my strength lasts… But it must! This work shall be the best and the biggest of all the ones I have written,' Ibsen said, and his voice quivered from inspiration and ardour to start working.

However, the human cloak was not strong enough for the fiery soul that Ibsen possessed at that time. The 'great work' he dreamt of finishing was never completed. (1928, 5.)

1. The 17 May celebrations in Norway commemorate the signing of the constitution on that date in 1814.
2. *Catiline* was received with silence by most of the Norwegian public except for a small and positive review in a student journal written by Paul Botten Hansen, a student three years older than Ibsen.

2
Early Plays:
from *Catiline* to *The Pretenders*

When Ibsen wrote his early plays, the Norwegian theatre was dominated by artists from Denmark and Sweden. It was not until the 1860s that Norwegian actors began to appear on the stage of the prestigious Christiania Theater.[1] Ibsen published *Catiline*, his first play, under the pseudonym Brynjolf Bjarme in 1850. He wrote his next two plays while studying in Kristiania: his one-act drama *The Burial Mound* was accepted for performance within days of being submitted to the Christiania Theater in 1850; the satirical *Norma* was published anonymously in 1851 but had to wait another 143 years for its premiere in Trondheim.

Ibsen's theatrical apprenticeship began in earnest when he moved to Bergen to join the first genuinely Norwegian theatre company, Det norske Theater; this professional company had taken over Komediehuset (the old Bergen Theatre) from an amateur dramatic society in 1850. The following year Ibsen, aged twenty-three, became its resident dramatist. He was responsible for providing a new play for each of the five seasons that he worked with the company. A new production of *The Burial Mound* was staged soon after he arrived, and four new plays premiered in subsequent seasons: *St. John's Night*, which he later disowned, was staged in January 1853; *Lady Inger* was performed in 1855 and published in a journal in 1857; *The Feast at Solhaug*, which followed in 1856, proved to be the most popular with Bergen audiences; and finally, *Olaf Liljekrans* was staged in 1857. During the five years of his residency, the theatre presented 122 plays, most of which were comedies, farces and dramas that echoed the repertoire choices of theatres in Copenhagen and Dresden. Ibsen had visited both cities at the expense of his Bergen employer.

A picture of the workings of Det norske Theater can be gleaned from its standard employment contract for actors, which stipulated the amounts to be deducted from wages for the following transgressions: bringing dogs into the theatre; missing rehearsals; failure to memorise lines; missing cues; being drunk or smoking during rehearsal or performances; quarrels and physical fights; offending female modesty during conversations with actresses; and spreading disparaging rumours about the theatre. Ibsen's day-to-day responsibilities at the theatre extended far beyond his role as playwright; he was a stage instructor with control over the design and production management of sets, costumes, lighting, and sound. His stage plans show his attempts to replace the open, painted wings of perspective scenery with closed wings representing intimate interiors with real furniture. Details for the staging of fifty-three plays are recorded in his production books, and these plans, together with the costume designs for *Olaf Liljekrans,* are held in the theatre archive at the University of Bergen.[2]

A second, more experienced director with the company was responsible for coaching the actors on the delivery and inter-pretation of the dialogue, but Ibsen's jurisdiction over the stage included the movements and gestures of the characters and the arrangement of tableaux. A rare insight into Ibsen's innovations in stage movement can be gleaned from a review of the com-pany while it was touring to Trondheim in 1856: 'It deserves to be remarked that the actors have abandoned the stiff and unnatural old-fashioned custom of running right down to the footlights or turning to the audience whenever they have any-thing to say' (qtd. in Meyer 1967, 78). His dislike of 'actors being marched to the foreground' of the stage stems from these early years in Bergen (to Harald Holst, 21 November 1878).

In 1857, Ibsen accepted the position of artistic director of the Kristiania Norske Theater (the Kristiania Norwegian Theatre) and found himself at the centre of debates about the importance of theatre in Norway's emerging national culture. Foreign artistic control of the Christiania Theater was on the wane: the company was beginning to employ Norwegian actors and build a repertoire of Norwegian plays. Despite his commitment to the Kristiania Norske Theater, Ibsen submitted his next play, *The Vikings at Helgeland*, to the Board of the Christiania Theater. It was accepted for production, but when the management failed to schedule the play, Ibsen withdrew the script and premiered it at his own theatre. By 1862, the Kristiania Norske Theater was struggling; its most experienced actors were joining the Christiania Theater, and audience numbers were declining. At the end of the year, the theatre was declared bankrupt, and it closed. Like his best actors, Ibsen became a temporary employee of the Christiania Theater, where he worked primarily as a literary advisor. His next play, *The Pretenders*, premiered at that theatre in 1864 and proved to be the most successful of his early works, but *Love's Comedy*, which he completed in 1862, created such a furore on publication that is was another ten years before it was performed.

After having worked for a decade as a director and having written ten plays, seven of which had been performed, Ibsen found himself seriously in debt. His later ambivalence about working as a director or manager of a theatre company is not surprising, considering how close he came to financial ruin. On 28 December 1867, he wrote in a letter to his fellow Norwegian playwright Bjørnstjerne Bjørnson, who was contemplating returning to a directing career:

> [...] Are you really going back to work in the theatre again? There is undoubtedly a need for you there, but there is a much greater need for you to continue your writing. If your taking up theatrical work merely meant wasting time, merely meant that all the poetic visions, moods and images were put aside for the time being to reappear again later, it would not matter so much. But such is not the case. Other ideas may come, but the ones in between die unborn. For a writer, working in the theatre is equivalent to repeated, daily abortions. This is a crime, according to civil laws; I do not know if God is more lenient. Think it over, dear Bjørnson! The gift of writing is not a privilege, it is a responsibility.

Although the eleven years Ibsen had spent in theatres at Bergen and Kristiania provided very little financial remuneration, they were a rigorous training in the craft of playwriting. He had worked from source material as varied as Roman history, the sagas, folk ballads, and early Norwegian history. He had experimented with a range of theatrical genres and employed comedy, tragedy, and satire to create epic, historical, contemporary and music dramas. He had actively participated in the staging of six of his plays and had contributed to the staging of over a hundred others. While Ibsen's first ten plays account for only 584 of the 20,440 production events recorded in IbsenStage, this extraordinarily rich theatrical apprenticeship deeply influenced his theatre practice, particularly regarding his dramaturgical use of gesture and stage movement, settings, costume and lighting design.

This chapter opens with a brief chronology written by Ibsen about his early dramas, which is followed by statements on individual works arranged by title. The longest extracts come from prefaces to second editions of plays published after Ibsen had been recognised as a significant Norwegian writer. These prefaces provide insights into the circumstances surrounding the composition and sources of inspiration of *Catiline*, *Norma*, *The Feast at Solhaug* and *Love's Comedy*. A few references to *The Vikings at Helgeland* can be found in the preface to *The Feast at Solhaug*, but there is a paucity of information from Ibsen on *The Burial Mound* and *Lady Inger*.[3]

28 October 1870 to Peter Hansen
(Danish journalist, translator, literary and theatre historian. Ibsen provided the following biographical notes for an anthology of Scandinavian writers edited by Hansen.)

Everything of an artistic nature that I have brought forth has its source in a mood and a situation in real life; I have never written something because, as we say, I have 'found a good subject'. I shall now confess chronologically.

Catiline was written in a small provincial petit bourgeois town, where it was beyond my power to express all those things fermenting inside me except through crazy tricks and riotous pranks, which incurred the displeasure of all those respectable burghers who were unable to enter the world I was struggling with on my own.

Lady Inger is the result of a hastily embarked-upon and violently broken-off love affair, to which a few lesser poems are also related, such as 'Field Flowers and Potted Plants', 'A Bird Song', etc., printed in *Nyhedsbladet* (and to which I call your attention in passing).[4]

The Vikings at Helgeland I wrote as an engaged man. I have used the same model for Hjørdis as I did later for Svanhild in *Love's Comedy*.

Only when I got married did my life take on a more profound dimension. The first fruit thereof was a longer poem, 'On the Highlands'. The urge for liberation which permeates this poem, however, did not get its full expression until *Love's Comedy*. This book caused much gossip in Norway; my personal affairs came under discussion, and my own reputation suffered in people's eyes. The only one who approved of the book at the time was my wife. She is exactly of the kind of character I need—illogical, but with a strong poetic instinct, a magnanimous mindset, and an almost violent hatred of all things petty. My countrymen failed to understand all this, and I did not care to make my confession to such people. So I was excommunicated; everyone was against me.

This awareness that everyone was against me, that there were no longer any outsiders I could say believed in me, necessarily produced a feeling that found its release in *The Pretenders*, as I know you will understand. Enough about this.

Just as *The Pretenders* was published, Frederik VII died and the war began. I wrote a poem, 'A Brother in Need'. Of course, it had no effect in the face of the Norwegian Americanism which had repelled me at every point.[5] So I went into exile!

Catiline (1850)

Premiered 3 December 1881, Nya Teatern, Stockholm.[6]

Preface to the Second Edition (1875) of Catiline.

While preparing for my [university entrance] examinations, I read Sallust's *Catiline*, together with Cicero's Catilinarian orations. I devoured these documents, and a few months later my drama was finished. As my book shows, at that time I did not share the interpretation of the two ancient Roman writers concerning the character and conduct of Catiline, and I am still inclined to believe that after all, there must have been a measure of greatness or eminence in a man whom Cicero, the indefatigable counsel for the majority, did not find it expedient to tackle until affairs had taken such a turn that there was no longer any danger involved in the attack. One should also remember that there are few individuals in history whose renown has been more completely in the hands of their enemies than that of Catiline.

[…]

During my visit home last summer, and particularly since my return here, shifting images of my literary life have appeared before me more clearly and more sharply than ever before. Among other things, I brought out *Catiline* again. I had almost forgotten the details of the book's content; however, on re-reading it I found that it nevertheless contained a great deal which I could still acknowledge, especially remembering that it is my first literary enterprise. A great many things which my later writings have concentrated on—the contradiction between ability and aspiration, between will and possibility, the simultaneity of tragedy and comedy in humankind and in the individual—already appear here in vague innuendoes, and so I conceived the plan to prepare a new edition as a kind of jubilee version; a plan my publisher approved with his usual readiness.

[…]

I therefore decided to revise this, my youthful drama, in a way I believe I could have written it even then, if I had had more time at my disposal, and under more favourable circumstances. On the other hand, I have not touched the ideas, the concepts and the development of the whole drama. The book has remained the original version; but now it appears in a completed form. (HIS, vol. 1, 130–3.)

The Burial Mound (1850)

Premiered 26 September 1850, Christiania Theater (Oslo).[7]

7 September 1897 to Julius Elias
(German translator and historian of art and literature. Elias edited a German-language edition of Ibsen's collected works.)

Today I am sending you *The Burial Mound*, which I have finally succeeded in laying my hands on. After reading it through, I find that there is quite a lot of good material in this small piece from my youth, and I thank you sincerely for forcing me to include it in the collection.

Norma (1851)

Premiered 5 November 1994, Studentersamfundets Interne Teater (The Students' Association's Internal Theatre), Trondheim.[8]

Preface to Norma; or, A Politician's Love

I found myself at the public gallery in the Parliament the other day. The matter under discussion was of the usual nature, so I can no longer remember what it was about. When Schydtz happened to be speaking, and I therefore had nothing to pay attention to, I gave my imagination free rein, and abandoned myself to comfortably floating between the realms of reality and unreality, to which we entrust ourselves in relaxed moments when the soul feels tired or the world around us envelops us in its soporific veil. This is what I was thinking: in these 106 heads, some with wigs, some without, is the quintessence of all the excellence, of all the intellectual talents which old Norway can exhibit. [...] Here you will find genius, eloquence, patriotism, liberalism piled up in a compact mass [...] My contemplations continued in this direction for a few hours, until Schydtz had finished, and my undisturbed flight of thoughts was thus interrupted.

In the evening I went to see *Norma*, and suddenly a light dawned on me: 'The Parliament is a dramatically talented corporation!' I will not even try to explain to myself or my readers the chain of reasoning that brought me to that conclusion, for who does not know the force of tunes, who does not know that music can cut through the Gordian Knot's thread of thoughts with Alexander's sword, push us forward with the speed of lightning onto the spiral wanderings of logic, and place us at a point we had least expected? But the closer I considered the matter, the clearer and more obvious it seemed to me. Holmboe is the respectable father of the play; Motzfeldt, Lange, and Harris the old, contrary uncle who has lost the feeling for life's poetry, but who it is still good to keep in reserve, no matter how much his prosaic worldly wisdom is hostile to the young lovers' fanciful plans and castles in the air. The Opposition on the whole is the coquette, whom every young hothead enjoys courting but is usually reluctant in the end to take as wife (especially when her rival may well bring him a more sizeable dowry). Stabell is obviously the hero of the intrigue; he is one of these genuine dramatic characters Heiberg refers to, 'whom one has to arrive at by guesswork rather than information, and who finally, at the end of the play, stands where one would have least expected at the beginning'.

It was these observations that moved me to compose the opera *Norma; or, A Politician's Love*, whose printed text is enclosed, and which I herewith offer to the Parliament for performance at one or other festive occasion. The Parliament must organise the music itself, and as it is comprised of virtuosi on all possible instruments, from trumpets to drums to bassoons, this should pose no problem [...]

St. John's Night (1853)

Premiered 2 January 1853, Det norske Theater, Bergen.[9]

19 September 1897 to Julius Elias

The play is a miserable product, which does not really origi-
nate from my hand. It is built upon a loose, fraudulent draft,
which I in my time received from a student friend, reworked
and put my name to, but which I now find it impossible to
acknowledge. [...] Far from explaining any of the rest of my
authorial production, it stands totally outside it, and has no
relation to any of it; I have therefore regarded it as unwritten
and non-existent for many years past.

Lady Inger (1854)

Premiered 2 January 1855, Det norske Theater, Bergen.[10]

The Feast at Solhaug (1856)

Premiered 2 January 1856, Det norske Theater, Bergen.[11]

The Vikings at Helgeland (1858)

Premiered 24 November 1858, Kristiania Norske Theater
(Oslo).[12]

Preface to the Second Edition (1883) of The Feast at Solhaug.

I wrote *The Feast at Solhaug* in Bergen in the summer of 1855,
that is, about twenty-eight years ago. [...] I had written *Lady
Inger* the previous year. My work on this drama obliged me to
immerse myself in the literature and history of Norway during the Middle Ages, especially in the latter part of the period.
I did my utmost to live and breathe the manners and customs
of those times, the people's emotional lives, their thoughts and
ways of speaking.

However, it is not particularly attractive to linger over this
period for too long, nor does it offer material particularly suitable for dramatic treatment.

Thus I soon turned to the saga period itself. However, the
sagas of the kings and, on the whole, the more exacting

historical traditions from this distant age did not fascinate me; I was unable at the time to exploit the wars between kings and chieftains, parties and clans to any dramatic purpose. That was to come later.

On the other hand, in the Icelandic family sagas I found what I required to give human form to the moods, concepts and thoughts that filled me at the time, or of which I had at least a relatively clear idea. I had not been familiar with these Old Norse literary contributions to the personal histories of our saga period; I had hardly heard them mentioned. Then by chance N.M. Petersen's excellent translation—as far as the style of the language is concerned—fell into my hands. From these family chronicles, with their varying relationships and scenes between man and man, woman and woman, in short between human being and human being, I encountered a personal, resonant, vivid life; and from my living with all these fully rounded, single, individual women and men, the first raw, hazy outlines of *The Vikings at Helgeland* were formed.

I can no longer say how many details of the drama I worked out then. But I remember well that the two characters I first got a glimpse of were the two women who later became Hjørdis and Dagny. I knew there had to be a great feast in the play, with ardent and fateful altercations. I also wanted to include everything of character, passions and reciprocal relationships I could imagine were most typical of life in the saga period. In a word—I wanted to reproduce dramatically what had been re-written in epic style in the *Volsunga Saga*.

I made no complete, coherent plan at the time. However, I knew clearly that such a play was to be my next written enterprise.

But then a number of things intervened. Most were of a personal nature and these were probably the strongest and most conclusive; but I also believe that it was of some significance that at the time I was closely studying Landstad's collection of *Norwegian Ballads* that had been published a couple of years previously. I could more readily reconcile the moods in which I found myself with the literary romanticism of the Middle Ages than the more factual nature of the sagas, better with verse than prose, better with the verbal music of the ballad than the impersonal language characteristic of the saga.

Thus it happened that the fermenting, formless sketch of the tragedy *The Vikings at Helgeland* temporarily transformed itself into the lyrical drama *The Feast at Solhaug*.

The foster sisters Hjørdis and Dagny, the two female characters in the planned tragedy, became the sisters Margaret and Signe in the completed lyrical drama. The latter two sisters' derivation from the two saga women is easily discerned once your attention is drawn to it. The family resemblance is unmistakeable. The tragedy's as yet loosely conceived hero, the Viking chieftain Sigurd, widely travelled and well-received at royal courts, was transformed into the minstrel knight Gudmund Alfsøn, who has likewise been travelling for a long time in foreign countries and lived in the King's household. I changed his relationship with the two sisters in accordance with the altered circumstances of time and situation; however, the position of both sisters towards him remained essentially the same as in the tragedy as originally planned and later completed. The fateful feast, which it had been so important to portray in my first draft, became the stage on which the characters performed; it became the background against which the action stood out, and, on the whole, conveyed to the image the fundamental tone at which I had aimed. Yes, the play's ending eased and softened the work in harmony with its art as drama rather than tragedy; but orthodox aestheticians might still dispute whether a residual touch of tragedy remains at the end of drama, testifying to its origin.

I shall not enter further into this subject, however. I wanted only to maintain and establish that the play before you, like all my dramatic works, is an inevitable result of my life at a certain point. It has its origin within, and not from any outer influence or inspiration.

This, and no other, is the true account of the genesis of *The Feast at Solhaug*.

Olaf Liljekrans (1857)

Premiered 2 January 1857, Det norske Theater, Bergen.[13]

Recollection from John Paulsen
(Norwegian author.)

Ibsen once said to me about his work during his younger years, that if the lyric-romantic *Olaf Liljekrans*, inspired by the folk-song genre, was not good for anything else, at least it would be suitable for an opera libretto. In fact, at one stage he had attempted to rewrite it as such. He called his new opus *The Mountain Bird* and appealed to the composer Udbye in Trond-heim to compose the music; however, the whole thing fell through for unknown reasons.

I told Grieg this, and Grieg approached Ibsen, who drew his attention to his old drama. But *Olaf Liljekrans* did not tempt Grieg. He wanted something new and fresh, something that could inspire him; and apparently nourished the secret hope that Ibsen would write something exclusively for him. (1913, 16.)

18 July 1861 to M.A. Udbye
(Norwegian composer and organist.)

I take the liberty to enclose the first scenes of an opera libretto and to enquire whether you would be willing to compose the music. As your name as a composer is held in higher esteem than everyone else's in the country, I would see it as an honour and a certain guarantee of the work's success should you agree to accept this suggestion. I shall greatly look forward to receiving a few lines from you regarding this matter. The rest of the manuscript could be dispatched shortly.

Love's Comedy (1862)

Premiered 24 November 1873, Christiania Theater (Oslo).[14]

Preface to the Second Edition (1867) of Love's Comedy.

The present work was written in the summer of 1862, and the first edition appeared in the winter of that year.

But I made the mistake of publishing the book in Norway. Both time and place were unfortunate choices.

The play provoked a storm of resentment, more violent and more widespread than most books can pride themselves on in a society whose prevailing majority usually regards literary matters as being of little concern.

The reception did not surprise me, however. 'The healthy realism' that we Norwegians are entitled to attribute to ourselves, at least as far as the realism is concerned, if not its health, brings us quite naturally to see justification in the status quo, and that the present solution to every problem is correct. This approach provides a sincere feeling of well-being, though not too much clarity.

When I lashed out at love and marriage to the best of my ability in this comedy, it was only natural that the majority would bellow on behalf of love and marriage. Most of our critics and readers have only imperfectly acquired the intellectual discipline and training required to see through misapprehensions. But it is not my business to give them a course. A preface is no ABC.

30 April 1872 to Edmund Gosse
(English poet, author and critic.)

Love's Comedy should really be considered as a forerunner to *Brand*, as I there portray the prevailing contradiction in our society between reality and the claim of the ideal in everything concerning love and marriage. The book aroused a violent and bitter storm in Norway when it came out [...]

24 October 1872 to Hartvig Lassen
(Norwegian editor and literary manager at the Christiania Theater.)

The reservations I entertained at one stage about the play being performed have long since disappeared. Many indications have convinced me that the public has now opened its eyes to the truth that the core of this work rests on an unconditional moral foundation, and as far as the play's artistic structure is concerned, I am now more than ever of the opinion that this is immaculate; at least, it is not surpassed by any of my other dramatic works. Altogether, I consider *Love's Comedy* among the best of my creations.

16 December 1872 to Andreas Isachsen
(Norwegian Actor. Worked with Ibsen at Det norske Theater in Bergen and at the Kristiania Norske Theater. Joined Christiania Theater in 1865.)

I must steal a moment of my very busy time to write a few lines to you about *Love's Comedy*, whose production will surely come up soon. I ask you to take care of this play in the best possible way concerning both concept and design. But first of all, I ask you to ensure quite strictly that the play is performed in an appropriate way as far as the *interaction of the actors* is concerned.

In this respect, I ask you to inform the esteemed actors of the following:

I regard this play as one of my best, and the reception it will receive from an audience is utterly dependent on the way it is being performed.

It is necessary that each actor knows his or her role by heart at the first rehearsal.

It is necessary that each actor knows the *whole* play and not just the scenes he or she is in. If this is not complied with, the actors will not fully understand the characters they are to portray.

The dialogue in my play is full of particular vocal points, allusions, hints, etc. Each of these must be understood; but they must be depicted with *finesse* and not so emphatically that they are jerked out of their organic relationship with the rest of the dialogue.

The dialogue must be performed with energy, lightness and the highest degree of *truthfulness* in the intonation.

What was often missed in my time at the Kristiania Norske Theater was the natural variety in the fast and slow speed of dialogue, according to the content. The natural softness and strength of the voice was missed, and especially the increasing pace which happens when a human being is affected—anger, indignation, disgust, etc. In my time, many tried to achieve this effect by *shouting louder*. But this had no effect. There is no other way to express increasing feeling other than by increasing the energy with which the dialogue is delivered.

Finally, I want to add that in all good theatres in Europe, a play is only regarded as properly rehearsed when it can be played without a prompter.

I would like these points to be imprinted in the actors' hearts, with my warm greetings. I am secure in the hope that each of them, both from love of their art, and as a personal favour to me, will do their best.

I do not doubt that you, my dear friend, agree with me on the above, and that you will take care that it will be observed.

Recollection from Bolette Sontum
(Eldest daughter of Dr Christian Sontum, Ibsen's doctor.)

The only other remark I can recall him ever making about his own plays was in discussing *Love's Comedy* with my mother. 'But Svanhild should not have engaged herself to Guldstad,' she protested. 'Console yourself, dear friend,' he replied. 'The next day she will have a rendezvous with Falk!' My mother was fortunate enough to enjoy his boyish love of little jokes. He especially loved to tease her about her enthusiasm for his characters. (1913, 252.)

The Pretenders (1864)

Premiered 17 January 1864, Christiania Theater (Oslo).[15]

9 May 1870 to Peter Heise
(Danish composer.)

My question to you is this: would you consider composing the music for the play? The first act needs an overture and introductions, church music and a celebration march; the second, dances; prayers and lullabies in the third; melodramatic accompaniment to the battle scenes in the fourth; and lastly, there is the women's choir in the finale.

16 June 1870 to Peter Heise
I was extremely pleased to have it confirmed that you agree to compose the music for *The Pretenders*. I cannot deal with the Latin text for the choirs in the first act, but I shall soon send you a kind of translation from memory; similarly, I shall write words for the women's prayer at the end of the play (plus the monk's words in the third act).

  After further consideration, I quite agree with you that there should be no music for the battle scenes; on the other hand, I thank you sincerely for the suggestion to treat the ghost scene melodramatically.

14 June 1876 to Ludvig Josephson
(Swedish actor and theatre manager. Artistic director of the Christiania Theater from 1873 to 1877.)

I travelled to Berlin at the beginning of this month to attend the [German-language] premiere of *The Pretenders*, which was magnificently performed by Meiningen's Court Players. The play was received with great applause and I was repeatedly called to the curtain. I do not think the Berliner critics were particularly pleased, most of whom are playwrights themselves. Still, the play had a run of nine nights, and would have had a longer run if the Meiningen Players did not have to finish their season on the fifteenth.

21 September 1876 to Johan Herman Thoresen
(Norwegian senior civil servant and brother of Suzannah Ibsen. Thoresen managed Ibsen's finances in Kristiania.)

I have also received an official invitation to Vienna, where *The Vikings at Helgeland* is about to be produced at the Burgtheater [K.K. Hof-Burgtheater was the Austrian Court Theatre], and also to Schwerin, where *The Pretenders* is to be performed. *The Vikings at Helgeland* is also being rehearsed at the theatres in Dresden and Leipzig, and is still being performed to enthusiastic audiences in Munich. The honorarium from all the German and Austrian theatres is 10 per cent of the gross income of each performance in the author's lifetime, and the same to his heirs for the first fifteen years after his death. So you can see that it pays to write for the stage here. I also have a finished manuscript for the German first edition of *Lady Inger*, which has already been accepted for production in Meiningen and Munich, and will be printed during the coming winter.

1. The history of Ibsen's relationship with this theatre is the subject of Chapter 7; his early critical writings which contributed to the debates on the development of Norwegian theatre and its importance to national culture can be found in Appendix 1.
2. Ibsen's costume designs for *Olaf Liljekrans* can be found online at HIS: ibsen.uio.no/VAR_VKostymeOL_tegn.xhtml?tema=art&visFaks=Ja ibsen.uio.no/VAR_VKostymeOL2_tegn.xhtml?tema=art&visFaks=Ja ibsen.uio.no/VAR_VKostyme6_tegn.xhtml?tema=art&visFaks=Ja Click on the 'faksimile' icon to access designs.
3. Premiere of *Lady Inger*: ibsenstage.hf.uio.no/pages/event/77874; premiere of *The Burial Mound*: ibsenstage.hf.uio.no/pages/event/77870.
4. Ibsen includes the following author's note: '*The Feast at Solhaug* is a study which I no longer admit to; but this play, too, had a personal origin.'
5. Ibsen's reference to Americanism probably reflects the association between American culture and materialism.
6. ibsenstage.hf.uio.no/pages/event/78075
7. ibsenstage.hf.uio.no/pages/event/77870
8. ibsenstage.hf.uio.no/pages/event/80944

9. ibsenstage.hf.uio.no/pages/event/77871
10. ibsenstage.hf.uio.no/pages/event/77873
11. ibsenstage.hf.uio.no/pages/event/77875
12. ibsenstage.hf.uio.no/pages/event/77885
13. ibsenstage.hf.uio.no/pages/event/77883
14. ibsenstage.hf.uio.no/pages/event/77943
15. ibsenstage.hf.uio.no/pages/event/77898

3

Closet Dramas:
from *Brand* to *Emperor and Galilean*

Ibsen left Norway for Italy in 1864, thus beginning twenty-seven years of voluntary 'exile'. A grant from the Norwegian authorities made the journey possible, but Ibsen's finances were in a terrible state and the costs of travelling with his wife Suzannah and son Sigurd were prohibitive. A campaign to increase his writer's stipend was launched by fellow playwright Bjørnstjerne Bjørnson; as a result, Ibsen's initial grant was more than doubled. Not only could he travel en famille to Italy, he could also visit Copenhagen and Berlin. Ibsen's journey was both a liberation and an inspiration, and years later he would mythologise his first view of Italy:

> I [...] crossed the Alps on the ninth of May. The clouds hung like great, dark curtains over the high mountains, and we drove under them through the tunnel and found ourselves suddenly at *Mira Mara* [Miramare Castle], where the beauty of the South, this peculiar bright light, shining like white marble, suddenly revealed itself to me, and influenced all my later work, even if all its content was not beautiful. (HIS, vol. 16, 513.)

He felt he had 'escaped from darkness into light, from the fog through a tunnel into sunshine' (ibid.). The 'darkness' that oppressed him was both professional and financial: despite his considerable success as a dramatist, director and public intellectual, he felt the lack of public recognition made manifest in his penury. The 'light' lying before him was the possibility of reshaping his life as an artist.

Ibsen's journey coincided with the end of the Dano-Prussian war. In Berlin he witnessed the triumphant return of German soldiers parading through the streets with confiscated Danish cannons from the Dybbøl fortifications. This scene of cultural humiliation made a strong impression on Ibsen: for many years, he was prone to drunken diatribes against Sweden and Norway for abandoning Denmark during the war. Ibsen arrived in Italy during the struggle for independence led by Garibaldi, a leader whom he admired (cf. Meyer 2012; Rønning 2006, 125–36). It is possible that his disappointment at the Scandinavians' lack of unity (in contrast with the Italians' struggle for unification) increased his sense of cultural and intellectual independence.

Leaving Norway also meant leaving the day-to-day practice of making theatre, and Ibsen never joined another theatre company. His next two works, *Brand* and *Peer Gynt*, were *books* intended for a readership, rather than plays written for performance. Ibsen called them 'dramatic poems', in other words closet dramas for the reading public. *Brand* was published by Gyldendal, Scandinavia's leading publishing house, in Copenhagen in 1866. Only two of Ibsen's previous ten dramas had been professionally published in Norway, and the arrangement with Gyldendal gave him access to the whole of the Scandinavian book market. Bjørnson was the figure behind the publishing contract. He told Frederik Hegel at Gyldendal that Ibsen was working on a drama based on historical material. Hegel agreed to publish the work despite some misgivings: he found the first part a polemical work on contemporary life rather than an historical study; and he was worried that the inclusion of Norwegian words and phrases might prove difficult for Danish readers. Even so, *Brand* generated unprecedented sales for a serious work of fiction, and it was reprinted four times within a year of its publication. Within twelve months 3,173 copies had been sold, producing royalties of 1,035 riksdaler. As this represented a considerable sum, Ibsen's economic problems were over. Financial security changed his persona; from his outer appearance to his handwriting, he assumed a disciplined, almost dignified 'bourgeois' appearance.

Brand and *Peer Gynt* stand out in Ibsen's oeuvre as his two great verse dramas. He describes composing them in a state of inspiration, writing 'both morning and afternoon, which I have never been able to do before' (to Bjørnstjerne Bjørnson, 12 September 1865). Both works are long and immensely rich texts which draw on contemporary reality (unlike all of Ibsen's early dramas except *Love's Comedy*). Neither drama was suitable for performance in its published form, but Ibsen welcomed their production, and when the opportunity arose he offered theatre managements advice on cutting the texts for performance. He also arranged for Edvard Grieg to compose a musical score for *Peer Gynt*. The production history of these two verse dramas reveals that they have been performed in multiple genres with the most diverse ideological and political agendas. They are often interpreted as existential dramas because of their focus on extraordinary *individuals*; but they are also strongly political texts that critique the abuses of religion and national chauvinism. This concentration on the relationship of individuals to larger political forces was to become a trademark of many future Ibsen plays. Ibsen once said that Brand resembled himself in his best moments, but it is Peer that has come to be loved and cherished by global readers and spectators. Today *Peer Gynt* is more popular than ever on stages as far afield as Burkina Faso, Zimbabwe, China, India, Berlin and Oslo.

With *The League of Youth* Ibsen returned to writing for performance as well as publication; he continued to use a contemporary setting and combined it with strong satirical and political strains. Ibsen was an individualist with clear anarchistic and idiosyncratic tendencies, and he wrote a series of political satires: *The League of Youth* is preceded by *Norma* and followed by *An Enemy of the People* and *Rosmersholm*. A contempt for political life with its conformism, intrigues and trickeries is evident in each of these works. Ibsen's anti-hero in *The League of Youth*, the charming but hypocritical opportunist Stensgaard, was interpreted by some contemporaries as a portrait of Bjørnstjerne Bjørnson, which offended his old friend. The play lacked the success of his two preceding verse dramas and is rarely performed today, but it does contain several strong comic scenes, and the female characters have elements that reappear in the important women in Ibsen's later plays.

By the time *The League of Youth* was published in 1869 Ibsen had moved to Dresden, where he was to live for the following six years. His next drama, *Emperor and Galilean*, was profoundly influenced by German culture, philosophy and public life. Ibsen considered this double drama of two five-act plays to be his 'major work', possibly because it took him four years to prepare, compose, and write this gargantuan text, and perhaps because of its central position in his oeuvre. *Emperor and Galilean* concerns the struggle between paganism and Christianity in the Roman Empire. Julian 'the apostate' is the protagonist in this somewhat overpopulated text. Emperor from AD 361 to 363, Julian was an immensely complex personality; he was a successful military commander, an intellectual, a social reformer, a theosophist—and a 'doubter'. While Ibsen was accused of preaching 'atheism' in his double drama, the dominant critical reading interprets the text as a depiction of the necessary, world-historic victory of Christianity. Toril Moi has argued that *Emperor and Galilean* represents Ibsen's final break with idealist aesthetics and a turn towards what she calls 'modernism' (2006, 188–91); indeed, Ibsen's insistence on the importance of his decision to write in prose suggests that he saw the drama as a realistic work of art reflecting the contemporary world of here and now. Not all readers and theatre producers have agreed with him, but the play has had some interesting stagings in the last decades, including an adaptation in Beirut (2013) in which conflicts between religion and politics were highlighted in the performance.[1]

28 October 1870 to Peter Hansen
Dybbøl fell as I arrived in Copenhagen. In Berlin, I saw Kaiser Wilhelm make his entry with trophies and booty. Those were the days when *Brand* began to grow inside me like an embryo. The work of unification in Italy had been completed through a boundless spirit of self-sacrifice by the time I got there, while at home—! Add Rome, with its perfect peace, cohabitation

with the carefree world of artists, a life which can only be compared with the ambience of Shakespeare's *As You Like It*, and you have the premise for *Brand*. It is a complete misunderstanding to believe that I have described Søren Kirkegaard's life and times. (I have read very little of S.K., and understood even less.) That Brand is a clergyman is actually immaterial; the demand, all or nothing, applies to all areas of life, to love, to art, etc. Brand is myself in my best moments, just as certainly as I have used self-analysis to bring to light many of Peer Gynt's and Stensgaard's characteristics.

While I was writing *Brand*, I had a scorpion in an empty beer glass on my desk. Now and then the animal became ill; then I would throw it a piece of soft fruit, which it furiously attacked and emptied its poison into; then it became well again. Does not something similar happen with us poets? The laws of nature also apply to the inner, spiritual world.

Peer Gynt followed *Brand* as if of its own accord. It was written in Southern Italy, on Ischia and in Sorrento. Being so far away from future readers makes you ruthless. This poem has much of its origins in my own youth; with certain necessary exaggerations, my own mother was the model for Aase. (Just as she was for Inga in *The Pretenders*.)

The environment has a great influence on the forms in which the imagination creates. Cannot I, rather like Christoff in *Jakob von Tyboe*,[2] point to *Brand* and *Peer Gynt* and say: 'See, this was the ecstasy of wine'? And is there not in *The League of Youth* something reminiscent of 'Knackwurst and beer'? That does not mean I am reducing the value of the play; it means my point of view has changed, because I am now writing in a society well-organised to the point of boredom. What will happen, then, when I come home to live again! I must seek deliverance in a remote subject, and so I am thinking of getting started on 'Emperor Julian'.

Brand (1866)

Premiered 24 March 1885, Nya Teatern, Stockholm.[3]

12 September 1865 to Bjørnstjerne Bjørnson
(Norwegian playwright, director, novelist and public intellectual.)

Everything is well now, and it really has been all the time, with
the exception of certain periods when I have been at my wits'
end, not only as far as money was concerned but because my
work was at a standstill. Then one day I went to St. Peter's
Basilica—I had an errand in Rome—and there, what I wanted
to say suddenly struck me in a strong and clear form. Now I
have thrown overboard everything I have tormented myself
with for a year without getting anywhere [the epic version of
Brand], and in the middle of July I started something new
which progressed in a way nothing ever has before. New in the
sense that I started to write it then, but the material and the
mood and tone of it have been weighing heavily on me since
the many deplorable political events at home made me examine myself and our national life, and reflect on things which
earlier had barely touched me, or which I have never thought
seriously about. It is a dramatic poem, the subject is contemporary, the matter serious, five acts in rhyming verse (no *Love's
Comedy*). The fourth act is soon finished, and I feel I can write
the fifth in eight days. I work both morning and afternoon,
which I have never been able to do before.

It is delightfully peaceful out here [Ariccia, near Rome], no
acquaintances, I read nothing but the Bible—it is powerful and
strong!—If I were to describe at this moment how I have most
profited from my journey, I should say that it consists in having
purged myself of the aesthetic, as seen in isolation and claiming
authority in itself, which used to have such power over me.
Aesthetics in this sense seems to me now to be as great a curse
to poetry as theology is to religion. You have never had to
struggle with the aesthetic in this sense; you have never walked
around looking at the world through a frame created by your
hands. —Is it not a tremendously joyful gift to be able to write?
But with it comes a great responsibility; and I am now serious
enough to understand this and to be hard on myself.

An aesthete from Copenhagen once said when I was there: 'Christ is really the most interesting phenomenon in the history of the world.' The aesthete enjoyed Christ the way a glutton enjoys the sight of an oyster. However, I have always been too strong to become such a mollusc, but I wonder what the cerebral asses might have made out of me if they had had me to themselves. And it was you who prevented them, my dear Bjørnson.

[…] if you can use my new work [at the Christiania Theater, where Bjørnson was artistic director from 1865 to 1867] that would be a different matter; it is a dramatic work, but how far it is stageable in other respects is something for you to decide.

4 May 1866 to Michael Birkeland
(Norwegian national archivist, historian and politician. Birkeland supported Ibsen's application for a Poet's Scholarship in 1866.)

Rome is wonderful, marvellous, beautiful. I have an ability to work, and such strength that I could slay bears with my own hands. I was struggling with this poem in my mind for a year before it stood forth clearly; but once I had it, I wrote from morning till night and finished it in less than three months. It is impossible to write about Rome, especially if one knows it inside out like I do. I have wandered through most of the Papal State on foot at different times, my knapsack on my back. The danger of being robbed is not as great as you imagine at home. […]

You say the scholars are troubling their heads over 'quantum satis' [a phrase used by Ibsen in *Brand*]. In my time, it was good Latin; although medical Latin. Any doctor or medical student would be able to inform you that it is a standing formula for prescriptions of a substance, not according to a specific weight but to the necessary or sufficient amount. Therefore it is *the Doctor* who first uses the expression in the text, and it is the memory of it that makes Brand repeat it. Whether 'caritas' is a classic expression, I would not know; but it is used in modern Catholic Latin (in contrast to 'amor' = earthly love) to describe heavenly love, with its essence of mercy; as it is in Italian: carità.

26 June 1869 to Georg Brandes

Brand has been misinterpreted, at least as far as my intention was concerned (to which you may well reply that the intention is not the critic's concern). The misinterpretation is obviously rooted in the fact that Brand is a minister and that the problem is related to religion. But both these circumstances are quite inessential. I would be more than capable of forming the same syllogism about a sculptor or a politician as about a priest. I could have found an equally satisfactory expression for the feelings that drove me to create it if I had dealt with Galileo, for instance, instead of Brand (with the difference, obviously, that he would have had to stand his ground and refuse to admit that the earth stood still).

15 July 1869 to Georg Brandes

I must maintain what I said about *Brand*. Surely you do not want to blame me for the possibility that the book may conceivably give sustenance to pietism. You may as well reprimand Luther for introducing philistinism to the world; this was never his intention, and thus he has nothing to regret.

From William Archer to his brother, Charles Archer

I spoke to him about Kierkegaard, and he declares it is nonsense to say that Brand has anything to do with Kierkegaard. He says he always draws from models to some degree, and that a man who formed a sort of model for Brand was a certain Pastor Lammers. This man left the State Church, taking any number of people with him; then saw he was on the wrong track but neither could nor would take his followers back into the fold, and so left them in the wilderness and came abroad. Ibsen knew him in Dresden. However, he can't have been by any means an exact prototype of Brand, for Ibsen says he was full of the joy of life, went to the theatre, and was something of a painter and musician. (Qtd. in 1906, 8.)

Recollection from William Archer

He spoke of the mission which the Government had assigned him in his youth, to travel through the country and collect folk-songs. As a matter of fact, he picked up no folk-songs at all, but brought back a store of folk-tales—all told him by one man, however. On the other hand, he gathered many impressions, which he afterwards used in *Brand*. He came to one valley where the parsonage had just been destroyed by an avalanche. The pastor and his wife were living in one room of a peasant's house. The wife, who had just given birth to a child, occupied a screened-off corner, while the husband transacted all the business of the parish in the remainder of the room. The scenery of *Brand* was mainly suggested to him by a side valley off the Geiranger Fjord—the Sunnelvsfjord, I think he said. He also spoke of coming down from the Jotunfjeld at a place where he looked straight down upon a steeple in the valley hundreds of feet below, and could see no possible way of descent. It appeared, however, that there was a path cut in the face of the precipice, and by this he made his way down, in company with a Catholic priest and a sick woman tied to a horse. (1906, 18.)

Recollection from Arnt Dehli
(Dehli was the masseur employed to assist Ibsen during the final years of his life.)

I can tell you that he firmly denied that Lammers was the model for Brand. 'I have never known Lammers,' he said. And he did not hide the fact that it was Christopher Bruun, the pastor of Johannes Church, he was thinking of when he wrote *Brand*; he told me that once, when we met Bruun and stopped to talk with him. And Ibsen added that Bruun's sister, whom he met in Rome, was the model for Agnes. (HU, vol. 19, 228.)

Recollection from P.A. Rosenberg

My next meeting with Ibsen was at Dagmarteatret's party in connection with his seventieth birthday. Martinius Nielsen had staged *Love's Comedy* and played the main role in *Brand*, which

I had adapted and directed for the stage. Both plays premiered in Denmark on this occasion. Ibsen was invited, of course, and saw *Brand* performed for the first time in his life. He seemed to be moved, and dried his eyes several times during the scenes in the fourth act. 'Do not bawl!' he mumbled to himself. After the performance, which lasted until midnight, he asked to meet Martinius Nielsen and my wife, who had played both Svanhild and Agnes. My humble appearance was also requested; we spent three unforgettable hours with him. Besides Riis-Knudsen, Mrs Oda Nielsen was also present, and Sven Scholander turned up later. Ibsen was in a lively mood and spoke continuously, something that was unusual for him. His joy over the production seemed to be genuine, and I also know that he later praised it unconditionally to various people. About Martinius Nielsen's performance he said, 'This is *my* Brand, the way I have imagined him.' He was also full of praise over Agnes, and he demanded to sit between her and Mrs Oda the whole evening [...]

I sat right across from Ibsen at the table [...]. When Martinius Nielsen had poured the champagne and given a speech about the guest of honour [...], Ibsen said slowly to me: 'They speak about my philosophy in this country. I do not *have* a philosophy. They sometimes call me an advocate of truth. I cannot see that I have advocated one single truth. Have I?'

[...]

'You have not cut much in *Brand*,' he said. I hesitated. As it was, I had had to cut over a third of the play.

'Can I see the prompter's book?' I brought it to him, my heart trembling. Page after page was crossed out.

'What the hell,' he mumbled, while he was leafing through the book. 'Yes, it seems I had forgotten most of it myself.' (HU, vol. 19, 215–19.)

Peer Gynt (1867)

Premiered 24 February 1876, Christiania Theater (Oslo).[4]

5 January 1867 to Frederik Hegel
(Ibsen's Scandinavian publisher and close associate for twenty years. HIS holds 280 letters from Ibsen to Hegel.)

I can finally tell you that my new work is well under way, and that I will finish it early this summer, unless something untoward happens. It is a long dramatic poem, and the main character is one of the Norwegian people's half-mythical and adventurous characters from more *recent* times.

8 August 1867 to Frederik Hegel

It might interest you to know that Peer Gynt is a real person who lived in Gudbrandsdalen, most probably at the end of the last century or the beginning of this. His name is still well known among the peasantry up there, but not much more is known about his exploits than what is to be found in Asbjørnsen's 'Norske Huldre-eventyr'.[5] Thus I have not had much to build the poem on, but that has given me all the more creative freedom.

9 December 1867 to Bjørnstjerne Bjørnson[6]

What kind of hell is it that keeps coming between us? It is as if the devil himself casts his shadow over us. I have received your letter. There can be no sense of betrayal from the mouth of someone who writes as you did. Certain things cannot be fabricated. I had written an answer, from a highly grateful heart. One should not be thankful for praise; the only thing to be truly grateful for is to be understood. But now my answer is useless; so I tore it to pieces. An hour ago I read Clemens Petersen's review in *Fædrelandet*. If I am to answer your letter *now*, I have to start in a different way: I must acknowledge that I have received your honourable letter of such and such a date, and the review in the aforementioned paper. —If *I* were in Copenhagen and had a friend there as close to me as Clemens Petersen is to you, I would have beaten the life out of him before I had allow him to commit such a tendentious offence against truth and justice. Clemens Petersen's article is built on a lie; not because of what he says, but what he refrains from saying. And there is much here that he *deliberately* refrains from saying. You are welcome to show him this letter. As surely as I know that he has a deep and serious relationship with what really makes it worth living in this world, just as surely do I know that this article will one day sting and burn his soul; because to conceal the truth is just as much a falsehood as to openly lie. Clemens Petersen has a great responsibility, because Our Lord has burdened him with a heavy task. —Do not think I am a blind, conceited fool! I can assure you that in my quiet moments, I probe and dissect and rummage around in the innermost corners of my own self; and where it stings the worst, too. —My book *is* poetry; and if it is not, then it shall become so. The concept of poetry in our country, in Norway, shall bow and conform to the book. There is nothing stable in the world of concepts. The Scandinavians of our century are not Greeks. He says that the Strange Passenger represents the concept of Angst! If I were about to be executed and could save my life by coming up with such an explanation, it still would not occur to me; such a thing never entered my mind. I chucked in the scene as a caprice. And is not Peer Gynt a human being with a complete and individual personality? *I* know that he is. And is not the Mother? We could learn many things from Clemens Petersen, and I have learnt much from him. But there is something he could benefit from learning himself, and where I, even if I cannot teach it to him, have the advantage over him; and that is what you in your letter call 'faithfulness'. That is the very word! Not faithfulness to a friend, a cause or anything like that, but towards something infinitely higher.

However, I am glad for the insult inflicted upon me. There is a divine help and ordinance in it; I feel my strength growing with my anger. If there is to be war, let there be war! If I am not a writer, or poet, then I have nothing to lose. I shall try my luck as a photographer. I shall deal with each and every one of my contemporaries up there, one by one, the way I have with the language reformers.[7] I will not spare the child in the mother's womb, nor the thought or emotion behind the word of any living soul who deserves the honour to be included. — Dear Bjørnson, you are a warm, blessed soul, who has given me far more of what is grand and wonderful than I can ever repay. But it is this very trait in your nature that can as easily be your curse as your good fortune. I have a right to tell you this because I know that beneath the crust of nonsense and debauchery, I have always taken life seriously. Do you know that I have shunned my own parents, my whole family, because I could not bear to continue a relationship based on only a half understanding between us?

What I am writing here is probably quite incoherent but summa summarum it is this: I do not *want* to be an antiquarian or a geographer; I do not *want* to cultivate my talent for Monrad's Hegelian Idealism. In short, I do not want to listen to good advice.

24 February 1868 to Frederik Hegel

How is *Peer Gynt* going? In Sweden it has been very well received, from what I can understand from the reviews; but do the sales reflect this?

I have learnt that the book has caused a storm in Norway, which does not worry me in the least; however, both there and in Denmark they have found much more satire than I intended. Why can they not read the book as a poem? For that is how I have written it. The satirical sections are fairly isolated. But if contemporary Norwegians recognise themselves in the character of Peer Gynt, as it seems they do, it is the good citizens' own affair.

15 July 1869 to Georg Brandes

I cannot agree with you regarding those particular parts of *Peer Gynt*; of course I bow to the laws of beauty but I do not care for its by-laws. You mention Michelangelo: in my opinion no one has sinned more against the rules of beauty than he, but everything he has created is still beautiful because it is full of character. I have never really warmed to Raphael's art; his characters belong to a time before the fall of man and all things considered, a Southern European has a different aesthetics than we do. He wants formal beauty; to us, even formal lack of beauty may be beautiful through its inherent truth. But to battle over this with pen and ink is futile; we must meet.

30 April 1872 to Edmund Gosse

Peer Gynt is *Brand*'s opposite; many consider it my best book. I do not know if you will find pleasure in it. It is wild and formless, ruthlessly written, in a way I only dared to write far from home; it came into existence during my sojourns on Ischia and in Sorrento during the summer of 1867.

21 September 1882 to Georg Brandes

My parents on both sides belonged to the most respected families of their time in Skien. The town's longstanding Member of Parliament, district court judge Paus, and his brother, district recorder Paus, were my father's half-brothers and my mother's cousins. My parents were just as closely related to the Plesner, von der Lippe, Cappelen and Blom families, thus to almost all the patrician families who dominated the town and surrounding areas at the time [...]

In *Peer Gynt* I have used the circumstances and memories of my own childhood as a kind of model in my descriptions of life in 'the rich Jon Gynt's house'.

16 June 1880 to Ludwig Passarge
(German civil servant, author and translator.)

I am pleased to learn that you have found a reputable publisher for your translation of *Peer Gynt*. But with my best will, I am unable to explain the many allusions in the book which may be incomprehensible to German readers; because for me, as a foreigner, it is impossible to judge what needs explanation and what does not [...]

Neither am I able to offer further explanations about the circumstances which gave rise to *Peer Gynt*. For such a portrayal to be understandable, I would have to write a whole book about it, and the time is not yet ripe for that. Everything I have written is most intimately connected with what I have lived *through*—if not *experienced*. To me, each new piece of work has served the purpose of a spiritual liberation and cleansing process; for you are never without responsibility for, and are always complicit with, the society to which you belong. Therefore I once wrote the following lines as a dedication at the front of a copy of one of my books:

> To *live* is to war with trolls
> in the vault of the heart and the brain
> To *write*—that is to hold
> doomsday over oneself.

You do not know the word 'pusselanker', and that is only natural because the word is not used in the written language. It means 'small children's tripping legs or feet', and the expression is only used by mothers and wet nurses when they are babbling with their little children.

The meaning of the lines you ask about is as follows: in order to gain access to hell, Peer Gynt pleads that he has been a slave dealer. To this, 'The Thin Man' responds that there are many who have committed worse things; for instance, suppressed the spiritual, the will and the mind among their fellow beings; but if such things are done 'half-heartedly', that is, without daemonic seriousness, it does not qualify to get them into hell, only into the 'casting-ladle'.

Recollection from Vilhelm Bergsøe
(Danish author and zoologist. In 1867, he was Ibsen's companion in Sorrento and Ischia and wrote a detailed account of their daily walks.)

IBSEN. Can you portray a man on stage who is running
  around with a casting-ladle?

BERGSØE. Yes, why not?

IBSEN. But it must be a big casting-ladle—one in which
  you can re-cast human beings.

BERGSØE. That would look pretty comical.

IBSEN. Yes, that is what I think too; but then I do not think
  it is really written for performance. (1907, 212.)

23 January 1874 to Edvard Grieg
(Norwegian composer and pianist. IbsenStage holds 893
records of *Peer Gynt* where Grieg's score was used.)

I intend to adapt *Peer Gynt*, which is soon coming out in its
third edition, for the stage. Do you want to compose the necessary musical accompaniment? I shall briefly suggest to you
how I think of adapting the play.

The first act will remain intact, with only a few edits in the
dialogue. I want Peer Gynt's monologue on pp. 23, 24 and 25
either to be treated melodramatically or in part as a recitative.
There must be much more made out of the scene in the wed-
ding yard, p. 28, by means of a ballet, than is suggested in the
book. To this end, a special dance tune must be composed,
which will continue softly right up to the end of the act.

In the second act, the scene with the three herd girls,
pp. 57–60, must be treated musically at the discrimination of
the composer, but there must be devilry in it! I have imagined
that the monologue on pp. 60–2 should be accompanied by
chords; that is, as in melodrama. The same is true of the scene
between Peer and the Woman in Green, pp. 63–6. Likewise,
there has to be a kind of accompaniment to the scene in the
Hall of the Mountain King; in which, however, the dialogue
will be considerably shortened. The scene with The Bøyg,
which should be performed in its entirety, must also be accompanied by music; the bird voices must be sung; the ringing of
bells and the singing of psalms are heard in the far distance.

I need chords in the third act, but sparingly, for the scene
between Peer, the woman and the troll urchin, pp. 96–100.
Likewise, I have imagined a soft accompaniment from the top
of p. 109 to the bottom of p. 112.

Almost the whole of Act Four will be omitted from the performance. In its place I have imagined a large-scale musical
tone picture which suggests Peer's roaming in the wide world;
American, English and French melodies could sound throughout as alternating motifs, swelling and fading. The chorus of
Anitra and the girls, pp. 144–5, should be heard from behind
the curtain, along with the orchestral music. During this, the
curtain should be raised and we should see the tableau

described at the bottom of p. 164 as a distant dream picture, in which Solveig, as a middle-aged woman, sits singing in the sunshine against the house wall. After her song, the curtain should come slowly down, the music continues in the orchestra, and then it should change to depict the ocean storm which opens the fifth act.

The fifth act, which is now titled the fourth or an epilogue in the performance, must be considerably shortened. Musical accompaniment is needed from pp. 195–9. The scenes on the capsized boat and in the churchyard are to be left out. On p. 221, Solveig is singing and the postlude continues to accompany Peer Gynt's following speeches, then it moves into the choral music on pp. 222–5. The scenes with the Button Moulder and the Troll King are to be shortened. On p. 254, the church people are singing on the forest path; the ringing of bells and distant singing of psalms are suggested in the music during what follows, until Solveig's song ends the play, and the curtain falls as the singing of psalms once more sounds closer and stronger.

17 November 1885 to Theodor Andersen
(Danish actor and director based in Copenhagen.)

Yesterday I returned the copy of *Peer Gynt* I was sent and I hope it has found its way into your hands.

I approve of the deletions you have made, and, as you see, I have made further cuts to the dialogue.

Should the rehearsals indicate that even further edits are desirable, either in the scenes you point to in your letter or at other places in the play, I ask you to do whatever is necessary according to your best judgement.

From what I hear, Josephson made a mistake in the staging of the play in Kristiania, as he let the three herd girls be played as ordinary, dolled-up, pretty young girls. That is not how I had imagined them. There should be something wild, reckless, witch-like about these figures. I would like them to be played by skilful character actresses of voluptuous, daemonic beauty.

19 May 1880 to Ludwig Passarge

Allow me first to offer you my warmest thanks for the friendly interest with which you treat my literary activity. Your understanding of *Peer Gynt* coincides totally with what I intended when I wrote this book, and of course I can only be pleased that it has found a translator who, with full clarity, has penetrated into the innermost purpose of literature.

Nonetheless, it was still a surprise to learn that you regard this work as suitable to be translated and published in German. I must admit I have grave doubts myself. Among all my books, I regard *Peer Gynt* as the one which will be least understood outside the Scandinavian countries. I ask you to consider that most of your prospective German readers do not possess the necessary background to understanding the book. You yourself no doubt have an accurate knowledge of Norwegian nature and Norwegian life; you are familiar with our literature and our ways of thinking; you know people and characters up there. But are not all these things necessary in order to acquire a taste for this poem? This is why I have such grave doubts, which I have not wanted to keep back from you; although of course, I must assume that you scrupulously considered everything I have pointed out here before you decided to take on such difficult and extensive work.

25 May 1890 to Bjørn Bjørnson
(Norwegian actor, theatre manager, playwright, and son of Bjørnstjerne Bjørnson.)

The Bøyg, I think, should preferably be portrayed as grey, compact, rolling masses of fog. A clever scene painter and a machinist would be able to depict this with the help of moving gossamer material.

Recollection from William Archer

He wrote *Brand* and *Peer Gynt* (which appeared with only a year's interval between them) at very high pressure, amounting to nervous overstrain. He would go on writing verses all the time, even when asleep or half awake. He thought them capital for the moment; but they were the veriest nonsense.

Once or twice he was so impressed with their merit that he rose in his nightshirt to write them down; but they were never of the slightest use. At Aricca he used to get up at four or five in the morning and go for a long walk; then, when he came back, he was in good trim for writing.

He began *Peer Gynt* at Ischia and finished it at Sorrento. He set to work upon it with no definite plan, foreseeing the end, indeed, but not the intermediate details. For instance, he did not know that Peer was to go to Africa. 'It is much easier,' he said, 'to write a piece like *Brand* or *Peer Gynt*, in which you can bring in a little of everything, than to carry through a severely logical (konsekvent) scheme, like that of *John Gabriel Borkman*, for example. (1906, 18.)

The League of Youth (1869)

Premiered 18 October 1869, Christiania Theater (Oslo).[8]

31 October 1868 to Frederik Hegel

My new work is proceeding quickly. I have been struggling with it in my thoughts all summer without really writing anything. Now the full draft is finished and written down; the first act is completed, the second act will be finished in eight days, and I hope that by the end of the year the whole play will have been written. It is a prose piece and intended exclusively for the stage. The play's title is *The League of Youth; or, Almighty & Co.*, a comedy in five acts. It deals with conflicts and trends in contemporary life and, although set in Norway, will be just as suitable for Denmark. I find myself in a happy and reconciled state of mind, and write accordingly; this time the dear, admirable man G. Brandes will have no reason to reprimand me for unlawful intercourse with the muses. I would like you to send me a copy of Brandes' *Æsthetiske Studier*, and charge me for it. While still in Rome I heard that he was writing a treatise on the comic, a concept with which I must confess I am not, theoretically speaking, fully conversant, and which I would like to see clarified, especially by someone such as Brandes.

22 December 1868 to Frederik Hegel

I also thank you very much for Brandes' book *Æsthetiske Studier*, which has been a true goldmine for me, especially the parts regarding the comic. Brandes is a remarkable man for seeing so clearly, deeply and coherently, and if it were possible, I would claim that his ability to express his ideas lucidly to the reader, above all so that they stay in one's memory, is even greater.

26 June 1869 to Georg Brandes

In my new comedy you will find ordinary everyday life, no strong emotions, no deep feelings, and above all no isolated thoughts. Your just reproach concerning the authorial presence in unconsidered lines in *The Pretenders* has had its effect. […]

But now I am anxious to hear your thoughts about my new work. It is written in prose, and as a result it has a strong realistic colouring. I have taken particular care with the form and, among other things, have achieved the feat of doing without a single monologue; yes, without a single 'aside'. However, all this proves nothing, of course; and therefore I beseech you: should you have a free moment, would you please be so kind as to read it and let me know your verdict; no matter what your verdict may be, you will do me a great favour by expressing it to me here in my solitude. […]

15 July 1869 to Georg Brandes

I am beginning to suspect that I should not have asked you to read my new comedy. On closer reflection, I believe that what truly interests you in literature are those tragedies or comedies that take place in the individual's inner life, and that you care little or nothing about the true circumstances of real life, whether political or whatever. In that case, you may well ask as regards my play: What is Hecuba to me? But this time I had no wish to express anything but what the work itself contains, and so it must be judged accordingly. Besides, you yourself are not without a certain responsibility; for in a sense you egged me on to take this direction through a remark in your aesthetic writings. More about this when we speak.

It is a misunderstanding to assume that I believed you do not like strong emotions or deep feelings; on the contrary, I wanted to warn you against expecting what you would not find.

19 June 1869 to Lorentz Dietrichson
(Norwegian poet, academic, and historian of art and literature. In 1869, he became a professor at the Royal Swedish Academy of the Arts.)

As you will see, the play is a simple comedy, nothing more. Some people in Norway might say that I have portrayed real persons and conditions. However, that is wrong; I have, of course, used models, something which is just as necessary for the writer of comedies as for the painter and sculptor.

It seems to me that the play would be suitable in Sweden as well; that is, in the real Sweden. Whether it fits the theatre there is something for you to decide. It is, at any rate, quite easy to stage; it requires no expensive set, all it requires is an honorarium to the translator. So therefore, my dear friend, please do your utmost to have it produced.

14 December 1869 to Frederik Hegel

The reception which *The League of Youth* has received pleases me very much; I was prepared for opposition, and I would have been disappointed if there had been none. But what I was not prepared for was that Bjørnson, from what I hear, has felt himself under attack in the play. Is this really the case? He must surely see that it is not him personally but his pernicious and lie-ridden political circle which served as my models. However, I shall write to him today or tomorrow, and I hope that the affair, despite all the differences, will end in reconciliation. […]

4 January 1870 to Jonas Collin
(Danish zoologist.)

They are judging my new work from the political rather than the aesthetic point of view. From the attacks I have laid eyes on, it appears that phrase-mongering, hollowness and roguery are regarded in Norway as national characteristics which must not be interfered with.

10 February 1870 to Jens Peter Andresen
(Norwegian lawyer and Chair of the Christiania Theater Board from 1866 to 1871.)

First of all, I must thank you for being the first who has expressed my own opinion of *The League of Youth* clearly and lucidly. It is exactly as you say, that the politics in the play, 'so far as one can say there is any', have been immaterial to me. But of course, I needed a plot through which the characters could develop, and then it seemed closest to hand to choose situations and conditions which one may say are typical, to a certain degree, of our society. If I have hit the mark with someone in particular, it has been inadvertently; and it would have been a much worse complaint against the work if one could claim that the play's characters and circumstances found no equivalent reality to our own. These days, comedy must, in my opinion, have a strong realistic quality. At any rate, the writer of comedy, like any artist, must use a model. But there is a big difference between the model's head and a portrait.

3 September 1877 to Marcus Grønvold
(Norwegian artist. Grønvold met Ibsen in Munich in 1877.)

But should you find yourself in the vicinity of the Court Theatre [Königliches Residenz-Theater in Munich] one of these days, you would do me an extraordinary favour if you could find the director Jenke, and ask him from me to change one point in *The League of Youth* which I have already mentioned briefly to him. As you probably remember, Aslaksen often speaks about 'the local conditions'; Strodtmann has translated this literally with 'lokale Verhältnisse' which is wrong, as in German it does not have the comical connotations of narrow-mindedness.

Emperor and Galilean (1873)

Premiered 5 December 1896, Leipziger Stadttheater.[9]

10 June 1869 to Frederik Hegel

At last I am going to embark on the vast, and long-planned work, *Emperor Julian*; I feel that my conception of it has now grown sufficiently distinct, and that, once I begin, it will progress effortlessly. Regarding this, may I ask a great favour of you? In the spring of 1866, *Fædrelandet* published an excellent article in three parts by Listow, which gives a condensed overview of Julian's life. If it is at all possible for you to obtain this for me, I would be extremely grateful.

7 July 1899 to Roman Woerner
(German literary historian and translator of *Emperor and Galilean*.)

[…] I have not used a particular historical work as a basis for *Emperor and Galilean*. I do not know Tillemont's work; but I have gone through and made extracts from various historians of the Church, and in that respect I owe a debt of gratitude to the German library on the Capitoline Hill. I mainly consulted Ammianus Marcellinus for the historical material, and I found him most useful.

26 February 1888 to Julius Hoffory
(Danish philologist and translator. Professor at the University of Berlin from 1887.)

Emperor and Galilean is not the first work I have written in Germany, but I suppose the first I have written under the influence of German intellectual life. When I arrived in Dresden from Italy in the autumn of 1868, I brought the sketch for *The League of Youth* and wrote the play that winter. During my four years in Rome I made numerous historical studies and wrote quite a few notes concerning *Emperor and Galilean*, but I did not make any clear plans for its overall structure, and even less did I write anything down. My outlook on life was still that of a Scandinavian national, and I could not yet accommodate the foreign material.

Then I experienced Germany's great progress, the year of war and the development that followed. To me, all this carried within it a power of transformation. Until then, I had understood world history and human life from a national viewpoint.

24 September 1871 to Georg Brandes

In all, there are times when the whole world history appears to me as nothing but a big shipwreck; all that matters is to save oneself. —I have no expectations as to special reforms. The case is that the whole human race has gone astray. Or is there really any substance in the present situation? The whole line of generations seems to me like a young man who has failed to stick to his cobbler's last and has gone to act in the theatre. We have made a fiasco of our roles both as lovers and heroes; the only thing we have shown a spot of talent for is the naïve comical. But with our more highly developed self-consciousness, we are no longer fit for that. I do not believe all this is any better in other countries; the masses are removed from all understanding of higher things, both abroad and at home.

And so I was going to try to raise a banner! Oh my dear friend, that would have turned into a story, like the one when Louis Napoleon stepped ashore in Boulogne with an eagle on his head. Later, when the hour of his destiny struck, he did not need any eagle. My work on *Julian* has, in a certain way, made me a fatalist; still, this play does become a banner of a kind. However, do not fear that the work will be of a tendentious nature; I look at the characters, at their conflicting plans, at *history*, without dabbling with the 'moral' of it all—assuming that you do not mistake history's moral for its philosophy; since the latter will certainly shine through as the final verdict on those who struggle and those who are victorious. But all this can only be elucidated in practice.

14 October 1872 to Edmund Gosse

I am working daily on *Julianus Apostata*, and hope to have the whole work finished by the end of this year. As soon as the book has been published I shall take the liberty to send it to you, and I do wish that it will meet with your approval. I am putting a part of my spiritual life into this book; what I depict, I have lived through in other ways myself, and the chosen historical theme also has a closer connection with our own time's movements than you would first believe. I see this as an imperative demand of any modern treatment of such remote material, if it is to arouse any interest as a piece of creative writing.

23 February 1873 to Ludvig Ludvigsen Daae
(Norwegian historian and classical philologist.)

[…] I really wanted to know the correct Greek spelling; not to use it in its pure form mind you, but to be able to decide how far I dare legitimately go in changing the Greek names to Scandinavian ones. You see, I aspire towards a certain conformity and I am reluctant to let the many names contrast or clash with each other. As I now use the abridged, naturalised forms Julian, Gregor, etc., I cannot spell Basileios in pure Greek. As the Romans have changed this name to Basilius—could I not change it to Basilios? That would be so much more desirable, as the name (in my play) is frequently mentioned in connection with the man's birth place, Cæsaræa, and I do not dare to touch the spelling of this word because the Roman title Cæsar appears so often in the book.

My dear friend, you will now have a clear view of my position, which, although not philological, is still, I believe, one I am able to justify. What I as a foreigner want to avoid are the Greek diphthongs *ai*, *ei* and *oi*. Thus I would like to write Ædesios, Basilios, Ødipos.

Moreover: Can I write Cæsarios, or was the man (a brother of Gregor of Naziang) called Cæsarion? For the aforementioned reasons, I do not dare to exchange the letter C with K (obviously!). Do I dare to write: Emperor Konstanzios? Was the name of the city Pergamon? Was the name of the Dog Star Sirios? Is Hilarion the correct Greek form?

Should there be something in the above too witlessly barbaric, please do me the great favour of sending Hegel the necessary corrections; but sparingly, for it is extremely important to me to stick to the principle, as far as it can be defended in any way with subtle arguments.

So Eunapios has written his book in Latin; my bookshop owner here assured me it was in Greek. I am happy to see that the biography contains nothing in conflict with what I knew beforehand and have employed.

The drama I am now publishing will be my major work. It is titled *Emperor and Galilean*, and comprises 1) *Cæsar's Apostasy*, 2) *Emperor Julian*. Each of these is a big drama in five acts. The play is about a struggle between two irreconcilable powers in the life of the world; a struggle that will forever repeat itself, and because of this universality I call the book 'a World Historical Drama'. In the character of Julian, as in most of what I have written in my more mature years, there is more of what I have lived through in my own spiritual life than I would care to reveal to the public. But at the same time it is a wholly and fully realistic work; I have seen the characters in front of my eyes in the light of their own time—and I hope my readers will as well.

6 February 1873 to Frederik Hegel

Do not let the term 'world drama' frighten you! It is in league with 'folk drama', 'family drama', 'national drama', etc., and is apposite; for my play is dealing with both heaven and earth.

[…]

This play has been my Herculean task; not in the writing itself, for that was an easy task, but in the effort it took to put myself freshly and lucidly into such a distant and foreign era. I was truly pleased to learn from your second to last letter that there is a prospect of good sales, because several years of my life have been sacrificed to this book. I dare to predict that we will both get pleasure from it.

20 March 1873 to Adolf Strodtmann
(German poet, literary historian and translator.)

[…] I have not changed my disposition re Germany, and will never do so. I am, like most Norwegian Scandinavians, a pan-Germanist. I consider Scandinavianism as merely a transitional phase towards the amalgamation of the whole large Germanic tribe. If I were to become aware that in the end we would remain an isolated Scandinavian union, I would never dip my pen in an inkwell to promote that cause.

You will also see from the enclosed poem, which is no more than eight months old, that I have not relinquished my understanding of the world historical function of Germany in our century; what I have expressed in it, I will still adhere to and express at every opportunity.[10]

8 September 1873 to Georg Brandes

I hear from Norway that Bjørnson, although he cannot know the book, has declared it to be 'atheistic', adding that it was obvious I had to arrive at that position. What the book is or is not, I have no wish to look into; all I know is that I have vividly experienced a fragment of the history of humankind, and what I saw, I wanted to recount.

30 January 1875 to Georg Brandes

Accept my warmest gratitude for finding room for *Emperor and Galilean* in your journal. And I have much to say to you in that connection; however, expressing it in writing means I must limit myself to the comment that I find an inner contradiction in your condemnation of the determinism expressed in my book when I compare your disapproval thereof with your approval of something similar in P. Heyse's *Kinder der Welt* ('Children of the World'). For in my opinion, it makes hardly any difference whether I say about a person's character that 'it runs in his blood' or that 'he is free—subject to the laws of necessity'.

15 January 1874 to Edmund Gosse

I am especially grateful for your obliging review of my new drama. There is only one point I would like to discuss briefly with you. You believe that my play should have been written in verse and that it would have benefited from that. Allow me to contradict you on this point; for the play is, as you will have observed, constructed in the most realistic style; the illusion I wanted to bring forth was that of reality; I wanted to evoke in the reader the impression that what he read was something that had really happened. If I had used verse, I would have worked against my own intention and the task I had imposed on myself. The many everyday and insignificant characters I have deliberately included in the play would have become indistinct and indistinguishable from each other if I had allowed them all to speak in a tempo of rhythmic verse. We no longer live in Shakespeare's time, and among the sculptors there is already talk about painting the statues in natural colours. Much can be said about this, both pro and contra. I have no wish to see the Venus de Milo painted, but I would rather see the head of a negro made in black than in white marble. On the whole, the form of the language must comply with the degree of idealisation which pervades the representation. My new play is not a tragedy in the ancient sense; I wanted to depict human beings, and therefore I did not want them to speak the 'language of the gods'.

10 September 1874 speech to Norwegian Students' Union and Choral Society[11]

When Emperor Julian stands at the end of his life and everything collapses around him, there is nothing that assaults his spirit so profoundly as the thought that all he has won is this: to be remembered with esteemed appreciation by clear and cool heads, while his adversary lived on, rich from the love of warm living hearts. This feature has been born from something lived *through*; it has its origin in a question which I sometimes have asked myself while down there in my solitude.

24 September 1887 Banquet Speech at Grand Hotel, Stockholm

It has been said that I too have played a prominent part in creating a new era in our countries.

However, I believe that the times we now live in could just as well be described as a conclusion to an era, and that something new is about to be born from it.

For I believe in fact that natural science's theories about evolution are also valid in regard to aspects of spiritual life.

I believe that we are about to enter an era in which the concept of the political and social will cease to exist in their present forms, and that from them both a unity will grow, which for the time being will carry the conditions for the happiness of humanity within it.

I believe that poetry, philosophy and religion will merge into a new category and become a new life force which, moreover, we who live now can have no clear idea about.

On more than one occasion it has been said of me that I am a pessimist.

And so I am, in the sense that I do not believe in the perpetuity of human ideals.

But I am also an optimist, in the sense that I fully and wholly believe in the reproductive ability of ideals, and in their capacity to evolve and develop.

Particularly, and more precisely, I believe that the ideals of our time, as they perish, tend towards what I in my drama *Emperor and Galilean* have implied with the term '…the third Kingdom'.

1. ibsenstage.hf.uio.no/pages/event/94659
2. *Jakob von Tyboe, eller Den stortalende soldat* (1725; 'Jakob von Tyboe, or the Bragging Soldier') was written by Ibsen's favourite playwright, Ludvig Holberg.
3. ibsenstage.hf.uio.no/pages/event/78142
4. ibsenstage.hf.uio.no/pages/event/77960
5. Peter Christen Asbjørnsen published numerous legends in *Norske Huldre-Eventyr og Folkesagn* (1845, 1848, and 1870; 'Norwegian Popular Legends and Stories of the Hidden Folk').
6. Bjørnson adored *Peer Gynt*. He wrote an enthusiastic letter to Ibsen on 18 November in which he praised the book; he also gave it a positive review in *Norsk Folkeblad* (23 November 1867). Clemens Petersen's review appeared in *Fædrelandet* (20 November 1867). The latter claimed that *Peer Gynt* was not

'poetry' because it failed to conform to conservative idealist aesthetics, thus lacking 'harmonious, conclusive, clear and certain depiction of the Ideal'. At that time, Petersen was Scandinavia's most influential critic; he was also a close friend of Bjørnson.

7. Ibsen never sympathised with the language reformers' efforts to construct a new Norwegian built on dialects and the Old Norse heritage. In *Peer Gynt* he ridiculed the language reformers in the fourth act through the character of HuHu, the 'language reformer from the Malabar Coast'.

8. ibsenstage.hf.uio.no/pages/event/77906

9. ibsenstage.hf.uio.no/pages/event/78771

10. Ibsen is referring to his poem *Ved tusenårs-festen* ('At the Millennial Celebration').

11. The march organised in Ibsen's honour stopped in the street outside his windows. The students sang a song written for the occasion with humorous references to Ibsen's own writings: 'It is easy to breathe on the top plains', finishing with the words 'Welcome home is the power which shall pull you / To your country and your waiting people'.

4
Middle Plays:
from *Pillars of Society* to
An Enemy of the People

Ibsen's fortunes as a playwright changed around the time of his fiftieth birthday in 1878. He wrote four plays in the middle years of his career which secured his future as an international dramatist. First there was the box-office success of *Pillars of Society*; then what was to become his most performed play, *A Doll's House*; followed by *Ghosts*, which cemented his reputation as an avant-garde playwright; and finally, *An Enemy of the People*, a play that has been adapted to critique systems of political power and sites of pollution all over the world.

The phenomenal commercial success of *Pillars of Society*, particularly in German theatres during 1878, continues to intrigue scholars (Dingstad 2016; Hanssen 2016). Until his breakthrough into the German theatre, most productions of Ibsen's plays were presented by Nordic theatres. IbsenStage records forty-six German productions of *Pillars of Society* for the year 1878; the average annual number of productions of all his plays during the previous twenty-seven years is less than seven. Although lack of copyright protection reduced Ibsen's income from the German productions of *Pillars of Society*, the popularity of the play renewed his commitment to writing for performance.[1] In *Pillars of Society*, as Mark Sandberg has persuasively argued, Ibsen 'not only engaged profoundly in the present moment' but 'fundamentally shifted his valuation of the past' (Sandberg 2015, 134). He was never to return to historical settings, or to the overt referencing of folk and classical sources that dominated his early plays. To reinforce his argument, Sandberg quotes Ibsen's narrator from the poem 'To the Accomplices':

> Thus have I turned my view and my mind
> away from the soul-deadened saga of our past,
> away from our lying dream about a future dawning,
> and enter into the hazy world of the present. (Ibid.)

The present as represented in Ibsen's next play, *A Doll's House*, chimed with the most debated social issue of his time: the emancipation of women.[2] *A Doll's House* did not enjoy the immediate success of *Pillars of Society*, but the role of Nora proved so popular with English, German, Russian, Italian, French, Portuguese and Japanese actresses that they had toured the play across five continents by the end of the century (Holledge et al. 2016). *A Doll's House* made Ibsen a world dramatist. Today *A Doll's House* has been performed in thirty-five languages in eighty-seven countries, thirty-nine of which are outside Europe; the play still averages 1.6 new productions a week in this century. Ibsen was adamant that Nora was taken from life; in fact, he claimed that all his characters portrayed 'real living people' (Motzfeld 1911, 4). The more successful he became, the more his acquaintances saw themselves in his plays. Laura Kieler's life-story has parallels with the plotline of *A Doll's House*. Kieler had written a novel entitled *Brands døtre: et livsbillede af Lili* ('Brand's Daughters: A Life Portrait of Lili') in response to *Brand*, and it was through this novel that Ibsen made her acquaintance. Her husband had developed tuberculosis, and without his knowledge she had borrowed money to pay for his recuperation in a warmer climate; when her husband found out about the loan, he temporarily committed her to an asylum. Eventually, she resumed her marriage and pursued her career as a writer. Extracts from Ibsen's letters to Kieler are included in this chapter.

Ghosts, Ibsen's next play, reinforced public perception of Ibsen as a dramatist of controversial social issues. The opprobrium that greeted the publication of *Ghosts* made the play a cause célèbre within the Independent theatre movement.

The Freie Bühne performed *Ghosts* in Berlin in 1889,[3] the Théâtre Libre performed the play in France in 1890,[4] and the Independent Theatre performed it in London in 1891.[5] These performances were given almost ten years after the publication of the play in 1881; the first ever performance of *Ghosts* was given by a Danish company in Chicago (1882).[6] The following year, the Swedish actor manager August Lindberg began a Scandinavian tour of the play that was to continue for fifteen years. In all, Lindberg produced seventeen plays by Ibsen between 1878 and 1914.[7] Ibsen attended two German performances of *Ghosts*: a matinee performance at the Residenz-Theater in Berlin (1887),[8] and a performance at the private theatre of Georg II, Duke of Saxe-Meiningen (1889).[9] Frustratingly, he did not record his impressions of these performances.

A 'peaceable play' is how Ibsen described *An Enemy of the People* to Hegel in January 1883. The play, which he had written during the furore surrounding *Ghosts*, was published late in 1882 and premiered less than two months later at the Christiania Theater in Norway. In his comments on *An Enemy of the People*, Ibsen placed great importance on 'making the audience believe that they are sitting and listening and watching something which happens out there in real life' (to Lindberg, 2 August 1883). IbsenStage holds 1,395 records of *An Enemy of the People*. It is Ibsen's fourth most popular play, and it has been produced on five continents.

The social dramas written by Ibsen between 1878 and 1882 have stimulated considerable critical debate about his political views. A series of extracts from Ibsen's letters and speeches, as well as some reminiscences from his acquaintances, are included in this chapter because they refer to his views on social democracy and the emancipation of women. Ibsen's public statements have fuelled both sides of a debate that revolves around his intentions in creating the character of Nora: did he set out to represent an emergent female subjectivity tied to modernity, or the struggle of all human beings attempting to achieve self-realisation? The first extract comes from a letter to Bjørnstjerne Bjørnson in which Ibsen comments on a failed attempt to introduce a Married Women's Property bill in the Norwegian parliament. Two speeches follow in which he refers directly to the social position of women: in the first, he represents women and workers as the 'nobility' of the nation; in the second, he claims he is 'not even fully aware of what the Women's cause really is'. The reference to 'Women's cause' comes from a speech given at a banquet in his honour hosted by the Norwegian Women's Rights League in 1898. The speech has been cited in numerous scholarly articles, but the context of the banquet is rarely discussed. Ibsen knew that his audience would be drawn from the political establishment. The founders of the League included several former Norwegian Prime Ministers, important figures in the leadership of the Party, as well as the editors of the large Liberal newspapers.

The distance Ibsen maintained between himself and all political parties is evident in an interview published in the *Pall Mall Gazette* in which he states he 'never was or ever would be a Social Democrat' (13 August 1890, 6). The interview was in response to a lecture on Ibsen that George Bernard Shaw had given to the Fabian Society, in which he made a connection between *A Doll's House* and the Social Democratic platform on the emancipation of women. A letter from William Archer to his brother Charles provides the backstory to this interview. The last extract that relates to Ibsen's views on the emancipation of women comes from Camilla Collett, who is often referred to as the first Norwegian feminist. Her somewhat unflattering description of Ibsen as a patriarch was written seven years before the publication of *A Doll's House*; ten years later, Ibsen acknowledged the importance of Collett's work as a pioneer of social progress in a letter celebrating her seventieth birthday.

The final extracts in this chapter come from four letters to Georg Brandes in which Ibsen expresses his views on the role of the state, the meaning of freedom, and the importance of minority vanguards in the shaping of public life.

Pillars of Society (1877)

Premiered 14 November 1877, Odense Theater.[10]

An early note on Pillars of Society

The keynote through the whole play must be constituted by the women, living a kind of shyness in the midst of the male bustle, with its narrow objectives expanded with a confidence that provokes and impresses at the same time. (HU, vol. 8, 154.)

23 October 1875 to Frederik Hegel

My new play is advancing quickly; I shall have the first act finished in a couple of days, and that is always the most difficult part of a play for me. The book's title will be *Pillars of Society*, a play in five acts. This work can, in a way, be seen as a counterpart to *The League of Youth*, and will stir up several of our time's more significant issues.

29 July 1877 to Frederik Hegel

I believe I may say with certainty that we will both gain satisfaction from this work; it is new and modern in every respect, and as far as artistic composition is concerned, perhaps the best of all of my works.

20 September 1877 to King Oscar II
(King of Sweden and Norway from 1872 to 1905. He awarded Ibsen the Order of Olaf in 1873.)

To write and print this work at this particular time seemed a relevant thing to do for the current age. Recently, from other quarters, and through literature, there have been attacks on institutions which are integral to our whole nation's past, and on whose preservation our people's welfare and progress depend. Therefore I believed that it could be beneficial to steer the general public's views and thoughts in another direction, and show that lack of truth in a society is not embedded in institutions but in the individuals themselves. It is the human being's inner life, the life of the soul, which must be cleansed and set free; it is not the outer freedoms which should be coveted, but on the contrary, the spiritual, personal liberation, and this can only be acquired and appropriated by the human being himself, if his course of life has truth as its basis and point of departure.

Nothing of this is directly stated in this book; but it is my hope that the reader will say it to himself and adopt this view which is at the core of my writing.

30 September 1877 to Elise Aubert
(Norwegian author of novels and short stories.)

Allow me with these lines first of all to thank you and your husband for your most pleasurable company in Stockholm; and then allow me to enclose a copy of my new book, which I wanted you especially to be able to read before it falls into the claws of the masses. I have tried to hold it back for as long as possible; because each time I hand a book over to the bookshop, I have a feeling which I imagine parents must have when they give away their daughter in marriage. It is like a kind of jealousy; you think you no longer fully own what is no longer yours alone.

A Doll's House (1879)

Premiered 21 December 1879, Det Kongelige Teater (the Royal Theatre), Copenhagen.[11]

19 October 1878 Notes for the Modern Tragedy

There are two kinds of spiritual law, two kinds of conscience, one in the man, and quite a different one in the woman. They do not understand each other; but in practical life, the woman is judged according to the law of men, as if she were not a woman but a man.

The wife in the play is in the end at a loss, not knowing what is right or wrong; her natural feeling on the one side and her belief in authority on the other leave her utterly bewildered.

A woman cannot be herself in our contemporary society, it is an exclusively male society, with laws written by men and with prosecutors and judges who judge female behaviour from a male point of view.

She has committed forgery, and it is her pride; she did it out of love for her husband, to save his life. However, this husband stands with all conventional honourableness on the law's ground and looks at the matter with male eyes.

Agony of the soul. Crushed and bewildered by belief in authority, she loses faith in her moral right and her ability to raise her children. Bitterness. A mother in our contemporary society; just as with certain insects, she goes away to die when she has fulfilled her duty to reproduce. Love of life, of home, of husband and children and family. At times, womanlike, she shrugs off her thoughts. Sudden return of angst and fear. She must carry everything alone. The catastrophe is approaching inexorably, inescapably. Despair, struggle and destruction.

[The following was added later in the margin:]

Krogstad has behaved dishonestly, which made him wealthy, but now his prosperity is of no help; he cannot retrieve his honour.

4 July 1879 to Edmund Gosse

I have lived here in Rome with my family since September and during this time have devoted myself to a new dramatic work, which will soon be finished, and which will come out in October. It is a serious play, a family drama really, dealing with current conditions and problems within marriage; the play will be divided into three rather long acts.

2 September 1879 to Frederik Hegel

As this work touches upon problems which must be acknowledged as particularly current, I think you may expect large sales, and I assume you will risk nothing by preparing a rather big edition, so that the book will not be sold out just as the demand is at its liveliest.

15 September 1879 to Frederik Hegel

This much is in any case certain: I cannot remember that any of my books have given me greater satisfaction in the development of the details than this particular one.

October 1879 to the Board of Kungliga Dramatiska Teatern (The Royal Dramatic Theatres), Stockholm

I have the honour herewith to submit my new dramatic work, *A Doll's House*, a play in three acts, respectfully enquiring whether the Board of Kungliga Dramatiska Teatern would consider this play for performance at its dramatic theatre.

In case the Board agrees to proceed, I would like to request that Nora's role must be offered to Mrs Hwasser, as I have great expectations of her performance in this role. I would also be grateful if the elegance and courteous ease which Mr Fredrikson possesses could be put to use in the role of Lawyer Helmer, just as I believe that Doctor Rank's role would be in the best of hands with Mr Elmlund, should Mr Schwartz be unavailable.

16 November 1879 to the Board of the Christiania Theater

It seems to me that my new play [*A Doll's House*], as far as the casting is concerned, is especially suited to Christiania Theater's ensemble of actors. I do not want to offer any suggestions; the casting of the roles should of course always be left to the Board of Directors; but perhaps I may be allowed to mention how I have imagined the casting of the play

[...] The nurse has really only one scene; but for several reasons, I attach great importance to that scene. Besides, I do not believe that many differing opinions about the casting will arise between the administration and me.

The play demands, to a high degree, a natural form of acting and a fast but thoroughly prepared treatment of the dialogue. I hope the director will realise the importance of this, and that he, as well as the actors, will spare no effort when it comes either to studying the roles or staging the play.

3 January 1880 to Erik af Edholm
(Theatre manager and Swedish Officer of the Crown attached
to the Royal Dramatic Theatre in Stockholm.)

It is quite rightly the case, as you assume, that my play's title, *Et
dukkehjem* ('A Dollhome') is a new phrase, which I myself have
made up, and I am very pleased that they will render the phrase
in Swedish in a direct translation.

 The expression 'det vidunderlige' ('the wonderful'), which
Mrs Hvasser [sic] also had the kindness to write to me about,
in Swedish, as far as I can understand, can best be translated as
'det underbara'. The word is a favourite expression that Nora
often makes use of; already in the first act she talks about 'hvor
vidunderlig dejligt det er at leve og være lykkelig' ('how wonderful it is to be alive and happy'), etc.

 Helmer certainly wants to be able to win Nora back. As far as
she is concerned, she can only say that at that moment she does
not and cannot know anything about that; the instant she walks
away from her home is when her life will really begin. You ask if
she plans to get herself new dolls. No. Nora's relationship to
Doctor Rank shows her moral purity in that respect. A further
question being asked is what will happen to the children; who
shall raise them. To that the answer is that there is a big adult child
in the play, Nora, who must go out into life to raise herself, and
as a result, perhaps, will once become fit to raise the small ones—
or perhaps not; no one can know that. But this much is certain,
that with the view Nora has attained of her marriage during that
final night, it would be immoral of her to continue her married
life with Helmer; she cannot do that, and therefore she leaves.

 It is impossible for me to believe that there is anything
offensive in the way in which Helmer expresses his sensuality
after the ball, at any rate it is impossible to leave this out in the
portrayal of such a marriage; it would have been dishonest to
suppress anything here, and I am quite certain that I have not
portrayed the reality any worse than it is in numerous cases.
Moreover, Mr Fredrikson will, with his usual noblesse, know
how to keep this scene within the correct boundaries.

[…]

In Denmark, as you may know, this new play of mine has caused an extremely strong commotion; the parties stand violently head to head; the whole large edition of the book, 8,000 copies, sold out in the course of a fortnight and a new edition has already been printed. However, the conflict is not about the play's aesthetic value, but the moral problem it poses. I knew beforehand that this would meet with objection from many quarters; if our Nordic general public were so far advanced that everyone agreed about this problem, it would have been unnecessary to write the book.

17 February 1880 to the Editor of Nationaltidende

[…] Immediately after *Nora* was published, I received a message from my translator and business manager for the North-German theatres, Mr Wilhelm Lange in Berlin, that he had reason to fear that another translation or 'adaptation' of the play with a changed ending would be published, and that several North German theatres would most likely prefer it.

To prevent such a possibility I sent him a proposal for a change to be used in case of absolute necessity, in which Nora does not manage to leave the house but is forced by Helmer over to the children's bedroom door; here they exchange a couple of lines, Nora sinks down at the door and the curtain falls.

I have myself described this change to my translator as a 'barbaric act of violence' against the play. Thus it is entirely against my wishes to use it; but I entertain the hope that it will not be employed by too many German theatres.

18 February 1880 to Heinrich Laube
(German author, critic, and director at the Stadttheater in Vienna where he presented *A Doll's House* for three nights in 1881.)

You find that the play's ending does not conform to the category we know as 'drama'. But, my dear director Laube, do you really place such a great value on so-called categories? I believe, however, that the dramatic categories are malleable, and that they must be adjusted according to the existing facts of literature, not the other way around. This much is certain, at least, that the play, with the present final scene, has had an almost unprecedented success in Copenhagen as well as in Stockholm and Christiania.

I did not write the changed ending from conviction, but only at the request of a North-German impresario and an actress who is guesting there as Nora. I enclose a copy of this change, from which you will hopefully recognise that the effect of the play can only be weakened by using it. [According to the press reports, Laube used the alternative ending for the second and third performance.]

I therefore suggest that you disregard the changed ending, and bring the original version to your audiences.

The Change:

(See p. 90 in the printed book)

NORA. That we could make a real marriage out of our lives together. Farewell. (*Begins to leave.*)

HELMER. Well then—go! (*Seizes her arm.*) But first you shall see your children for the last time!

NORA. Let me go! I *will* not see them! I *cannot*!

HELMER (*draws her towards the door, left*). You *shall* see them. (*Opens the door and says softly.*) Look, there they sleep, so carefree and calm. Tomorrow, when they wake up and call for their mother, they will be—motherless.

NORA (*trembling*). Motherless...!

HELMER. As you once were.

NORA. Motherless! (*Struggles with herself, lets her travelling bag fall, and says.*) Oh, this is a sin against myself; but I cannot forsake them. (*Half sinks down by the door.*)

HELMER (*joyfully but softly*) Nora!

(*The curtain falls.*)[12]

14 April 1880 to Frederik Hegel

Down here [in Munich], *A Doll's House* has caused the same stir as at home. People have passionately taken sides for or against the play, and it has hardly ever happened before in

Munich that a dramatic work has been so passionately discussed as this.

17 April 1880 to Wilhelm Lange

I was very pleased to learn that Mrs Niemann will already be able to start performing in *Nora* in May, and even more pleased that she has finally decided to perform the play unchanged. This is definitely the only right thing to do. I have experiences here from Munich to support me in this. I doubt there is any other play here which has put the audience in such a powerful emotional state and triggered such passionate discussions as this one. And the reason is essentially the play's ending.

23 January 1891 to Moritz Prozor

(Lithuanian-Polish-Russian diplomat and translator of Ibsen into French. Prozor's alternative ending, which is mentioned in this letter, has been lost.)

I see with regret that Mr Luigi Capuana has caused you quite considerable trouble by his suggestion to change the final scene of *A Doll's House* for use in the Italian theatres.

I do not doubt for a moment that your version would be patently preferable to Mr Capuana's suggestion. The point is, however, that I cannot possibly undertake to give my direct authorisation to any kind of change to the play's conclusion. I can almost say that the whole play is written exactly for the sake of the final scene.

And added to this, I believe Mr Capuana is wrong when he fears that Italian audiences would not be able to understand or approve of my work if it is performed in the theatres in its original form. At least this should be tried. Should it really become clear that it does not work, then Mr Capuana may, on his own responsibility, use your edited ending, but without such a step being formally sanctioned or authorised by me.

In my letter to Mr Capuana, which was sent yesterday, I expressed myself briefly about this matter, and I hope that he drops his reservations until experience has confirmed that they really are justified.

In its time, when *A Doll's House* was quite new, I was forced to give my consent to a change of the ending for Mrs Hedwig Niemann-Raabe, who was to play 'Nora' in Berlin. But at the time, I had no choice. As an author, I had no legal rights in Germany and thus could do nothing to prevent it. And besides, the play was available to the German public in its original form; that is, undistorted, as the German edition was already printed and available in the bookshops. The version with the altered ending did not last long in the repertoire. The unchanged version is still being played.

Recollection of John Paulsen[13]

As a whole, the presentation [at the Königliches Residenz-Theater in Munich] was good—Mrs Maria Ramlo, who played Nora, was particularly excellent—and after the performance, Ibsen thanked all the actors warmly. One was tempted to believe that it was a perfect performance in Ibsen's eyes. But later, when I spoke to Ibsen in his home about the production, which I praised highly, he had more than a few complaints. It was not just that a couple of the performers had only partially understood their roles, but he was also unhappy with the colour of the wallpaper in the living room—it did not create the mood he had wished for. He even complained about tiny matters such as Nora's hands not being right (I cannot remember whether they were too big or too small). (Qtd. in Østvedt 1976, 183.)

11 June 1870 to Laura Petersen (Kieler)
(Norwegian/Danish author.)

Please accept my most sincere gratitude for the courtesy you have payed me by dedicating your book (*Brands døtre: et livsbillede af Lili*) to me.[14] However, if you expect me to express an opinion about the work, I would find myself in a somewhat embarrassing situation. You want the book to be understood as one of edification, or religion, and I am not in a position to judge that kind of literature. What has appealed to and interested me is the character description together with your unmistakable talent for creative writing. But whether this is praise in your eyes, I would not know.

[...]

Are you thinking of pursuing the career of an author? For that, you need something more than natural talent. You must have something to write about, a depth of life experience. Without that, you do not create, you only write books. Now, I know very well that a life of loneliness is not a vacuous life. But the human being is, in the spiritual sense, a long-sighted creature; we see most clearly at a distance. Details disturb; you have to get a distance between yourself and what you want to judge. Summer is best described on a winter's day.

26 March 1878 to Laura Kieler

I neither can, nor will in any way recommend 'Ultima Thule', the manuscript you sent to me, to Hegel. You will not remain anonymous in the small Danish circles, and such a rushed and in every respect botched piece of work would destroy your literary name and credentials for a long time, and rightly so. The whole story is without a trace of probability, credibility and reality. I can understand that you might have written something like this; but I find it incomprehensible that your husband did not resolutely oppose the publication of something so unfinished. Surely he must see it as his duty and obligation to protect your talent; this must be his natural inclination. He cannot possibly do anything but encourage you to work slowly and deliberately, and only proceed with fully matured plans. But then you act irresponsibly towards yourself by not following his advice. You write in your letter about conditions which make this hurried work necessary. I do not understand that. In a family where the husband is alive, it can never be necessary that the wife, such as you, drains her spiritual heart-blood. Neither do I understand that you are allowed to. Your letter must hide something which totally changes the context; that is the impression I have by reading it several times. If I am wrong, if matters really are how you describe them, then you must pull yourself together and put an end to this. It is inconceivable that your husband knows all about it; so you must tell him; he must take upon himself the worries and concerns which now torment and haunt you into anxiety.[15]

2 August 1878 to Frederik Hegel

A sad catastrophe happened to Mrs Laura Kieler, as you probably know. Her husband informed us quite briefly that she was admitted to a mental hospital. Do you know anything else about these circumstances and whether she is still there?

8 October 1878 to Frederik Hegel

P.S. Should you have any information to impart re Mrs Kieler the next time you write to me, I should be extremely interested.

1 July 1890 to Fredrika Limnell
(Swedish philanthropist and pioneer feminist.)

I am not totally clear about what Laura Kieler actually aims at when she tries to get *me* involved in these disputes. A statement from me like the one she wants, namely 'that she is *not* Nora', would be both meaningless and ridiculous, as I have never alleged the opposite. If untruthful rumours have been spread up there in Copenhagen that at an earlier point in her life something happened which has a kind of likeness with the promissory note in *A Doll's House*, then she herself or her husband, preferably together, are the only ones who, through an open and resolute denial, can destroy the false rumours.[16] I cannot comprehend that Mr Kieler did not adopt this solution a long time ago as something that would have immediately put an end to this slander.

I am genuinely sorry that I cannot comply with your request that I intervene in this. But I believe that you, by considering this matter more closely, considering all aspects of it and keeping the details in mind as far as these may be known to you, will agree with me when I say that the best support I can offer our mutual friend is to remain silent and stay out of it.

Ghosts (1881)

Premiered 20 May 1882, Aurora Turner Hall, Chicago.[17]

Working notes for Ghosts

The play will be like an image of life. Faith undermined. But it is not possible to say so. 'The Orphanage'—for the sake of others. They will be happy, but this, too, is just an appearance. Everything is ghosts.

A main point: She has been a believer and a romantic; this is not totally erased by the standpoint she later gains: 'Everything is ghosts.'

To marry for external reasons, even religious or moral, brings a Nemesis upon the offspring.

She, the illegitimate child, may be saved by marrying—the son—but then—?

[…]

These contemporary women, mistreated as daughters, sisters, wives, not brought up in accordance with their talent, kept away from their calling, robbed of their inheritance, embittered in their minds,—these are ones who become the mothers of the next generation. What is the result?

The keynote will be: Our strong flourishing intellectual life in literature, the arts, etc; and then in contrast: the whole of mankind gone astray.

The complete human being is no longer a product of nature, he is an artificial product, just like wheat, and fruit trees, and the Creole race and the thoroughbred horses and dogs, vines, etc.

The fault lies in the fact that all humankind has failed. When human beings demand to live and develop humanly, it's megalomania. The whole of humankind, and especially the Christians, suffer from megalomania.

Here we erect monuments over the *dead*; because we have duties towards them; we allow lepers to marry; but their offspring—? The unborn—? (HU, vol. 9, 136–7.)

23 November 1881 to Frederik Hegel

Ghosts will most likely cause alarm in some circles; but, so be it. If it did not, it would not have been necessary to write it.

22 December 1881 to Ludwig Passarge

My new play has now come out and has aroused a terrible uproar in the Scandinavian press. I receive letters and newspaper articles for and against it on a daily basis. A copy will be sent to you shortly; however, I believe it would be totally impossible to get this play produced by a German theatre at this moment; I hardly think they would dare to stage it in the Scandinavian countries in the near future. However, 10,000 copies of the play have been printed, and it looks very likely that a new impression will be required before long.

24 December 1881 to Erik Bøgh

(Bøgh worked as a literary advisor at the Royal Theatre in Copenhagen from 1881 to 1899. He advised against the acceptance of *Ghosts* for production.)

What pleases me amid all the opposition is that the Danish papers' opinions, as far as I have seen, have been made in a civilised, humane and polite tone, without all the journalistic crudities they seem to consider indispensable in that certain other country in the North [Norway]. Nor in Copenhagen would such recensions be written by anonymous theologians. On the whole, Denmark has more and more adopted the laudable custom that writers sign their name. And that is welcome. To me it seems something quite bandit-like to direct an attack against someone named, while concealing one's own name. I do not understand how anyone with a sense of honour can stoop to such a thing.

3 January 1882 to Georg Brandes

Yesterday I had the great pleasure of receiving from Hegel your excellent and perspicacious, and to me so complimentary, review of *Ghosts*. Please accept my warmest and most whole-hearted gratitude for this inestimable favour you have once more shown me! Anyone who reads your article must surely have their eyes opened to what I have intended with my new book, if they want to see it at all. For I cannot free myself from the thought that an exceptionally large number of the false interpretations published in the papers have been offered against better judgement. But I do believe that in Norway this utter nonsense has, in most cases, been unintentional; and it has an obvious explanation. Because up there, the reviews are partly in the hands of a few more or less disguised theologians; and these gentlemen are usually utterly incapable of writing rationally about literature. The weakening of their powers of judgement, which, at least in the case of the average person, is an inevitable result of a prolonged pursuit of theological stud-ies, reveals itself especially in their judgement of human character, human actions and human motives. Practical busi-ness judgement, however, does not suffer so much from those studies. Therefore the ecclesiastical gentlemen are very often excellent municipal servants; but they are unquestionably our worst critics.

6 January 1882 to Sophus Schandorph
(Danish novelist and poet.)

I was quite prepared for the uproar. If certain of our Scandina-vian reviewers have no talent for anything else, at least they have an incontestable talent for thoroughly misunderstanding and misinterpreting the authors whose books they accept to judge.

[...]

They try to make me responsible for the meanings expressed by certain of the play's characters. Yet there is not in the whole book a single opinion, a single utterance, which may be laid at the door of the author. I made sure of that. The method, the very technique upon which the book was based simply, of itself, prohibited the author's presence in the dialogue. My intention was to provoke in the reader the impression of experiencing something real. But nothing would more effectively counteract this intention than injecting authorial opinions into the dialogue. And do they not believe at home that I possess enough dramaturgical judgement to realise this? Yes, I have realised it, and I have acted accordingly. In none of my plays is the author so much of an outsider, so utterly absent, as in this one.

Then it has been said that the book preaches nihilism. Not at all. It does not preach anything. It merely points to the nihilism which is fermenting below the surface, at home as elsewhere. And that is how it must be. A Pastor Manders will always provoke some Mrs Alving or other. And just because she is a woman, she will, once she has started, go to great extremes.

28 January 1882 to Otto Borchsenius
(Danish author and editor.)

Of course, this play may be somewhat daring in several respects. But I thought the time had come to move a few frontier posts. And it would be so much easier for an older writer like myself to execute that business than the many younger authors who might wish to do something similar. I was prepared for a storm to roll over me; but one cannot veer from one's course because of things like that.

16 March 1882 to Frederik Hegel

As far as *Ghosts* is concerned, I think the disposition of the good people at home will become more understanding, and within a short time. But all these dilapidated old fuddy-duddies who have attacked my writing the way they have will eventually receive a shattering verdict in the literary history of the future. People will know how to trace the anonymous poachers and marauders who have ambushed me with arrows of abuse in Professor Goos' huckster journal and other similar places. My book belongs to the future. Those fellows who have hollered over it do not even have a genuine relationship with their own contemporary reality.

And that is why I have taken this side of the matter with such cold-bloodedness. I have made many studies and observations during the storm, which I shall make good use of in future writings.

22 June 1882 to Jonas Lie
(Norwegian lawyer and author.)

Thank you too for the letters which pleased me so much when the war against *Ghosts* was raging at its worst. It did go as you wrote then; the storm has subsided, and there are many signs of a more sober-minded view of the book. In Sweden it has produced a whole literature of brochures and journal articles. The Norwegians showed themselves to be the most cowardly of all as usual; and the most cowardly among the cowardly were, of course, the so-called liberals. They ran for their lives to disavow the merest suspicion of any form of agreement with me.

Anecdote quoted by Francis Bull
(Norwegian professor of literature.)

They say that King Oscar II, at a party for Ibsen at Stockholm's castle in 1898, said to the guest of honour: 'But you should not have written *Ghosts*, Ibsen! It is not a good play; but *Lady Inger*, now, that is a good play.' Ibsen became self-conscious and quiet, Queen Sophie tried to save him from the embarrassing situation by talking about other things, but after a long pause Ibsen burst out: 'Your Majesty, I *had to* write *Ghosts!*' (HU, vol. 9, 13.)

24 June 1882 to Sophie Adlersparre
(Author and leading figure in the Swedish women's rights movement.)

In the middle of the storm of ill will and objections raised against my latest drama from so many directions, and the abundance of misinterpretations it has been subjected to, I could not have wished for more welcome support than the interpretation and elucidation from such a richly gifted and highly esteemed woman.

I feel assured that you, with your lecture, have made hundreds of spectators and readers regard my work with clearer eyes than before. Your lecture deals with so many of the issues I wanted to air; and it is all presented in a form which has greatly pleased me, and at the same time deeply honoured me. It would be too complex to enter into details. I shall only remark on one thing: I totally agree with you that I do not dare to go further than I do in *Ghosts*. I myself have felt that the general conscience in our home countries refuses to permit it, and I do not feel a particular incentive to go any further. An author does not dare to distance himself so far from his people that there is no longer any understanding between them and him. But *Ghosts* had to be written; I could not stop with *A Doll's House*; after Nora, Mrs Alving simply had to come.

2 August 1883 to August Lindberg
(Swedish actor manager.)

[…] I have had grave doubts about how to answer your suggestion of obtaining the rights to stage *Ghosts* in Copenhagen and Stockholm.

I can with some certainty predict that the royal theatres in those capital cities will ask in the near future for permission to perform this play. But it is a matter of course that the conditions I can then expect to obtain will be far less favourable if the play has already been performed there.

On the other hand, I entertain the hope, strengthened by the information from you, that you will give my work an interesting and sophisticated production; and I do not doubt that the play's spirit and tone will be understood, respected and depicted without reneging on the full, ruthless truthfulness it requires.

I will therefore confine myself to placing the following terms: 500 kroner for the rights to stage it in Copenhagen; 400 for the same rights in Stockholm. These honoraria shall, as usual, be paid in advance to Gyldendal [Ibsen's publisher] (Councillor Hegel) in Copenhagen.

Should you agree to these conditions, no other director will be given the right to stage the play if this should collide with your interests.

13 November 1886 to Duke Georg II of Meiningen[18]
(The innovations introduced by Georg II at the Saxe-Meiningen Theatre had a profound impact on European nineteenth-century theatre practice.)

I have received the information from your highness about the forthcoming production of my play *Ghosts* with great pleasure. Allow me to express my deepest thank you to you and your wife for the invitation. I shall certainly not fail to be in Meiningen on time for the performance.

These days, the interior composition of the Norwegian country house usually does not express any particular national characteristics. The living room of the oldest family house of this type is sometimes covered with coloured, dark wallpaper. Below is the wainscoting of plain parquet wood. The ceilings as well as the doors and the window frames are all of the same white. The stoves are large, heavy and typically of cast iron. The furniture is rich, in the style of the first French Empire; but the colours are darker throughout.

This is roughly how I have imagined the living room in Mrs Alving's house.

5 January 1887 to Frederik Hegel

I leave the day after tomorrow, this time I go to Berlin, where *Ghosts* is to be performed at the Residenz-Theater on Sunday the ninth. I would rather stay at home; however, after the many invitations I have received, I cannot refuse to put in an appearance, especially as *Ghosts* has become a burning literary and dramatic topic in Germany.

6 May 1890 to Rodolphe Darzens
(French author. He translated *Ghosts* for the Théâtre Libre in Paris.)

The word 'håndsrekning' [helping hand] does not have a double meaning. It merely denotes an obliging assistance in case of need. Osvald reflects that he must be assured that there is someone who is willing to give him the poison if he should be unable to take it himself.

From William Archer to his brother, Charles Archer

Then of course we got on *Gengangere* [*Ghosts*]. He [Ibsen] said: 'The people in the North are terrible. I write a play with five characters and they insist on putting in a sixth—namely Ibsen. There never was a play with less utterance of personal opinion in it.' Then he went on to say that his idea had been to show, in Fru Alving, how a badly educated, badly trained woman was certain to be driven, by men of Pastor Manders' way of thought and feeling, into opposite extremes. [...] Then I asked him right out: 'How do you figure to yourself what occurs after the curtain falls? Does she give her son the poison or not?' He laughed, and said in his unctuous, deliberate drawl: 'That I don't know. Every one must work that out for himself. I should never dream of deciding such a difficult question. Now, what do *you* think?' I said that if she did not 'come to the rescue', it was no doubt the result of a genganger, a ghost, still 'walking' in her—always assuming, I added, that the disease was ascertained to be absolutely incurable. He said he thought the solution perhaps lay there: that the mother would always put off and put off 'coming to the rescue,' on the plea that while there is life, there is hope. (Qtd. in 1906, 7.)

An Enemy of the People (1882)

Premiered 13 January 1883, Christiania Theater (Oslo).[19]

16 March 1882 to Frederik Hegel

I can inform you that for the moment I am fully preoccupied with the preparations for a new play. This time it will be a peaceable play, which may be read by the cabinet ministers and wholesalers as well as their ladies, and which the theatres will not have to retreat from. It will be a very easy task for me to complete, and I shall make sure I finish it in the early autumn.

21 June 1882 to Frederik Hegel

I completed my new play yesterday. It is called *An Enemy of the People* and is in five acts. I am still uncertain whether I should call the play a comedy or a drama; it has many characteristics of a comedy about it, but also a serious fundamental idea.

9 September 1882 to Frederik Hegel

I had fun working on this play, and I have feelings of loss and emptiness now that I have finished it. Doctor Stockmann and I got on excellently with each other; we agree on so many subjects. But the doctor's head is messier than mine, and besides, he has quite a few other peculiarities which make people accept things from his mouth which they probably would not accept from mine.

Recollection from P.A. Rosenberg

Martinius Nielsen said: 'The Doctor [Ibsen] has after all said that the strongest man in the world is he who stands most alone.'

'Now wait a second', Ibsen answered, '*When* did I say that?'
'In *An Enemy of the People.*'
'Is it not Stockmann who says that line?'
'Ye-es…'
'I am not responsible for all the nonsense he comes up with.'

'No, but one does, through the course of action in the play, get a distinct impression of where the Doctor's sympathies lie,' Nielsen said.

'Do you think you can know that?' Ibsen answered, 'You might be wrong.'

'Very well,' Nielsen answered, 'but the Doctor has in at least one place uttered his meaning, his sympathies and antipathies.'

'Where?' he asked sharply.
'In the lyrical poems.'

Ibsen paused for a moment, and then said with an unfathomable smile: 'Yes, those small devils should never have been put in print.' […]

'No you see,' Ibsen said, 'I can be likened to a chemist, who has familiarity with substances and awaits the result. Often my characters surprise me by doing or saying things I had not expected of them; yes, they can sometimes turn my original plan upside-down, those Satans. A writer must *listen* into his work; you see, it is a complete misunderstanding that he can "command the poetry"; on the contrary, it is the poetry that commands him.' (HU, vol. 19, 217.)

13 December 1882 to the Board of Kungliga Dramatiska Teatern (The Royal Dramatic Theatres), Stockholm

I expect that the translation [into Swedish] will be done by a skilled literary person, and that the play's rehearsals and staging will be carried out with the utmost care. Similarly, I must insist that all the minor roles in the fourth act, at the people's meeting, will be performed by real, accomplished artists and not by subordinate persons at the theatre. The more characteristic, authentic figures in the crowd, the better.

A Swedish newspaper, which printed a précis of the play's content, has misunderstood one of the characters, something I now direct your attention to. The newspaper describes 'Captain Horster' as an 'old' man, an 'old' friend of the doctor's, etc. This is totally wrong; Captain Horster is a *young* man; he is one of 'the young people' whom Doctor Stockmann says he likes to see in his house. The short dialogue between Horster and Petra in the fifth act must be played in such a way that we sense the beginning of a warm and sincere relationship between these two.

14 December 1882 to Hans Schrøder
(Norwegian educator and director of the Christiania Theater.)

Allow me to send you a few lines on the occasion of the approaching rehearsals of *An Enemy of the People*.

Naturally, it is not my intention to extend any influence either on the staging of the play or the casting from afar; however, a few words as to my thoughts about one or two things surely cannot hurt.

I dare take it as a given that Mrs Wolf and no one else will play Mrs Stockmann. Mrs Wolf is without doubt the one actress at the Christiania Theater who best possesses what is required to portray this character in the way in which I have seen and depicted it.

As for Hovstad's role, if you have an otherwise acceptable actor of not too heroic bodily proportions, he should be chosen. Hovstad descends from poor smallholder people, has grown up in an unhealthy home, with bad and insufficient nutrition, has suffered from the cold and worked hard all his childhood, and later, as a poor young man, he suffered much privation. Such living conditions leave their mark, not just on the inner personality and the outer physique. Heroic characters of plebeian descent are rare exceptions in reality. In any circumstance, Hovstad must have something heavy about him, something crumpled or stooping in his posture, something uncertain in his movements; but all this, of course, portrayed with full truthfulness.

Billing's lines are formed in such a way that they demand a dialect from the eastern part of Norway; not, for example, from Bergen. For he is more an east-Norwegian character.

A Danish critic has, laughably, been completely wrong about Captain Horster. The critic describes him as an old man, as Dr Stockmann's old friend, etc. This is of course, quite mistaken. Horster is a young man, one of the young people whose good appetite the doctor is pleased about, but who does not often come to his house because he does not like the company of Hovstad and Billing. Horster's interest in Petra must shine through finely and lightly in the first act and during the brief dialogue between him and her in the fifth act, we should sense that they stand at the beginning of a warm and heartfelt relationship.

Both boys must be rehearsed tirelessly until the differences in their natures are clearly portrayed.

I must ask that all available actors, without exception, are employed in the fourth act. The director must instil the greatest possible natural truthfulness here, and strictly forbid any exaggerated caricatures. The more characteristic and distinctively realistic the figures are, the better.

Throughout the play, and as far as every single role is concerned, the direction must relentlessly ensure that the lines are not misrepresented. They must sound exactly the way they are written in the book. A lively tempo is desirable. The last time I was at the Christiania Theater the delivery seemed dragging to me.

But above all, truthfulness; the illusion that everything is real and the audience is watching something which takes place in real life.

An Enemy of the People is not easy to stage. It demands an extremely well-rehearsed collaboration, therefore many diligently directed rehearsals. But I trust everybody's goodwill, and there is no shortage of artistic talents at the Christiania Theater.

24 December 1882 to Hans Schrøder

Morgenbladet has published a statement about the casting of *An Enemy of the People*. And on that occasion, I must once more trouble you with a few lines.

I see that Mr Gundersen is to play the Mayor. This actor's looks are certainly not suited for a character who cannot even think about eating a hot meal for supper, whose stomach is delicate, who suffers from bad digestion and lives on thin tea-water. Neither does it greatly suit a man who is described as good-looking, refined and meticulous. However, these deficiencies may partly be made up for by appropriate make-up and costuming. Therefore, Mr Gundersen must pay great attention to these two things.

Neither does Mr [Arnoldus] Reimers' physical build harmonise with a temperament like Dr Stockmann's; fiery people are usually more slight of build. So as far as Mr Reimers is concerned, the same request goes for him as for Mr Gundersen. He must make himself as thin and as small as possible.

I do not know Mr Hansson, but from everything I hear about him, I do not doubt he will be able to portray Hovstad's role satisfactorily.

However, I must object strongly to Mr H. Brun playing Horster. I refer to everything I said in my previous letter about this role, and request that it is given to Mr Schancke, and that he will be made acquainted with the way I want this role perceived and played.

I have no objection to the rest of the casting. Mr Selmer will certainly be right for Billing; this character's repetitive phrase 'damn me' must not be stressed, it must come out as just another expression he does not think about. I do not know Miss Gjems; but I place great importance on the role of Petra being performed correctly and with fully credible truthfulness.

12 June 1883 to Georg Brandes

As far as *An Enemy of the People* is concerned, I believe we would find much common ground once we had an opportunity to discuss it. Of course you are right when you say that we *must* all work to spread our ideas. However, I maintain that an intellectual vanguard-fighter *can* never gather the majority around him. In ten years' time, the majority may have arrived at the position Stockmann held at the public meeting. But of course, the doctor has not been standing still during those ten years; he will still be at least ten years ahead of the majority; the majority, the mob, the crowd, will never catch up with him; he can never be supported by the majority. Personally, at least, I can sense such a never-ending progression. Where I stood when I wrote my different books, there now stands a fairly compact crowd; but I am no longer there; I am somewhere else, further ahead, I hope.

2 August 1883 to August Lindberg

It is especially important to me that the translation is made with the greatest possible care. From what was told me by a competent and outstanding Swedish critic, this was far from the case with the translation of *An Enemy of the People* that was used by the Kungliga Dramatiska Teatern [the Royal Dramatic Theatres in Stockholm]. The Norwegian text was misunderstood in many places, and was rendered in a bad, heavy and forced language in other places, and with expressions and turns of phrase which do not exist in day-to-day spoken Swedish.

The language has to sound natural, and each character in the play has to have his or her characteristic manner of speaking; one human being does not express himself the same way as another. In that regard, much can be corrected during rehearsals; there it is easy to hear what does not sound natural and unforced, and thus what has to be changed and changed again until the line sounds totally true and authentic. The effect of the play depends to a large degree on making the audience believe that they are sitting and listening and watching something which happens out there in real life.

Ibsen on Politics

The Women's Question and Social Democracy

23 March 1884 to Bjørnstjerne Bjørnson[20]

If the majority of the Parliament had supported Berner's motion with honest intent, they would not have sent it out to the Municipal Councils for deliberation. They would not have asked the men for a declaration at all, only the women. To consult men in such a matter is the same as asking the wolves if they support increased protection for the sheep.

Oh no, the minority of our people, who possess all the political, communal and social privileges, will not voluntarily let them slip through their fingers or share them with the unprivileged majority. That is why I predict the result of the suffrage proposals with such certainty. None of them will attract a sufficient number of votes. Such things are not simply handed over by their owners, they must be fought for.

[...]

If I could have my way at home, all the unprivileged people would unite and form a strong, resolute and aggressive party, whose programme would be directed exclusively towards practical and productive reforms; a very wide extension of suffrage, the regulation of women's position, the liberation of public education from all sorts of medievalism, etc.

14 June 1885 speech to the Working Men of Trondheim

A majority of the ruling elite neither grants the individual freedom of belief or freedom of speech beyond an arbitrarily set boundary.

So there is much more to be done before we can say that we have reached true freedom. But I fear that our current democracy will not be able to solve these tasks. An element of nobility has to enter our public life, our administration, our representative bodies, and our press.

Obviously, I am not referring to the nobility of *birth*, nor that of *wealth*, nor the nobility of *knowledge*, not even that of *ability* or talent. I am thinking of the nobility of *character*, the nobility of will and spirit.

Nothing else can liberate us.

This nobility, which I hope our people will be given, will come to us from two sources. It will come to us from two groups, which have still not been irreparably damaged by party pressures. It will come to us from our women and from our workers.

The transformation of social conditions which is now under way in Europe deals primarily with the future positions of workers and women.

This is the transformation I hope for and wait for, and which I will work for and shall continue to work for all my life, with all my heart.

26 May 1898 speech to the Norwegian Women's Rights League

I am not a member of the Women's Rights League. My works have not been written with a conscious political tendency in mind. I have been more a poet and less a social philosopher than everyone seems inclined to believe. Thank you for the toast, but I must renounce the honour of having worked consciously for the Women's cause. I am not even fully aware of what the Women's cause really is. To me, it has been a human cause. And if you read my books carefully, you will understand that. It is desirable to solve the Woman Question, along with other problems; but it has not been the whole intention. My task has been the *portrayal of human beings*. And when this portrayal is fairly accurate, the reader will invest it with his or her feelings and moods. They ascribe these feelings to the author; but no, that is not so. They nicely re-write it, each according to their own personality. Not only those who write, but also those who read create; they are co-writers, often with more imagination than the author himself.

[...]

It is up to the mothers to awaken a conscious feeling of *culture* and *discipline* through arduous and slow work. This must be created in the human individual before we can lift the people to a higher level. It is the women who shall solve the Human Question. They will do it as mothers. And only as such can they do it. Here lies a great task for the women.

13 August 1890 interview quoted in the Pall Mall Gazette

[Ibsen] declared that he never at any time had belonged to the Social Democratic Party. He never had studied the Social Democratic question, nor does he intend to join the Social Democratic Party at a future date. In fact, he declared he never was nor ever would be a Social Democrat. He was surprised to find his name used as a means for the propagation of the Social Democratic dogmas. If a mere accidental coincidence of certain tendencies or principles involved in his book *Nora* with regard to matrimonial and woman questions are [sic] identical with or cover certain planks of the Social Democratic platform, his *Nora* is not, he explained, an abstract hypothesis conceived to demonstrate certain party dogmas, but was taken from life.[21] Nora existed; but he never intended to lay down a hard and fast rule that all women in a similar position to Nora should or must act like Nora (p. 6).

From William Archer to his brother, Charles Archer

You would see from Shaw's letter which I sent to you that Ibsen was supposed to be infuriated at having been classed as a Socialist by G.B.S. He explained to me, however, that his rage existed only in the imagination of the *Daily Chronicle* interviewer. What he really said was that he never had belonged, and probably never would belong, to any party whatsoever; but he expressed himself as pleasantly surprised to find that English Socialists, working on scientific lines, had arrived at conclusions similar to his. This the *Chronicle* interviewer (a Berlin Jew) twisted into an expression of unpleasant surprise that anyone should have the audacity to make use of his name in Socialist propaganda. The Old Man was quite put out about this, for the thing had got into the German and Danish papers too [as well as the *Pall Mall Gazette* in London]. While I was with him he received a letter from Vollmar, one of the Socialist leaders in the Reichstag, and a friend of his, asking him what the devil he meant by this seemingly contemptuous disclaimer, not only of Socialism, but of all sympathy with Socialism. Ibsen had already written a letter to Brækstad, intended for the English papers; and he forthwith sat down to write a German translation of this letter for Vollmar.

Fru Ibsen [Ibsen's wife, Suzannah] and he had an amusing little scene apropos of this incident. She said, 'I warned you when that man came from Berlin that you would put your foot in it. You should have let me see him; women are much more cautious than men in what they say.' Whereupon the Old Man smiled grimly, and said that wasn't generally supposed to be the strong point of the sex; adding that since the interviewer was going to lie about what he said, it didn't much matter whether he was cautious or not. Then Fru Ibsen suggested that he ought not to have seen him at all, and I closed the discussion by assuring her in that case he would have made up the interview entirely from his inner consciousness. (Qtd. in 1906, 15.)

23 February 1872 from Camilla Collett to her son, Alf Collett
(Norwegian author and pioneer of Norwegian feminism.)

He is an egotist from head to toe, and above all as a man in his relation to women. His situation at home has had no influence at all on him. Note all his heroes: *despots* every one of them in their dealings with women. Even for that repulsive creation Peer Grynt [sic] some noble woman has to stand by ready to drag him up out of the muck, i.e. sacrifice herself for him. Imagine our arguments, Alf! He'll remember it for sure. I don't think anyone, not even men, have ever said to him the kind of things I wasn't afraid to say. He listened… I can't make him out. For me he's the one among our geniuses whose life has had the *least* impact in bringing him to a truthful way of looking at things. Because of this and despite his talents, he's on the wrong track. He's always lived like a hermit. (Qtd. in Ferguson 1996, 234.)

17 January 1883 to Camilla Collett[22]

Ideas grow and proliferate slowly with us up there in the north; however unnoticeable, progress is being made. The Norway now in development will always carry traces of what your spirit has worked and paved the way for. You are one of the fighters whom posterity will place in the forefront of the road to progress, as necessary preconditions of its development.

On the Rule of the Majority

17 February 1871 to Georg Brandes

I will never agree to making liberty synonymous with political liberty. What you call liberty, I call liberties; and what I call the fight for liberty is nothing but the constant, living acquisition of the very idea of liberty. He who possesses liberty as something already achieved instead of something to seek after, to him it is dead and soulless, because the essence of the idea of liberty is surely that it constantly keeps expanding through acquisition. Thus, if someone stops during the fight and says: 'Now I have it', he demonstrates that he has lost it. But it is exactly this dead acceptance of a given acquisition of liberty which is characteristic of the political *state*; and that is what I said is not a good thing. Yes, it may certainly be a good thing to possess liberty of choice, of taxation, etc; but for whom is it a good thing? The citizen, not the individual. However, it is not at all a logical necessity for the individual to be a citizen. On the contrary. The state is the curse of the individual. How did the Prussian state buy its strength? By subsuming the individual under the political and geographical concept. The waiter is the best soldier. And on the other hand, the Jewish people: the aristocracy of the human race. How has it preserved itself in isolation, in poetry, despite all the brutality from the outside world? By not having a state to drag it down. If the Jewish people had remained in Palestine, it would long ago have perished in the name of its construction, just like all other nations. The state must be abolished! That is a revolution I will take part in. Undermine the idea of the state; establish voluntary, free will and its spiritual affinities as the only essential elements for a union—that constitutes the beginnings of a liberty worth something.

3 January 1882 to Georg Brandes

And what can one say about the current state of the so-called liberal press? These leaders, who speak and write about freedom and tolerance and who at the same time make themselves slaves of their subscribers' assumed opinions! I see more and more proof that there is something demoralising in the pursuit of politics and in joining parties. Under no circumstances could I join a party which has the majority on its side. Bjørnson says: the majority is always right. And as a practical politician I suppose he is bound to say that. I, on the other hand, must necessarily say: the minority is always right. Of course I am not thinking of the minority of the stagnationists who have been left behind by the great middle-party, which we call the liberals; I mean the minority that goes in front where the majority has not yet arrived. What I mean is that he is right who is in the closest alliance with the future.

[…]

To me, liberty is the highest and primary condition of life. At home, they do not worry too much about liberty, only about liberties, a few more or a few less, all depending on their party's standpoint. I also feel highly embarrassed by this rudimentary, this common nature of our public debates. The praiseworthy efforts to make our nation a democratic society have inadvertently moved a long way towards making us a plebeian society. The nobility of mind and spirit seems to be in decline at home.

1. Ibsen's strategies for controlling copyright in non-Scandinavian theatres are discussed in Chapter 6.
2. Following IbsenStage, we use William Archer's mistranslation *A Doll's House* rather than the literal translation *A Doll Home*.
3. ibsenstage.hf.uio.no/pages/event/78247
4. ibsenstage.hf.uio.no/pages/event/78275
5. ibsenstage.hf.uio.no/pages/event/88655
6. ibsenstage.hf.uio.no/pages/event/78077
7. Complete record for August Lindberg:
    ibsenstage.hf.uio.no/pages/contributor/431148
8. ibsenstage.hf.uio.no/pages/event/78163
9. ibsenstage.hf.uio.no/pages/event/78156
10. ibsenstage.hf.uio.no/pages/event/78003
11. ibsenstage.hf.uio.no/pages/event/75660
12. Translated from the German.
13. Ibsen attended rehearsals and saw the first night of this production at the Königliches Residenz-Theater in Munich on 3 March 1880:
    ibsenstage.hf.uio.no/pages/event/77203
14. Kieler's book, inspired by *Brand*, was titled, *Brands døtre: et livsbillede af Lili* ('Brand's Daughters: A Life Portrait of Lili').
15. It appears that Kieler took Ibsen's advice and burnt her manuscript; however, she later published two short stories both with the subtitle 'A Story from "Ultima Thule"'.
16. Rumours linking Keiler to *A Doll's House* began soon after the publication of the play. Her concern was not that her life had been one of the probable sources for the play, but the implication that she had committed forgery. Ibsen refused to become involved in the issue for the reasons he states in this letter.
17. ibsenstage.hf.uio.no/pages/event/78077
18. Translated from the German.
19. ibsenstage.hf.uio.no/pages/event/78084

20. Ibsen was one of the signatories to a public letter (together with Bjørnson, Jonas Lie and Alexander L. Kielland) that was sent to Parliament in support of Hagbard Berner's motion for a Married Women's Property Act. It stated that 'it is in the interest of society that the married woman as soon as possible stops being legally under-age'. Letter dated April 1884. Parliament decided to send the proposal out to all the Norwegian Municipal councils to get their opinion, and 505 of the 525 Councils decided that the status quo, in which married women were without financial independence of their husbands, was the natural order.

21. Originally published in Germany, this interview followed the German convention of using *Nora* as the title of *A Doll's House*.

22. On 23 January 1883 Camilla Collett was to celebrate her seventieth birthday. The occasion was celebrated by many women, but went largely unnoticed in the official, male Norwegian public. Collett took the men's silence as a demonstration, but was pleased to receive some letters from 'strong men who can stand alone', among them Ibsen. These letters were made public in the journal *Ny Illustreret Tidende*.

5
Late Plays:
from *The Wild Duck* to
When We Dead Awaken

The Wild Duck was the last play that Ibsen wrote in Rome; after a short visit to Norway, he moved to Munich (1885) where he lived for the next seven years. With his late plays, Ibsen settled into a rhythm of producing one new play every two years, the only interruption being the three years that separated *John Gabriel Borkman* (1896) from *When We Dead Awaken* (1899); this was a consequence of the major celebrations held in Kristiania, Copenhagen and Stockholm for Ibsen's seventieth birthday.

In 1891, Ibsen returned to Norway. Hildur Andersen helped him decorate and furnish his new Kristiania apartment on Victoria Terrasse (his closeness to her fuelled unfounded local rumours of a pending divorce). He wrote *The Master Builder* and *Little Eyolf* at Victoria Terrasse, before moving to his last home in Arbins gate. Increasingly he was treated as a celebrity, and his contribution to the development of Norwegian culture was publicly acknowledged at the opening of the new Nationaltheatret in 1899. At the opening ceremony, he shared the limelight with Bjørnson, and statues of both men were unveiled in front of the new theatre. He saw the last performance given at the old Christiania Theater: it was *Pillars of Society*; and the first performance at the new Nationaltheatret the night after the gala opening, *An Enemy of the People*. The following year, his health deteriorated, and after a series of strokes, he died in 1906.

The more successful Ibsen became, the less he wrote about his creative work in his letters (while the plays themselves became more self-reflexive). With productions assured in major European venues, there was no necessity for him to explain his intentions to artistic managements, translators or producers. This chapter relies on anecdotal reports from Ibsen's acquaintances to surmise his thoughts, particularly about his last four plays. The lack of evidence about Ibsen's creative intentions has led to speculation regarding the influence of his emotional life on the characters and relationships depicted in his late plays. Although he made it quite clear in an interview with *Politiken* in 1897 that he had 'never referred to particular persons in any of his plays' (qtd. in Seip 1936, 33), this chapter includes extracts from Ibsen's letters that suggest connections between his characters and an intimate circle of family and friends.

Although Ibsen argued that his oeuvre should be viewed as a 'continuous and coherent whole' ('To the Reader', March 1898), when he sent the manuscript of *The Wild Duck* to his publisher in 1884, he signalled that the play represented a significant new development as 'the approach and method differ in various respects from my earlier works' (Hegel 1884). Scholars have tended to define this methodological shift as the increasing use of symbolism within the realist dramaturgy of his late plays. In a discussion with Henrik Jæger, he suggested that the image of white horses in *Rosmersholm* was intentionally added to the play to introduce an element of mysticism to the work. Yet his views about the importance of incorporating layers of symbolic meaning within characterisations and dramaturgical structures can be traced right back to a theatre review from the 1850s. He argues that symbolic meanings within plays should wind 'hidden through the work like the silver vein in a mountain' and not 'be thrust into the light of day'. The audience can be trusted to discern these meanings from both the characterisations and the overarching dramatic idea; there is no need for actors to draw attention to the symbolic content by indicating: '"Look here, this is the meaning—this is the significance of what you see in front of you"!'[1]

In the late plays, the 'silver vein' of symbolism is increasingly present, but Ibsen was irritated by the interpretative games played by his critics. William Archer recalled him saying: 'that life is full of it [symbolism], and that, consequently, his plays are full of it, although critics insist on discovering all sorts of esoteric meanings in his works of which he is entirely innocent' (Archer 1952, 171). Ibsen kept on insisting that he could not be held responsible for what his characters said, and it is important to keep in mind that it is the characters who 'symbolise' their own existence, often with very negative effects on life, their own as well as the lives of those close to them. Ibsen's insistence that the silver veins in his work should not be 'pulled forth into the light of day' is clear from his correspondence with the artists contemplating productions of his late plays: he encourages them to draw on 'real life and real life only' when embodying his characters; the translators are asked to find unique modes of speech that reflect the social backgrounds of his characters; and directors are encouraged to create a mise-en-scéne that has 'the stamp of realism in every respect'. Despite these recommendations, his plays were produced using the symbolist performance techniques prevalent in late nineteenth-century European theatres, particularly in France, Germany, and Russia. Aurélien-Marie Lugné-Poë recalled that, as an adolescent, he used a 'monotonous, religious intonation' in his performance of *The Lady from the Sea*, but later claimed it was the result of youthful ignorance (Meyer 1992, 512). Herman Bang saw this performance and was convinced that Ibsen would have 'wept blood or stared into his hat' if he had been in the audience. When Lugné-Poë opened the Théâtre de l'Oeuvre in Paris with *Rosmersholm*, the symbolist elements in the production were far more sophisticated, but when Ibsen saw the touring performance in Kristiania, Bang recalls that he was 'a little upset' by the lighting because he did not want any 'stupid mysteriousness' in his plays (Lugné-Poë 1936, 81).

There are strong patterns within Ibsen's late plays created by the repetitive existential dilemmas faced by characters trapped within claustrophobic domestic worlds. The exploration of female desire, both in its expression and repression, is a major theme as are the frustrations of older men facing the diminution of their creative lives and their desire for rejuvenation; there are the dead children lurking in the shadows carrying the guilt from their parents' transgressions; and lastly, a collection of uncanny visitors are instrumental in disrupting the superficiality of the stage worlds. Narrative resolutions become increasingly illusive in these late plays; their endings tend to be open dramatic structures that invite artists to engage in further interpretative innovations.

None of Ibsen's eight late plays achieved the international notoriety of *A Doll's House* and *Ghosts*. The total number of IbsenStage records for the production histories of all these plays is 7,961, which is less than double the 4,184 records held for *A Doll's House* alone, but these late plays are arguably, Ibsen's finest works.

The Wild Duck (1884)

Premiered 9 January 1885, Den Nationale Scene, Bergen.[2]

12 June 1883 to Georg Brandes

I am currently grappling with the design of a new dramatic work in four acts. Over the years, various follies will amass themselves in one's mind, and one would of course like to find an outlet for them. But as the play is not going to deal with impeachment proceedings or the notion of absolute veto, not even with the topic of a new, purely Norwegian flag, I doubt the Norwegians will pay it much attention. Hopefully, it will find an audience elsewhere.

27 June 1884 to Theodor Caspari
(Norwegian author.)

I spent all winter pondering on some new follies, struggling with them until they assumed dramatic form, and during the last few days I finished a play in five acts. That is, the rough draft; and now comes the finer elaboration, the more energetic individualisation of the characters and their mode of expression.

27 August 1884 to Sigurd Ibsen
(Only child of Henrik and Suzannah Ibsen. Diplomat, politician, translator, and author.)

The German sculptor Professor Kopf from Rome has brought his thirteen-year-old daughter with him. She is as nearly perfect a model for the character of Hedvig in my play as I could hope for; pretty, with a serious face as well as nature, and a little gefrässig (greedy).

2 September 1884 to Frederik Hegel

With this letter I enclose the manuscript of my new play *The Wild Duck*, which has preoccupied me daily during the last four months, and it is not without a certain sense of loss that I must part with it now. The people in this play have, despite their many weaknesses, become dear to me during our lengthy daily interaction. But I do hope that they will also find good and kind friends in the larger reading public, and not least within the acting community; for they all, without exception, offer rewarding challenges to the actors. But studying and portraying these characters will not be an easy task; hence in regard to the theatres it would be desirable if the published play could be delivered to them reasonably early in the season. [...]

This new play has in certain ways a special place in my dramatic production: the approach and method differ in various respects from my earlier works. On this subject, however, I will not elaborate further. The critics will hopefully discover the points; they will at any rate find more than enough to argue about, more than enough to interpret. Moreover, I believe that *The Wild Duck* could perhaps tempt some of our younger dramatists to try new ways, something I would think desirable.

6 March 1891 to Victor Barrucand
(French author and journalist. He collaborated with Walther Halvorsen on a French translation of *The Wild Duck*; there is no record of this translation being used in performance.)

I also want to state that I am on principle against any translation undertaken by two or more people collaborating. *The Wild*

Duck presents quite special difficulties in the sense that one must be extremely intimate with the Norwegian language to understand the full extent to which every single character of this play has a characteristic, individual way of expression, which also demonstrates the character's class and education. When Gina speaks, for example, we must immediately hear that she has never learnt grammar and that she stems from the lower strata of society. And the same applies in different ways to all the other characters.

14 November 1884 to Hans Schrøder

I had imagined that Hjalmar must be played by Reimers. This role must be rendered without a trace of parody in the portrayal; not the slightest trace of him being conscious that there might be any touch of comedy in his lines. His voice could touch your heart-strings, Relling says, and that must be adhered to above all else. His sensitivity is genuine, his melancholy appealing in its way; not a hint of affectation. In all confidence, I would like to call your attention to Kristoffer Janson, who can be straight-out delightful when he talks the worst kind of nonsense. This is an indicator to the actor in question. Mrs Wolf should be a very good Gina. But where to find a Hedvig? I do not know. And Mrs Sørby? She must be attractive, bright, and not at all common. Could Miss Reimers solve that task? Or what about Mrs Gundersen? Gregers is the play's most difficult character as far as portrayal is concerned. Sometimes I think of Hammer, sometimes of Bjørn B[jørnson]; Old Ekdal can be given either to Brun or to Klausen; Relling to Selmer, maybe. I would rather the production is free of Isachsen, because he always walks around gesticulating like a weird actor instead of a normal human being; but he may be able to get something out of Molvik's few lines. Do not neglect the two servants; Pettersen could be given to Bucher, and Jensen to Abelsted, unless he is needed for one of the gentlemen in the dinner party. Yes, the guests! What to do with them? Ordinary extras cannot be used without spoiling the whole act. And what about the older Werle? There is Gundersen of course. But I do not know if he will be able to bring out what I want with this character, and in the way I want it.

In the ensemble acting and in the staging, this play demands natural truth and the stamp of realism in every respect. The lighting is significant as well; it differs in each act and is calculated to correspond with the basic mood that characterises each of the five acts.

22 November 1894 to August Lindberg

In answering your query, I hasten to tell you that *The Wild Duck*, like all my plays, is arranged from the point of view of the auditorium and not from the stage. I arrange everything in the same way I visualise it while I am writing.

When Hedvig has shot herself, she must be placed on the sofa with her feet in the foreground, so that her right hand holding the pistol can hang down. When she is carried out through the kitchen door I have imagined that Hjalmar holds her under her arms and Gina holds her feet.

I place great significance on the lighting in this play. I want it to correspond with the basic prevailing mood in each of the five acts.

Recollection from P.A. Rosenberg

Ibsen also spoke about Det Kongelige Teater's [the Royal Theatre in Copenhagen] production of *The Wild Duck*, which strangely enough did not meet with his approval. All we others admired Bloch's masterly staging, Mrs Hennings' lovely Hedvig, Olaf Poulsen's Old Ekdal and Miss Anthonsen's exceptional Gina. But Ibsen declared that they played it too much as a farce. 'It should be tragi-comedy,' he said, 'otherwise Hedvig's death becomes incomprehensible.' He only praised Mrs Hennings unreservedly. 'She *is* Hedvig,' he said, 'the others stand beside their characters.' (HU, vol. 19, 218–19.)

Rosmersholm (1886)

Premiered 17 January 1887, Den Nationale Scene, Bergen.[4]

Early working notes for 'White Horses'

He, the noble, refined nature, who has turned into a free-thinker and from whom all former friends and acquaintances have withdrawn. A widower; was unhappily married to a melancholy, half-mad woman, who finally drowned herself.

She, his two daughters' governess, emancipated, warm-blooded, somewhat ruthless, but yet refined. Is regarded in their social circles as the evil spirit of the house; is the object of misunderstanding and slander.

Eldest daughter; is about to perish from inactivity and loneliness; highly gifted without opportunity to use her talents.

Younger daughter; observant; dawning passions.

The Journalist; genius, vagabond. (HU, vol. 10, 444.)

From draft of Rosmersholm

She is a schemer and she loves him. She wants to marry him and pursues this goal relentlessly. He confronts her with it, she freely admits it. Then there is no more happiness in life for him. The daemonic is awoken by pain and bitterness. He wants to die, and she must die with him. She does. (HU, vol. 10, 485–6.)

2 January 1887 to Hans Schrøder

You believe Mrs Gundersen is the obvious choice to play Rebekka. This is not the case. Mrs G's strength lies in the great declamatory lines, and they do not exist in my play. How could she be able to handle the seemingly easy but overlayered conversations? And besides, dual natures, complex characters, do not come naturally to her. —Then you want Gundersen to play Rosmer. Please allow me to ask, how will it appear when Rebekka says she has been captivated by 'a wild, sensual desire' for him? Or when Brendel calls him 'my boy', etc? Or when Rector Kroll impresses and dominates him? Is G's personality compatible with this and much else? You must cast Rosmer's role with the most sensitive and subtle actor in the theatre's ensemble. —I have, of course, never wanted to see Ulrik Brendel in Johannes Brun's hands. That would be total madness. On the other hand, I have, after closer consideration, come to the conclusion that Brendel should be played by Mr Reimers, on the condition that he can be spared from Kroll's role. And I think he can, as I presume that the Rector would be played satisfactorily by Mr Hansson. —That the portrayal of Rector Kroll, this authoritative school-monarch, should be entrusted to Mr Bjørnson is hopefully just a joke, which I will not waste more time on now. However, if this monstrous thought is serious—if there exists such a total lack of criticism and self-criticism in the theatre's artistic leadership, I can unfortunately look forward to the rehearsals with fully justified distrust. Who is to explain the play's fundamental tone to the cast, with the interest, ardour and goodwill to observe that this is kept? Now, that is up to the theatre!

5 February 1887 to Hans Schrøder

Please forgive me for bothering you once more with a few words re *Rosmersholm*.

This is about Rector Kroll. From what the newspapers write, I must presume that this character has been misunderstood or incorrectly portrayed in the production at the Bergen Theatre [Den Nationale Scene].

True, I do not really fear that something similar will happen in Kristiania. However, it cannot hurt that I briefly suggest how I have seen this character.

Rector Kroll is an authoritative figure with a strongly developed desire to dominate, which a headmaster's position often entails. He is, naturally, of a good family. Major Rosmer's son does marry Kroll's sister, as we know. So the Rector has the manners of an affable senior civil servant. Despite a certain hot-temperedness, which erupts on occasion, his social tone is agreeable and obliging. He can be courteous when he wants to, or when he is with people he likes. But it should be noticeable that he can only appreciate people who share his opinions. The others irritate him, and he quickly becomes inconsiderate towards them, and then a hint of malice becomes discernible.

He has a distinguished appearance. He is neatly dressed in black. His coat reaches to his knees, but not any further. He wears a white neckerchief, large, of the older fashion, which can be wound twice around the neck. So no tie. His outfit explains why Ulrik Brendel at first takes him for Pastor Rosmer, and then for a 'fellow man of the cloth'.

In the first act, Rosmer also wears a black coat, but grey trousers and a tie or a cravat of the same colour. In the third and also the fourth act, however, he is dressed totally in black.

Rebekka must not have a hint of something commanding or masculine in her character. She does not *force* Rosmer onwards. She coaxes him. In her character there is something controlled, a quiet determination.

It would be difficult to mistake any of the other characters. Therefore I will not speak about them in more detail here, but I am, by the way, prepared to answer any questions put to me about one thing or another which may seem to be in doubt.

[…]

P.S. I take the liberty to request that my remarks are given to the respective actor word for word.

13 February 1887 to Bjørn Kristensen
(Norwegian Editor. Kristensen was Bjørnstjerne Bjørnson's nephew; when he wrote to Ibsen on behalf of his school debating club, he received this letter in response.)

The call to work certainly runs throughout *Rosmersholm*.

But beside this, the play is about the struggle that every serious human being has to conduct with himself to bring his life into harmony with his cognisance.

For the different spiritual functions do not develop evenly alongside each other in one and the same individual. The drive for acquisition hurtles forwards from one profit to the next.

On the other hand, the moral consciousness, 'the conscience', is very conservative. It has its deep roots in traditions, and altogether in the past.

From this comes the individual conflict.

But first and foremost, the play is of course a fiction about human beings and human destinies.

25 March 1887 to Sophie Reimers
(Norwegian actor. Reimers played Rebekka in the Christiania
Theater production that opened on 12 April 1887.)

I feel unable to answer your enquiry from down here, as it is expressed in quite general terms and without mentioning specific points.

In order to offer you any instructions I would have to be present and watch how you are building up the role.

The only advice I can give you is to read the play repeatedly and thoroughly, and carefully take note of what the other characters say about Rebekka. At least earlier, our actors often committed the big mistake of studying their roles in isolation and without properly seeing the character's position in, and in relation to, the whole work.

I have expressed myself briefly about Rebekka in a letter to the theatre director, and I shall ask him to tell you about my suggestions, should he not have done it already.

And besides, you must take your studies and observations of real life to help.

No declamation. No theatre intonation. No pomposity at all! Give each mood a credible, true-to-life expression. Never think about this or that actress you might have seen. Stay with the life that is going on around you, and portray a real, living person.

I do not think it is difficult to penetrate and understand Rebekka's character.

There are, however, difficulties in portraying and recreating this character since it is so complex.

However, I do not doubt that you will overcome these difficulties, if you only take real life, and real life only, as the basis and starting point for the expression of Rebekka's personality.

Recollection from Henrik Jæger

Tonight, Ibsen compared the people at home with tadpoles; in time they develop to become amphibians, but they still have the black tails dangling behind them; and the black tails they wriggle and wag are just obsolete ideas, which it will take them a long time to get rid of. It was something equivalent to what he had in mind with the white horses in *Rosmersholm*. As far as these white horses are concerned, he believes the current literature is developing an element of mysticism; that is the thought behind the white horses. (Qtd. in Midbøe 1960, 152.)

Recollection from Julius Elias[5]

He watched the dress rehearsal [at Stadttheater Augsburg on 6 April 1887], weeping and gnashing his teeth. Standing in the front stalls he winced in pain at every word uttered from the stage; clutching the plush of the orchestra rail with both hands, he incessantly groaned: 'Oh God, oh God.' In the third act, Johannes Rosmer had the grotesque idea of appearing in elegant piqué spats over highly polished calfskin boots. When the man came through the door, Ibsen staggered as if struck, clasping my arm: 'Look, just look…' The Rosmer he had given life to did not wear bright yellow piqué spats. Everyone was convinced that Ibsen would forbid the production at the last moment with one powerful word, when he suddenly straightened himself, and with a gesture, as if he was brushing away a bad dream, he said: 'I must abandon my original intentions—then it will not be too bad.' And he repeated this sentence to himself with quiet resolution. Thus, after having abandoned his original intentions, he found that everything worked satisfactorily. (1940, 403.)

Recollection from Aurélien Marie Lugné-Poë[6]
(French actor manager. Lugné-Poë produced and toured twelve plays by Ibsen with Théâtre de l'Oeuvre.)

While accompanying us to the door, he [Ibsen] said something further that I could not make out, though I caught, two or three times in passing, the name of Ulrik Brendel.

Having received a courteous welcome, friendly, but no more than that, as we were coming down the stairs from the master's rooms, I expressed my surprise to Herman Bang that Ibsen had said nothing about the previous evening's performance of *Rosmersholm*.

'Yes, yes,' said Bang, 'he was a little put out because Brendel, in the final scene, was lit for his entrance "by electric light". He does not want touches of stupid mysteriousness in his plays.'

My head was spinning as I left Ibsen's, and I did not recover my composure until, in the street, right in front of the door, I noticed a shop whose sign bore the name of one of his heroines (Mrs Helseth). (1936, 80–1.)

The Lady from the Sea (1888)

Premiered 17 February 1889, Christiania Theater (Oslo).[7]

Recollection from Henrik Jæger

The sea was company enough for him. 'There's something extraordinarily captivating about the sea,' he said. 'When you stand and stare down into the water, it's as if you see the life that moves around up here on earth, only in another form. There is coherence and resemblance everywhere. In my next work, the sea shall play a role.' (HU, vol. 19, 172.)

From draft of The Lady from the Sea

Life is seemingly light, bright and lively up there beneath the mountain shadow, and in the secluded monotony. Then the thought emerges that this kind of life is a shadow-life. No vigour; no fight for liberation and freedom. Only yearnings and desires. This is how the short light summer is lived there. And afterwards—into the darkness. Then the yearning for the life of the great world outside awakens. But what is won by that? Along with the changing circumstances, with the spiritual development, the demands and yearnings and desires grow. He or she who has reached the summit, craves the secrets of the future, and to take part in the life of the future and to have intercourse with distant worlds. Limitations everywhere. Thus the melancholy, like a subdued song of mourning over the whole of human existence and all human activity. A bright summer's day followed by the great darkness—that is all.

Has the path of human development taken the wrong direction? How did we come to belong on dry earth? Why not the air? Why not the ocean. The longing to possess wings. The strange dreams that one can fly and that one flies without wondering about it; how to interpret all this?

[…]

The pulling power of the sea. The longing for the sea. Human beings related to the sea. Bound by the sea. Dependent on the sea. Compelled to return into it. A species of fish formed a primeval link in the chain of evolution. Are rudiments from it still inside the human mind? In certain human minds?

The images of the teeming life in the sea and of the 'forever lost'.

The sea reigns with a power over one's moods that has the effect of will. The sea can hypnotise. Nature on the whole can. The great secret is the human will's dependency on 'that which has no will'.

16 November 1888 to Julius Hoffory

It has not been an easy task to translate this play, and I do not know anyone else but you who could have all that is required to solve it with complete satisfaction. An intimate knowledge of the Dano-Norwegian language, for instance, is necessary to recognise the tentative and second-rate, semi-educated nature of Lyngstrand's mode of expression, or the light touch of pedagogical pedantry which now and then appears in Arnholm's speech and turns of phrase. And similar linguistic subtleties and problems also occur in the lines of the other characters. Thus I am extremely grateful to you for taking this matter into your own skilled hands.

18 December 1888 to Hans Schrøder

You have hopefully been informed by my telegram of last Sunday that I agree with you about the casting of *The Lady from the Sea*. […]

I do not know Mr Schancke's work as an actor; but I hope he will succeed in finding and portraying the right manifestation of the unassuming, contented air which shines from Lyngstrand. Hilde is not easy to portray either. It should be understood that the daemonic streak which runs through her, largely has its origin in her childish, always unfulfilled longing to win Ellida's devotion.

Mr Hansson must not be misled by Bolette's and Hilde's remarks concerning his looks to portray Arnholm as really old or decrepit. He only seems like that to the young girls. His hair has thinned somewhat, and he is a little worn out from his teaching—that is all.

6 February 1889 to Hans Schrøder

Please forgive me for bothering you with a few words concerning a printing error, the only one to be found in *The Lady from the Sea*. On p. 193 this appears in a parenthesis next to one of Bolette's lines: 'halvt for sig selv' (half to herself). This is wrong. It should be: 'halvt fra sig selv' (half out of her mind). Should they have failed to guess the mistake during the rehearsals, please make the actress aware of it.

14 February 1889 to Julius Hoffory

So Mr Anno wants to exchange the name Bolette, uncommon in German, with Babette or another girl's name, on both the poster and in the production.[8] As my play is not set in Germany, I presume the reason given by him for the change can hardly be the only one, or the most weighty one. I suspect he has another reason, and therefore I have no objection to his wish. So Babette may be used in the play instead; assuming, of course, that German audiences will not find Arnholm's statement that the name is unlovely perplexing. Obviously, I cannot be certain about that, but trust you in this matter, too.

On the other hand, I must definitely object to the poster using 'Ein Seemann' [A Sailor] or 'Ein fremder Seemann' [A Strange Sailor] or 'Ein Steuermann' [A First Mate]. He is none of these. When Ellida met him ten years earlier, he was a second mate. Seven years later he let himself be engaged as a simple boatswain, thus as something much humbler. And now he arrives as a passenger on a tourist ship. He does not belong to the ship's crew. He is dressed as a tourist, not as an everyday traveller. No one must know *what* he is, just as no one must know *who* he is or what his real name is. This uncertainty is the main point of the method I have chosen in this case. Mr Anno must be kindly advised to pay special attention to this during rehearsals, or the fundamental mood of the presentation could easily be missed.

But if the expression 'Ein fremder Mann' [a strange man] has a comical flavour for the Berlin audience,—could the poster not use 'Ein Fremder' [A Stranger]? I have nothing against that. However, if this does not find approval, I would think that there is nothing else to do but give free rein to the potential jollities. Hopefully, they will not cause any serious or lasting damage.

I feel greatly reassured, my dear professor, knowing that you will keep an eye on the rehearsals; the final ones, at least. There may be a great many things concerning the foreign conditions which the director, Anno, is not fully aware of. And so, I am hoping for a good outcome.

According to a telegram from Kristiania, *The Lady from the Sea* was performed there for the first time, and to an extraordinary reception. I have still not heard from Weimar, where the play is supposed to be performed these days.

26 March 1889 to Julius Hoffory

I spent the […] week in Weimar. There, too, *The Lady from the Sea* was performed most admirably. The interpretation and rendering of the characters had a curious similarity to the one in the Schauspielhaus. But Wangel's character was not as finely prepared in the subtler details. Neither was Lyngstrand as incomparably truly felt and individualised. But I could not have wished for, or even imagined a better 'Stranger' than here—a tall, skinny figure with a hawk-like face, piercing black eyes and a splendidly deep and subdued voice.

Recollection from Magdalene Thoresen[9]
(Danish-Norwegian poet, novelist, short-story writer and play-wright. Thoresen was Suzannah Ibsen's stepmother and Ibsen's mother-in-law.)

While I was studying in Copenhagen, I met a young man, a wild, peculiar figure, a force of nature. He studied with me, and before the power of his tremendous, daemonic will I was forced to bow in the dust. He could have taken me with him into an intense, complete life of love—I still believe in that. He let me go, he might have regretted it later… I have never regretted that he let me go, as I met a better person because of it, and I have lived a better life. But as I said, I have always known that he could have brought out all the love contained in my very nature, and made it flower and bear fruit. So my days have been filled with a sense of longing and loss, search-ing high, searching low, always searching for a shadow. And the strength of my love did not vanish with the years, it just kept growing.

When my noble husband called me to be his wife and mother to the five poor children who were cavorting around him, he was already aware of the regrettable event in my rest-less life; for which I alone was responsible. But the past event, within which I was an ignorant weak creature without protec-tion, incapable of explaining my actions to myself or others—I asked him to regard as a closed book, to judge my character as the result of this whole struggle, and if he could find me wor-thy, wipe out all the rest. He did. If he had not, he would still have beaten his head against the wall; because I had become as silent as the grave. (1919, 98.)

3 May 1889 to Camilla Collett[10]

So allow me today to offer you my most whole-hearted grati-tude for your profound understanding of *The Lady from the Sea*. I felt quite assured beforehand that I could expect such an understanding from you, more than anyone. However, I was absolutely delighted to have this hope confirmed through your letter.

Yes, there are common points. Many of them, even. And you have seen them and felt them. That is, things that for me could only appear as a hint, a suggestion.

But it is many years now since you began, in one form or another, through your spiritual and intellectual life, to play a part in my writing.

Hedda Gabler (1890)

Premiered 31 January 1891, Königliches Residenz-Theater, Munich.[11]

From notes for Hedda Gabler

The pale, apparently cold beauty. Great demands of life and the joy of life.

He, who has finally conquered her, as a person, of modest background—but honourable, and a talented, broad-minded scientist. (HU, vol. 11, 497.)

7 October 1889 to Emilie Bardach[12]
(Austrian merchant's daughter. Ibsen met Bardach in Gossensass where her family was staying during the summer of 1889.)

A new work begins to dawn in me. I want to finish it this winter and try to transpose the hot summer atmosphere to it. But it will end in sadness. I can feel that. —That is my way.

15 October 1889 to Emilie Bardach

As usual, I sit here at my writing desk. I would like to work now. But I am unable to.

True, my imagination is working busily. But it constantly strays and wanders off. Away to places where it should not really be during working hours. I cannot suppress my summer memories. Nor do I want to. What I lived then, I keep reliving again and again—and yet again. To re-mould it all into a work of literature is impossible for me for the time being.

For the time being?

Could it succeed for me sometime in the future? And do I really wish that somehow it should, and could, succeed? In any case, not for the time being, I believe.

That I feel—that I know.

And yet it must happen. It most decidedly *must*.

But still, *will* it be possible? *Will* it?

20 November 1890 to Moritz Prozor

It gives me a strange feeling of emptiness suddenly to find myself separated from a work which has taken up my time and my thoughts exclusively for several months. However, it is also good that it has come to an end. For the incessant cohabitation with these fictitious people was beginning to make me more than a little nervous.

4 December 1890 to Moritz Prozor

The play's title is: *Hedda Gabler*. With that I wanted to imply that she, as a personality, is to be apprehended more as her father's daughter than her husband's wife.

In this play, it is not really my intention to deal with any so-called problems. My chief concern has been to portray human beings, human emotions and human fates based on certain current social conditions and opinions. When you have read it all through, my fundamental idea will become more clear to you than I can express here.

25 November 1890 to August Larsen
(Danish publisher. Larsen worked with Frederik Hegel at Gyldendal.)

Could you please correct something in the manuscript: in the dialogue between Hedda and Judge Brack in the third act, one of his lines says—'Common brawl between both ladies and gentlemen.' This should be changed to—'Common cockfight', etc.

27 December 1890 to Hans Schrøder

I have had the honour of receiving your friendly message that the Christiania Theater wants to perform my new play *Hedda Gabler* […]

Hedda must without doubt be played by Miss Bruun, who hopefully will strive to find dramatic expression for the daemonic sub-layers of the character.

14 January 1891 to Kristine Steen
(Norwegian teacher.)

Mrs Wolf wants to be relieved from taking on the role of the maid Berte in my new play, and believes that this part could be performed by any of the actresses in the [Christiania] theatre.

In this she is mistaken. There is no one else there who can portray Berte the way I want her to be portrayed. Mrs Wolf alone can do that. But she has obviously not taken the trouble to read the play through with attentive care. Otherwise I think she herself would understand that immediately.

Jørgen Tesman, his old aunts and the long-serving maid Berte together form an image of complete unity. They have a common mentality, common memories, common outlook on life. To Hedda, they appear as a hostile and foreign power directed against her fundamental essence. Therefore their portrayal must be one of reciprocal harmonisation. And this will be made possible when Mrs Wolf participates. But only then.

Out of regard for Mrs Wolf's sound power of judgement, I cannot seriously believe that she considers it beneath her artistic dignity to portray a maid. At least I have not considered it beneath my dignity to create this decent, simple, middle-aged person.

11 March 1891 to Cornelis Honigh
(Dutch translator of *Hedda Gabler*.)

The place you describe in my play is to be understood in the following way: Hedda, who feels that she is pregnant, cannot in any way trace a 'calling' within herself to take on the duties of motherhood. That is the 'claim', the demand, which she says no one must place on her. She would rather die. There is no question of any love affair with another man here.

19 January 1891 to Kaarlo Bergbom
(Co-founder of the Finnish theatre, Suomalainen Teatteri.)

It is especially important to me that the play is rendered in a correct and fluid translation. In other words, in a refined and natural spoken language. Not in a stiff bookish language. I do presume that there is a difference between these two things in Finnish as well.

The Master Builder (1892)

Premiered 19 January 1893, Lessingtheater, Berlin.[13]

Drafted July 1892 to an unknown recipient

Sunrise, transfusion of the young animal's blood. The airship that can be steered. Glimpse into the life of the Martians. (HU, vol. 19, 60.)

30 October 1892 to August Larsen

I am glad that I have finally finished this big work happily and satisfactorily. It feels like a release. However, it still leaves a sense of loss and emptiness.

Recollection from Ernst Motzfeldt
(Norwegian politician and Minister of Justice.)

Ibsen said: 'It is extraordinary how many profundities and symbols everyone ascribes to me. I have, for instance, received letters asking me if the nine dolls [of Mrs Solness] signify the nine muses, and the dead twins Scandinavianism and my own happiness in life. I have even been asked if the dolls are associated with something in a St. Paul epistle which I do not even know, or with something in the Book of Revelations. Why do people not just read what I write? It is merely about people. I do not write symbolically. I only describe people's inner life as

I know it—write psychology, if you like… I portray real, living people. Any significant personality will, in his inner life, to a degree also be representative of the general, of the common thoughts and ideas of the age. The portrayal of such an inner life may therefore seem symbolic. Those are the people I portray. And I have ample opportunity. I have constantly studied people and observed their inner lives. I have often walked with Hedda Gabler through the arcades of Munich. And I have also experienced much myself.

Solness and his wife are worthy people who do not suit each other, and thus they do not have a happy life together. They do not become what they could and ought to have been, according to their individual potential—despite not being actually unhappy, and despite having a mutual regard and a kind of affection and love for each other. They hold each other down, cripple each other. So their worst characteristics keep developing, and they begin to brood and ponder, they each go their own way, without sharing their thoughts with each other. On the other hand there is Hilde and Solness. They are not portrayed as extraordinary people, it is just that they feel spiritually akin, strongly attracted to each other, feel they belong together, and that a life together would certainly be immeasurably richer than what they have now, and also that they themselves would be better people (Hilde immediately makes him do for Brovik what he was unwilling to do before—did his wife try to make him do that?), and that their relationship would lift them up instead of pulling them down, and give life meaning. Then the collision comes—at a time when one still has a taste for life, a need for happiness, still feels unable to live a life deprived of joy, in dull resignation. And so they decide to build castles in the air and to live a spiritual life together. This lifts him up higher than before, to do things he has not been able to do for a long time (symbolically). But he stakes his life on it—and is killed. But was it so wrong, even if it cost him his life, when he did it for the sake of his happiness, and then really achieved it?'

During our conversation he said that it was wrong to think of unhappy love as two people who love each other but are forcibly separated. 'No, unhappy love is when two people who love each other get married, and then feel that they do not suit each other and cannot live happily together.' (1911, 4.)

13 February 1893 to August Lindberg
An excellent Hilde in every respect is absolutely necessary!

7 January 1893 to Hildur Andersen
(Concert pianist and musicologist.)
My wild forest-bird!

Where are you flying now? I do not know. Are you still circling above Leipzig? Or are you heading for the north? Closer to home? I know nothing. Now I want to go down to your mama and enquire about you. Perhaps there is also a letter for me there.

Where and when you receive these lines is uncertain. Or that is how it seems to me at the moment. I am also mostly writing them for my own sake, because I feel the need to send you something. Not be without 'Fühlung' [contact] with you, you understand. I have no newspapers today. At least not this morning. Later, perhaps; if I get to hear about you from your mama.

[...]

Oh, how I long for the princess! Long from the heights of dreams. Long to come back down to earth again and do what I said I would—so many many times!

A thousand heartfelt greetings meanwhile!

Yours, your master builder.[14]

11 February 1895 to Georg Brandes
I cannot resist my urge to send you a special thank-you for your [article on] 'Goethe and Marianne v[on] Willemer'. The episode in Goethe's life you describe there was unknown to me. I may have read about it a very long time ago in Lewis [sic], but then forgotten about it because the relationship was of no personal interest to me at that time.[15] Now the case stands

somewhat differently. When I think about the character of Goethe's production during the years in question, the rebirth of his youth, I think I should have seen that he was blessed by something as wonderful for him as meeting this particular woman, Marianne v. Willemer. Fate, chance, coincidence can certainly be quite caring, obliging forces now and then.

Recollection from Aurélien Marie Lugné-Poë[16]

He declared himself very pleased with the production, but was looking forward, he said, to the performance of *The Master Builder*, his most recent play. He was not surly, as he had been described to us, not even suspicious, but almost immediately he delivered that phrase in German which, at the time, I relayed back to Paris, and which was, for me, like a beam of light the next evening [when playing Solness]. 'French actors are better equipped than many others for performing my plays. It is not sufficiently understood: a passionate writer has to be performed with passion, no other way.'

[...]

In a single second, with one phrase, Ibsen had altered the whole character of our interpretation, which, till then, had been languid and rather sing-song. (1936, 80–1.)

Recollection from Herman Bang[17]
(Danish novelist. Bang provided Lugné-Poë with dramaturgical advice on the production of Ibsen's plays.)

This strange self-confessional play had not made an impression on the Nordic stages [...] Ibsen sat in his box. During the first act he was, as usual, motionless, and no one could say whether he heard or saw anything at all. And still it seemed to me as if something had made him wake up towards the end of the act. However, as the second act started its progress Ibsen got up. He stood in the back of his box, leaning against the wall, following every movement of the actors with his eyes. It was as if the eyes of the Master, by resting on them, increased the power and ability of the actors so that the love song on stage rose like a storm and raced forward—all the way till the curtain fell.

During the third act Ibsen leaned out over the balustrade of the box. Then I saw and knew that Lugné-Poë and Madame Bady had scored a victory. […] When I returned to the Grand that night Ibsen came to greet me. Only once have I seen him moved, and that was on this occasion. He stretched out both his hands to me; they were ice-cold, as though his excitement had drawn all the warmth from them. 'This', he said, 'was the resurrection of my play.' (1906, 1498–9.)

Little Eyolf (1894)

Premiered 12 January 1895, Deutsches Theater, Berlin.[18]

18 December 1894 interview with Norwegian newspaper Dagbladet

We went to see Dr Ibsen in connection with these statements [that 'The Rat Wife' in *Little Eyolf* originated from Goethe's poem *Der Rattenfänger* (*The Ratcatcher*)]. We asked the author if 'The Rat Wife' really was a reminiscence from his readings of Goethe.

— No, she is not, Dr Ibsen answered. I do not know Goethe's poem. I do know the Hamelin legend; but what I have used as a model are memories from Skien about a person who was called 'the rat wife'; by the way, she was called 'Aunt'. Besides, there are other places that have had similar figures.

— In Bergen there was also a 'Rat Wife' whom the street urchins used to shout at; it was just at the time when you, Dr Ibsen, were stage director at the Bergen Theatre [Det norske Theater] […]

The author hesitated, as if he was searching his memory for a moment.

— Yes, he said; it is very possible that some of the idea came from my time there, too […] But as I said, I decidedly remember the figure from Skien.

We told him that there was talk in town about the theatre's casting of the play. Many had thought that Mr Fahlstrøm, who has recently been on a study tour, would have been given Allmers' role.

— Yes, I do not doubt Mr Fahlstrøm's ability to interpret the words; but there are places in Allmers' role where a lyrical temperament erupts; where what lies behind the words can only be understood through the particular sound of voice… And so theatre manager Schrøder and I agreed to give this role to Mr Halvorsen. Casting is a difficult thing. You often have to harden your resolve in order to get it the way you want it… I believe I will be present at a couple of rehearsals. (HU, vol. 19, 203–4.)

Recollection from Bolette Sontum[19]

Ibsen and a few intimate friends, among them my mother and father, went to the first night's performance. [...] Ibsen was very nervous about the reception of *Little Eyolf*. He kept saying to my mother, who sat next to him, 'Do let's get out before the curtain comes down.' It was always a torture to him to see his own plays, for, though the acting was superb, he could hardly judge the merits of the characters, as they never seemed real to him through the medium of the actors after the vitality of his own imagination. *Little Eyolf* was received with great enthusiasm, and the curtain calls were many, but, though they clapped persistently, the audience were not able to make the author appear. Finally, the stage manager promised to give their congratulations personally to him.

Ibsen, meanwhile, was driving to the Grand Hotel in a shabby little sleigh as fast as one plodding horse could carry him through the streets. It was snowing heavily, a real Norwegian winter-night, the very sky seeming to melt down in soft white flakes.

When Ibsen reached the 'Grand', he was very much overcome by the performance and exceedingly nervous. He begged my mother to order the supper for him, and seemed like a child asking for protection. The hearty food and some good wine soon raised his spirits. When my mother, still full of the play, said, 'Poor Rita, now she has to go to work with all those mischievous boys!' Ibsen replied, 'Do you really believe so?

Don't you rather think it was more of a Sunday mood with her?' He really looked doubtful himself. (1913, 251–2.)

John Gabriel Borkman (1896)

Premiered 10 January 1897, Suomalainen Teatteri (the Finnish Theatre), Helsinki.[20]

Interview in the Copenhagen newspaper Kjøbenhavns Aftenblad

The main thing is that Mrs Borkman loves her husband. Initially she was not a hard and evil woman, but a loving wife who had become hard and evil from the disappointments she had suffered. She was disappointed by her husband first in love, then in respect of his genius. It is on this above all that the actress must lay emphasis. If Mrs Borkman had not loved her husband, she would have forgiven him long ago. Now she waits—in spite of her double disappointment, whose victim she has been—for the sick wolf whose steps she hears every day. Just as he waits for 'the world', so *she* waits for *him*. This emerges clearly from the dialogue; and it is this side of Mrs Borkman's character that the person interpreting her must above all emphasise. (Qtd. in HU, vol. 13, 26.)

17 December 1896 to Peter Hansen

What Mr Hennings claims concerning his conversation with me here is nonsense. I told him explicitly, in the presence of artistic director Schrøder, that there is *no* main role in my new play for Mrs Hennings; however, there may be one minor role. I was thinking of the role of Frida. For Ella, I would suggest Mrs Oda Nielsen. An actor who could play Rita should also be able to play Ella. Furthermore, she must be a credible twin sister to Mrs Eckard, who naturally has to play Gunhild.

The decoration painter [from Copenhagen] is very welcome and I shall assist him with anything I possibly can. They have a very capable painter at this theatre, and he, too, is pleased to be at Mr Petersen's disposal during his stay here.

When We Dead Awaken (1899)

Premiered 26 January 1900, Königliches Hoftheater, Stuttgart.[21]

13 June 1897 to Suzannah Ibsen
(Ibsen's wife.)

So I am feeling remarkably good—and in my solitude, plans for a new work have begun to hatch and germinate. I can already feel the basic ambience; but I can still see only one of the characters. Oh well, the others will emerge, too.

23 March 1898 speech at banquet to honour Ibsen on his seventieth birthday

[…] However, ladies and gentlemen, please do not believe that I […] plan to lay down my theatre pen for good. No, I intend to return to it, and keep a firm hold on it until the very last. For I have various follies in stock, which I have not yet found the opportunity to give expression to. Only when I have got them off my chest, may I think about quitting. And how easy it will be to quit then, as opposed to the time when I was in the middle of the beginning. How silent and empty it was around me then! How my fellow combatants were spread, apart, without reciprocity, without links! Many a time it seemed to me that once I myself had gone, it would be as if I had never been here. Nor my work either.

February 1900 to Gunnar Heiberg
(Norwegian journalist, playwright and theatre director.)

You were right. I was wrong. I have checked my notes. Irene is around forty years old.

3 January 1900 to Julius Elias

I cannot enter into a simple explanation of what I meant. Irene's intimations must be considered more as a kind of 'Wahrheit und Dichtung' [Truth and Poetry].

12 December 1899 interview with Norwegian newspaper Verdens Gang

What I have meant with the word 'epilogue' in this connection is simply that the play constitutes the epilogue to the row of dramatic works, which starts with *A Doll's House* and now concludes with *When We Dead Awaken*. This last play belongs to the experiences I have wanted to depict in this whole series of plays. It constitutes a whole, a unity, and with this I am now finished. If I write something hereafter, it will all be in a quite different context, perhaps in a different form also. (HU, vol. 19, 225–6.)

5 March 1900 to Moritz Prozor

You are essentially right in saying that the whole series of plays, which is concluded with the epilogue really started with *The Master Builder*. But I would refrain from saying anything more specific about this. I leave all comments and interpretations to you. (HU, vol. 18, 447.)

Recollection from Ernst Motzfeldt

He was already weakened by illness, but expressed in the course of the conversation that when he had had a short rest and settled a few business matters, he would start writing a new play. 'So,' I said, 'your last drama, which you yourself described as an epilogue, will not be your final work?' 'No, it is only a phase which is now completed. Now I want to start a new one.' [...] Then I asked could he please first provide some guidance or clue so we could fully understand the meaning of his writing in the phase he has now declared complete. He did after all know that a great deal of uncertainty prevailed concerning the fundamental idea of his writing [...] Ibsen said, 'No, it would not be right for me to do that. [...] Just as I myself claim full freedom, as far as the public is concerned, in the choice and treatment of my own material, so shall the public have full freedom to interpret what I write as they understand it. I have no right to deprive the public of that freedom.' This answer stopped me from any further questions. (1911, 4.)

1. See extract from: '*Lord William Russell* and its Performance at Christiania Theater', 20 December 1857 in this volume, p. 202
2. ibsenstage.hf.uio.no/pages/event/78128
3. This letter to Schrøder relates to the casting of the Christiania Theater production.
   ibsenstage.hf.uio.no/pages/event/78132
4. ibsenstage.hf.uio.no/pages/event/78164
5. ibsenstage.hf.uio.no/pages/event/78170
6. Ibsen attended a performance of *Rosmersholm* by the Théâtre de l'Oeuvre at Carl-Johan Teatret in Kristiania on 3 October 1894; the following night the company performed *The Master Builder*.
   ibsenstage.hf.uio.no/pages/event/78495
   ibsenstage.hf.uio.no/pages/event/78598
7. ibsenstage.hf.uio.no/pages/event/78221
8. Anton Anno directed *A Lady from the Sea* for the Königliches Schauspielhaus in Berlin.
   ibsenstage.hf.uio.no/pages/event/78226
9. Magdalene Thoresen was Ibsen's mother-in-law; her early life may have been a source for the character of Ellida (Ferguson 1996, 333).
10. Camilla Collett had communicated to Ibsen that she saw elements of herself in Ellida.
11. ibsenstage.hf.uio.no/pages/event/78298
12. The letters to Emilie Bardach have been translated from the German.
13. ibsenstage.hf.uio.no/pages/event/78423
14. Ibsen gave Andersen the manuscript of *The Master Builder* in November 1894, and a ring inscribed with the same date that he uses in the play for Hilda's arrival to claim her kingdom from Solness.
15. *The Life of Goethe* (1864) by G.H. Lewes.
16. See note 6. Recollection translated from the French.
    ibsenstage.hf.uio.no/pages/event/78495
17. Ibsen attended the performance of *The Master Builder* by the Théâtre de l'Oeuvre in Kristiania on 5 October 1894.
    ibsenstage.hf.uio.no/pages/event/78598
18. ibsenstage.hf.uio.no/pages/event/78633
19. Ibsen attended the Norwegian premiere at the Christiania Theater on 15 January 1895.
    ibsenstage.hf.uio.no/pages/event/78634
20. ibsenstage.hf.uio.no/pages/event/78776
21. ibsenstage.hf.uio.no/pages/event/79092

6

Copyright and Translation

The law protects the salmon in our rivers and the game in our mountains; our authors, however, appear to be classified with carnivores, we do our best to exterminate them.

(Letter to O. A. Bachke, 28 October 1871.)

I would not be able to approve of any translation not written directly from the original.

(Letter to Moritz Prozor, 3 March 1891.)

Your translation of my play *The Wild Duck* must never and nowhere be published or performed.

(Letter to unknown recipient, 8 June 1891.)

Scholars have bemoaned the fact that so much of Ibsen's extensive correspondence is devoted to matters of business, thus concurring with his own assessment that:

> letter writing has never been my strong suit. I am almost afraid that I have grappled for so long and so tenaciously with the dramatic form, in which the author must to a certain extent kill and submerge his own personality, or at least mislay it, that I may have lost quite a lot of what I value most in a letter writer

(To Karoline Bjørnson, 23 September 1884.)

Yet, viewed from another perspective, his business letters provide a fascinating insight into the strategies used by a nineteenth-century playwright to secure income from publication and performance. The first international copyright agreement, the Berne Convention, was drawn up in 1886. Norway signed the agreement in 1896, but as Ibsen published the Dano-Norwegian texts of his plays in Copenhagen, he was not covered by the Convention until Denmark signed in 1903 (D'Amico 2011, 149). Every country where Ibsen was published and performed was a new arena in which copyright had to be established, royalties maximised, and the quality of translations ensured. The strategies he used to secure these ends included: citing bilateral trade agreements; publishing his own translations; signing an agreement with a major European theatre agency; working with a publisher in London to secure British performance rights; joining the French Société des auteurs et compositeurs dramatiques; personally authorising translations of his work; and controlling simultaneous publications of his plays to maximise royalty protection in different nation states. On 2 January 1891, after nearly thirty years of fighting to protect his intellectual property in Europe, he wrote to his brother-in-law, Johan Herman Thoresen:

> I am very grateful for the information you sent me last summer re the supplementary article to the French commercial treaty. My French translator and representative, Count M. de Prozor, has made the decision valid on my behalf, so that my author's rights are now secured in France in every respect. I would like to mention that I have also arranged matters satisfactorily with England, from where I receive very ample honoraria. Something similar is the case here in Germany and in Austria, and of course we have the treaty with Italy. Therefore, I have no particular reason to complain.

Most of the extracts in this chapter relate to Ibsen's views on translation. IbsenStage data show that at least 145 people translated Ibsen's plays during his lifetime.[1] Thirty-one of these translators are mentioned in the Ibsen letters published in *Henrik Ibsen skrifter* (HIS): twenty-one of them were in direct correspondence with Ibsen. The translators known to Ibsen were translating his plays into German, French, English, Swedish, Dutch, Italian, Bohemian (Czech), Finnish, Italian and Russian. The remaining 114 translators do not appear in any of the surviving Ibsen correspondence. Among them were sixteen translators working in Swedish, nine in Finnish, six in

Dutch, six in German, three in Serbo-Croatian, two in Russian, five in English, three in Latvian, twelve in Bohemian (Czech), fifteen in Polish, six in Hungarian, four in Italian, two in Icelandic, two in Slovenian, three in Spanish, four in Greek, five in Bulgarian, one in Portuguese, and nine in French. Given that Ibsen signed a contract with a major German theatrical agency to sell the rights to the German translations of his plays across central and parts of Southern Europe, it is quite possible that he knew about the work of an additional fifty of the translators recorded in the pre-1906 IbsenStage production records. This leaves sixty translators with no known connection with Ibsen. Many of these individuals translated only one play for a single production; ten of them were associated as an actor or director with the performances in question.

Pillars of Society, *An Enemy of the People* and *A Doll's House* were the most popular choices for translation during Ibsen's lifetime. *Ghosts* and *The Wild Duck* came next, followed by *John Gabriel Borkman*, *Rosmersholm*, *Hedda Gabler* and *The Lady from the Sea*. There is a smattering of translations of the early plays: *The Feast at Solhaug*, *The Pretenders*, *Lady Inger*, *Love's Comedy* and *The Vikings at Helgeland*.

Ibsen used a similar strategy in every language market: he began by cordially responding to individuals interested in translating his work; he would then assess their skills, and over time build long-term business relationships with the most proficient. The clearest illustration of this strategy can be found in Ibsen's correspondence with his German translators, and it is extracts from these letters and their story of a twenty-eight-year-long negotiation that are the focus of this chapter.

There were no bilateral agreements to protect Ibsen's intellectual property in Germany, and his income from German-speaking theatres remained uncertain until the late 1880s (Fulsås 2008, 17 and 2009, 15). He attempted to control the German market by personally authorising translations, and although this had no legal authority, it did ensure the quality of the translation to the reading public and theatre companies. His first success in Germany was *Pillars of Society*, with sixty-two productions between 1878 and 1880 (Hansen 2017). One of the major translations used in these productions was an unauthorised and heavily edited text by Emil Jonas: Ibsen described it as a 'mutilation' (to Emil Jonas, 18 January 1878). To counter the use of unauthorised versions of the play by Jonas and others Ibsen financed a translation by Emma Klingenfeld (Fulsås 2008, 106–7).

Authorised translations of Ibsen's plays were published in Germany by S. Fischer in Berlin, and were marketed by Deutsche Genossenschaft dramatischer Autoren und Komponisten from 1878 to 1884. These translations were later marketed by the major theatrical agency Felix Bloch Erben, with which Ibsen signed a contract in 1887. The Leipzig publisher Reclam printed thousands of copies of Ibsen's plays without paying him. Ibsen received no royalties when theatres used these versions, but as mentioned in his correspondence below, he eventually entered a financial arrangement with the owner of the publishing house, Philipp Reclam.

Ibsen's main German translators were Marie von Borch, William Lange, Christian Morgenstern and Emma Klingenfeld. Their translations remained in the repertoires of German theatres for over a hundred years and they account for over eight hundred of the production records held in IbsenStage. They are the major figures in the story of Ibsen's translation into German, but there are many other fascinating characters with a role in this correspondence. These include Peter Friedrich Siebold, the commercial traveller whose Nordic interests embraced Ibsen's plays and reindeer hunting; Ludwig Passarge, the German civil servant and travel writer with a limited knowledge of Dano-Norwegian; Julius Hoffory, Professor of Scandinavian Philology and Phonetics; and Julius Elias, the editor of the German edition of Ibsen's *Collected Works* (1898–1904), which was the first to appear in any language.

To provide a context for Ibsen's correspondence with his German translators, this chapter begins with extracts from three letters written by Ibsen that explain the financial rationale behind his insistence on publication prior to the production of his plays. These letters also demonstrate his knowledge of the international dissemination of his work, and the lack of legal protection available to nineteenth-century writers. Ibsen received grants from the Norwegian parliament for over thirty years; the loss of income from translation was initially a major argument he used to secure these funds. As he became more successful and less dependent on this stipend, his major income streams were from Gyldendal, his Scandinavian publisher based in Denmark, and the productions of his plays in Nordic and German theatres.

The Copyright Context

5 October 1877 to Edvard Fallesen
(Danish officer, politician, and theatre manager attached to the Royal Theatre in Copenhagen.)

As Det Kongelige Teater [the Royal Theatre in Copenhagen] does not intend to pay me a percentage of the ticket sales, I am forced to seek the essential part of my income through book sales. The play is printed in a very large number of copies, and Hegel [the Gyldendal proprietor] has paid me a considerable honorarium for this first edition; he himself has had considerable expenditures when it comes to printing, paper, etc. So, I owe it to him as well as myself not to undertake arrangements which go against our mutual interests. In our countries [Norway and Denmark], the bulk of the book sales takes place in the last two months of the year; however, for a book published in Copenhagen to be available at the right time in more distant regions of Sweden and Norway, not to mention Finland and America, where a good many copies of my work also go, it must already be sent out around the middle of October. If this fails to happen, one cannot count on the book being sold out during the literary Christmas market, and the author must wait a whole year before a new print run is needed. This is what I dare not, or cannot, enter into; for then I would incur a financial loss which the honorarium proposed by Det Kongelige Teater cannot in any way compensate for. Besides, numerous orders have come in from bookshops around our countries, and they have received an assurance that they will have the book at a certain time. Nor can I avoid taking into account the reports that there are great expectations of this new work, and an author is always unwise to wait too long to meet such expectations, as he risks losing the public's interest before the book is released.

Another side to this matter is that I believe it is detrimental to a dramatic work first to be made available to the general public on stage. I believe this regulation within Det Kongelige Teater has had an unfavourable effect on dramatic production in Denmark. At least it remains a fact that this production has not shown any tendency to flourish since the introduction of the regulation. And this is easy to explain. In light of the current condition, a new play can never be understood and judged in isolation, in its pure state, in and for itself as poetic writing. The aesthetic judgement will always encompass both the play and the staging it is given; these two quite different things become muddled together and confused, and the public's main interest will usually be directed more towards the acting, the staging, the actors, than the play itself.

18 February 1882 to Hagbard Emanuel Berner
(Norwegian politician.)

[…] I learnt with great joy from *Dagbladet* that you have suggested to the Storthing [Norwegian Parliament] now in session to raise the Poet's Scholarships for Bjørnson and myself, and from a few statements in your letter I dare deduce that there is at least some probability that the case may be viewed positively by the National Assembly this year.

You have required further information about the losses which I believe Bjørnson and I have suffered through the lack of a literary convention in Norway's case. […]

In Finland, many or perhaps more accurately most of my dramatic works have been translated and performed in Swedish, as well as in Finnish.

I know for certain that *The League of Youth* has been translated and staged in Russia. From newspaper notices I have seen, this is very likely also to be the case with *A Doll's House*.

The last-mentioned play is also translated into Polish and has been produced in Warsaw. Likewise, a translation of my collection of poems was published there a few years ago; but when this was heavily edited by the Russian censor, it caused a new complete edition to be printed and published in Krakow; that is, in an Austrian territory.

The Vikings at Helgeland has been translated and staged in Hungarian. *A Doll's House* as well, apparently; at least, its production is being planned.

In England, there are two different translations of this play. *Pillars of Society* has also been translated into English and been performed in London.

It can be assumed with some certainty that there are translations of many or a few of my works in different countries of which I have no knowledge.

That I have not received any kind of honorarium for the translations and productions mentioned above is a matter of course.

As far as my literary affairs in Germany are concerned, I would like to offer you a brief overview.

The Vikings at Helgeland has been translated by Emma Klingenfeld at my expense, and printed and published by Theodor Ackermann in Munich, also at my expense and without my receiving an author's honorarium; besides, as commissioner, Ackerman gives himself 50 per cent of the profits from the copies sold. The Germans dare not in fact proceed as genuine publishers of the Norwegian dramatists' works, as, due to the absence of a convention, they can never be secured against competing editions.

Lady Inger is translated and published under the same conditions as *The Vikings*.

Pillars of Society likewise.

Besides, this last play has been translated in Berlin by Wilhelm Lange, who on his own account has organised productions by many German theatres, as well as its publication by Ph. Reclam in his Universal Library Series at Leipzig. Thus, Lange's translation could be sold for twenty pfennigs. My own, which is properly designed, costs two marks and thus suffers low sales. Furthermore, Mr Emil Jonas in Berlin has published an 'adaptation' of the play, which likewise is printed in a cheap edition and performed in many places in Germany.

The League of Youth is translated by Adolf Strodtmann in Berlin and published there by Duncker. The enterprise has nothing to do with me and of course I get nothing.

Another translation of this play is published by W. Lange. This enterprise, too, has nothing to do with me.

The Pretenders is translated by Adolf Strodtmann and published by Duncker; likewise *The League of Youth*. The theatre honoraria in both these cases go solely to the translator.

Brand is translated and published in two impressions by P.F. Siebold in Kassel.

Likewise, by Julie Ruhkopf in Dresden, and published in the Library of Foreign Classics by Kühtmann in Bremen.

Likewise, by Baron Alfred von Wolzogen in Schwerin, and published in Weimar.

Likewise, by L. Passarge in Königsberg, and published in Leipzig.

Peer Gynt is also translated by L. Passarge and published in Leipzig.

Most of my poems are translated by A. Strodtmann, and published in Berlin in his book: *Das geistige Leben in Dänemark* ['The Intellectual Life in Denmark'], etc, etc.

To prevent a repetition of the saga of *Pillars of Society*, when the manuscript of *A Doll's House* was ready, I entered into a contract with W. Lange about jointly publishing the play in German. He agreed to this and received the proof-sheets sent in instalments from Copenhagen. The conditions were that the translator should keep the whole of the honorarium from the sale of the book solely for himself. However, we should share the theatre honoraria equally between us. Thus, this play has given me a considerable income from the German theatres; but this method is useless for the future. To secure ourselves against competition from other translators, we had to make sure the play was published in German at the same time as the original. This, too, happened at Ph. Reclam in Leipzig. But he immediately seized the opportunity to send his cheap edition in great numbers to the Scandinavian countries where, at a cost of a mere twenty pfennigs, it was sold at considerable expense to the original edition, for which one must pay two kroner twenty-five øre. At the time, I received a report via business contacts that a single bookseller in Copenhagen had sold 600–800 copies of the German *Nora*. This means I can count yet again on having lost everything I earned through the honoraria from the German theatres. All of it as a result of us not having a copyright convention.

Ibsen and the Story of his Translation into German

10 February 1869 to Peter Friedrich Siebold
(German commercial traveller and first German translator of *Brand*.)

I am most grateful that you have chosen to translate *Brand* into German. The enterprise is certainly a difficult one; however, one can perform miracles in your beautiful mother tongue.

14 March 1869 to Frederik Hegel

A German, Mr Siebold, writes to me that he has translated *Brand*, and is arranging for its publication here [in Germany]. Do you know him? I must confess that I am not entirely confident about the undertaking. I do, however, plan to try and get my works circulated in Germany.

9 May 1869 to Peter Friedrich Siebold

I have to ask your forgiveness for a great many things. First, I must ask you to pardon the state in which I return your manuscript; unfortunately, in destroying some of my useless drafts I also happened to tear up your preface, and only discovered afterwards what had happened. I have not answered your esteemed letter until today because I have been waiting for answers regarding certain enquiries I have made in Leipzig. [...] My literary friends have advised me to approach the matter in the following manner. You are connected with the Leipzig *Illustrierte Zeitung* [*Illustrated News*]; were it possible for you to get them to accept a biography of me, then I would provide the required photographic portrait myself. [...] The biography should consist only of what is good and positive; the German critics will surely present objections later on.

If you find it advantageous, I should especially like you to mention what I had to struggle with during those earlier days. Would you also emphasise that several years ago, the Cabinet and the Storthing, in recognition of the position I hold in Norwegian literature, unanimously awarded me a salary for life, as well as ample travelling stipends, etc. Dear Mr Siebold, please do not misunderstand this as an effort to partake in any form of humbug, that would be against my nature; however, I have been assured that things like this are necessary. If my name is introduced to Germany in this way, it will be far easier for your translation to be published. If you then send it to me, I would travel to Leipzig with it myself, have the translation announced in some journal or other, talk with those concerned, and not give up until the book is published. The preface could then be made considerably shorter by referring to the biography. If you think this is a good suggestion, write to me. I shall have time at my disposal hereafter, and will do everything I can to advance an enterprise which is so much in my own interest.

28 May 1869 to Lorentz Dietrichson

[...] I want to presume on your friendship and ask you a favour.

The matter is this: a German literary person, P.F. Siebold in Kassel, has translated *Brand* and will publish the book in Leipzig this autumn. However, he or his publisher or both believe that the public should be prepared beforehand, and plan to publish my portrait, with a brief biography about my position in Scandinavian literature, my personal circumstances, etc, in a German journal, most likely *Illustrierte Zeitung*, as soon as possible. I have been approached about information; but

I do not feel I should concern myself with it, and of course Mr Siebold does not have sufficient knowledge of the subject. You will understand that this matter is of interest to me. Therefore, I turn to you, as my old friend. Dear friend, could you put something together that will suit the Germans? Write as favourably as your conscience will allow; the miseries of the wretched writer are no longer in vogue; inform them instead on how the Government and the Storthing have granted me a salary, that I travel, and live 'in dem grossen Vaterland' [Germany], etc.

15 June 1869 to Peter Friedrich Siebold

I have had the pleasure of receiving your friendly letter and the accompanying manuscript. I will read through the latter as quickly as possible. I do have some difficulty in deciphering your handwriting; however, I should be able to do it.

[…]

Many passages in your translation seem to me to be surprisingly well rendered. When I glanced over the pages I noticed a couple of lines which might possibly gain by compression; but as to how far this is possible in German, I naturally bow to your opinion.

28 February 1870 to Peter Friedrich Siebold

I hope the biography will be printed in the near future, and also that you will soon find a publisher [for the translation of *Brand*].

[…]

For my part, I am sorry that your description of the reindeer hunt will not be published in *Illustrierte Zeitung*. Because I am certain that you above all, with your intimate knowledge of our country and with your interests in the life of hunters, would deliver something particularly splendid.

6 March 1872 to Peter Friedrich Siebold

It was a double pleasure to receive your friendly letter after such a long silence. I am quite certain I wrote to you after the biography appeared in *Illustrierte Zeitung*; soon after the [Franco-Prussian] war broke out, I went to Copenhagen, and my attention was completely directed toward the great world events. [...] I thank you for making good your intention to introduce *Brand* to German readers. *I have not yet received the book*; I long to have it, although I do not in any way doubt that the translation will satisfy me. Besides, it was high time that your work was published, as here in Dresden another translation is finished and about to be sent to the printing press. This translation is by the novelist Julie Ruhkopf, who has sent me the manuscript for examination.

9 April 1872 to Michael Birkeland

The Paetel Brothers' Publishing House in Berlin has published *The Pretenders* and *The League of Youth* under the titles *Die Kronpretendenten* and *Der Bund der Jugend* in lovely editions and masterly translations by Adolf Strodtmann, who is a famous translator of Byron and Tennyson. A translation of *Brand* has also been published; another translation of this same book is announced from two other parties. Several translations of my poems are under way.

7 June 1873 to Julie Ruhkopf
(German author of books for young people and children.)

It is a special pleasure for me to be able to declare that I find the translation characterised throughout by the spirit of the poem [*Brand*], the way it is revealed in the original, as well as showing a complete understanding of all its details, all of which appear to be reproduced with the utmost faithfulness.

14 March 1876 to Julie Ruhkopf
(Ruhkopf's translation of *Emperor and Galilean* was never published.)

I would like to ask if you have found a publisher for your translation of this book [*Emperor and Galilean*]? If not, I suggest selling the translation to me, and I will cover the costs of having it printed. You will decide the price yourself, and the manuscript must be sent to me as soon as possible.

25 September 1877 to Emma Klingenfeld
(German translator of seven plays by Ibsen.)

When I last spoke to you, I forgot a few minor points I would like to direct your attention to before you begin the transcription of my play [*Pillars of Society*].

[…]

As far as names are concerned, I allow myself to suggest the following changes. The name Olaf should be changed to Oskar, Rørlund to Lundt, Tønnesen to Tönnsen, Vigeland should be written Wigland, Sandstad written Sandstadt, Dina Dorf should be changed to Dina Torp, which is a Swedish name, Krap written Krapp, and Aune should be changed to Auner.

I reached an agreement with Ackermann yesterday, and he is prepared to begin printing as soon as the first sheets are ready.

18 January 1878 to Emil Jonas
(German editor and author.)

In answer to your letter I must remind you about something you cannot be unfamiliar with; that as early as the beginning of November last year, I myself issued an original German edition of my play *Pillars of Society* at Ackermann's publishing house. A translation from your hand is thus quite superfluous, and I must decline most strongly an adaptation of the kind you describe.

What you write about your cuts in the first act is completely meaningless and testifies to the fact that you have never understood the work you believe yourself competent enough to adapt. Surely it must be obvious even to the most common literary fraud that in this play no role can be left out, and not a single line of dialogue cut. Also, the play has already been accepted by many German theatres in its unabridged and undistorted form.

Should you, despite what I have told you, still recklessly continue with your intention and thus from lack of skill distort and corrupt my work, I herewith let you know that I unremittingly will make this case the object of the comments it deserves in the Scandinavian press; it shall be known even in the highest places, and in time, you will experience the results that this will have.

I did not want to hold back this warning. There is still time for you to avoid the mistreatment of my work which you have threatened me with in your letter, and for your own sake, I advise you to consider carefully what you do.

Besides, my play will be performed in its undistorted form in at least two other theatres in Berlin, where it has already been accepted, so the audience will have ample opportunity to make comparisons. Should you still allow this botched piece of work to be presented to the general public, at least you owe me the satisfaction of printing on the [Berlin] Stadttheater's posters 'verstümmelt von Emil Jonas' ['mutilated by Emil Jonas'].

22 January 1880 to Frederik Hegel

I did see in one of the journals you sent me that *Nora* [the German title of *A Doll's House*] is advertised for sale up there [Denmark]; but I thought that you merely made me aware of this matter as a curiosity, as I simply could not imagine that anyone up there would buy the German translation unless perhaps to compare it with the original. Your message puts the matter in a different light, and I would therefore request that you immediately call on the authorities to act to stop this traffic, which is illegal and causing each of us damage. The German translation is, as a publishing enterprise, quite irrelevant to me;

I have not paid the translator any honorarium, and I receive no honorarium from the publisher; the translator must give me the necessary copies for use in German theatres; my involvement with this matter stops there. Obviously, we cannot forbid the German publisher to dispatch orders to Denmark; however, there should be no doubt that we can forbid Danish booksellers to offer this German translation for sale in Denmark. Our legislation contains clear provisions for such cases.

17 February 1880 to the Editor of Nationaltidende

In your honourable newspaper no.1360, I read a correspondence from Flensborg, from which I learn that *A Doll's House*, in German *Nora*, has been performed there, and that the play's ending at this performance has been changed—allegedly on my request.

The latter is utterly false.

[...]

As long as no copyright convention between Germany and the Scandinavian countries has been finalised, we Nordic authors are totally without any rights down here, just as the German authors are with us. Our dramatic works are thus regularly exposed to violent treatment both by translators and by managers, directors and actors at the smaller theatres. But having learnt from previous experience, if my works are threatened by something like that, I would prefer to execute the act of violence myself instead of giving my works over to treatment and 'adaptation' by less careful and less skilled hands.

17 April 1880 to Wilhelm Lange
(German scholar and translator of ten plays by Ibsen.)

I would be happy to agree with your suggestion concerning a new translation of *The League of Youth*. But before you let it be printed, please make use of the abbreviations and changes which I, together with the present director [of the Court Theatre in Munich] Mr Jenke, made in the Strodtmann translation. The Hoftheater library here [Munich] has a copy of the corrected manuscript; I shall try to borrow it and immediately send it to you. Our new printed edition may then be sent to the theatres in the version in which the play should be performed.

4 July 1883 to Emma Klingenfeld

I asked my publisher to send you the new edition of *The Feast at Solhaug*, because I thought it might possibly interest you to read through this work of my youth. That you are now working on translating the play is a great delight; I believe you are especially suited to this task and that the translation will succeed uncommonly well. I do not doubt that you will find a publisher, Reclam or another one, and perhaps you could also get your translation produced at some of the theatres in Germany and Austria. But if I may be so bold as to offer you some advice in this matter, I would like to suggest that you contact a theatre agent of good repute in Berlin who will take care of the business side on your behalf regarding the theatres. I apologise for involving myself in these matters that have nothing to do with me!

I hope that you *do not* translate the *preface* to the play, it would be of no interest to German readers; I doubt it would even be understood in Germany. However, I presume you share my opinion on this point.

That I did not send you my two latest plays, *Ghosts* and *An Enemy of the People*, was because these plays deal with problems which I presumed would be of less interest to you, and I feared that sending them might possibly be perceived by you as a request to translate these plays as well; a request which I felt you would not be able to accept with particular pleasure.

18 February 1886 to Ernst Brausewetter
(German author and translator of three plays by Ibsen.)

My main reason for not answering you before is that I hoped, on closer deliberation, you would come to recognise that your biographical and literary critical work could not be executed before you had acquired a thorough knowledge not only of the

Norwegian-Danish language, but of Scandinavian literature as a whole. Without such a foundation, the task you have set yourself could not be solved satisfactorily.

Now that you have been good enough to send me a translation of *The Wild Duck*, I must presume that in the meantime you have undertaken Nordic language studies. However, these studies have been far from thorough enough. The whole translation teems with misunderstandings, and I do not find that the original tone of the language is reproduced. In the original, every character has a specific, individual way of expressing him- or herself; in your translation, all the characters speak with an even, flat ordinariness.

I therefore beg you to put this effort aside for the time being. To publish the translation in its present form would cause me great damage, and I would be obliged to publicly protest.

30 October 1886 to Frederik Hegel

My new play [*Rosmersholm*] is being printed now, and I presume it will come out around the middle of next month.

[…]

On the one hand, to prevent the translation from damaging the original, and on the other hand, to make it difficult for competing translations, would you be so kind as to send Lange the printed sheets *one* act at a time, so when you have printed the second act, he receives the sheets of the first act, etc.? He does not know the title of the play, and the title page should be sent him last of all. […]

15 November 1886 to Franz Wallner
(German actor and author. Wallner performed the role of Osvald in *Ghosts* at the Berlin Residenz-Theater in 1887.)

I am very sorry to have to inform you that I am not able to provide any information about the agent for the translator of *Ghosts*. Moreover, I doubt whether the play has been placed with an agency. […] The translator M. von Borch is completely

147

unknown to me personally. However, the translation is very successful, and it would give me great pleasure if you could organise a production of the play at the Residenz-Theater.[2]

26 January 1887 to Frederik Hegel

Probably this very day a German translation of *Rosmersholm* is coming out in Berlin, done by M. v. Borch, who once translated *Ghosts*. W. Lange has hesitated so long to deliver his manuscript to Reclam that his competitor has beaten him to it. This case does not result in any pecuniary loss to me, as I have the same conditions with both translators.

4 February 1887 to Julius Hoffory

I wrote to Mrs v. Borch yesterday and informed her that, depending on a couple of further conditions re proofreading, I have nothing against her translation of *The Wild Duck* being issued by Mr Fischer's Publishing House instead of Reclam.

However, as far as *Lady Inger* is concerned, this is an old play, which came out in a German translation by Emma Klingenfeld ten years ago at Theodor Ackermann's publishing house here in Munich. The edition is not yet sold out, and under these circumstances, one should not be considering a new translation of this play for the time being.

22 April 1887 to Marie von Borch
(German translator of ten plays by Ibsen.)

I must ask you to please forgive me that only today I send you my most grateful thanks for your translation of *The Wild Duck*, and for the copy which you sent me.

This translation must undoubtedly be described as especially successful. It is, of course, not easy for me to make any decisive judgement with regard to the language. But from many competent readers with whom I have discussed the matter, I have received the confident and unanimous assurance that your work deserves all possible praise and acknowledgment.

[…]

You indicated in one of your letters that you would like to translate *Love's Comedy*. I have not yet given you an answer to this, but I would naturally receive your offer with great pleasure, if it could possibly be realised. But this endeavour would meet with great difficulties. This whole play is, after all, written in rhymed verse, which it would not be easy to reproduce in a translation.

24 May 1887 to Ernst Brausewetter

In answer to your esteemed letter, I would like to inform you that my play *The Wild Duck*, translated by M. v. Borch, was published by S. Fischer in Berlin several months ago, and the title page reads: 'the only German edition authorised by the author'.

That I, under these circumstances, cannot authorise the translation attempted by you is, obviously, a matter of course.

Besides, the publication of your translation at this point in time would to a large degree, and in several respects, damage my interests.

I must therefore request that you hold it back, at least for the time being.

I must also most decidedly ask that you do not publish any translation of *Emperor and Galilean*, as long as it has not been read through by me. This work is not suitable to be translated by a beginner, and besides, requires that the translator has a comprehensive philological training, without which the hint of Greek in the tone of this drama's language cannot be reproduced.

Moreover, it totally goes against all my intentions to let this great work come out in German so soon after the translations of *Rosmersholm* and *The Wild Duck*.

I and my regular, experienced translators proceed according to a plan made and carefully tested in advance, and I would not, without protesting sharply and publicly, put up with a spanner being thrown into this plan by uncalled for outsiders.

Of course, I appreciate the interest you show in my literary activity. However, the best way you can demonstrate this interest would be to hold back your translation of *Emperor and Galilean* until I inform you that the opportune time has arrived.

For the sake of convenience, I write this letter in Norwegian, as I presume that this language does not present any problems to you. And I feel assured that you, by considering this matter carefully, will acknowledge the validity of the reasons which move me to refuse, for the time being, your friendly offer of working as my translator.

8 November 1887 to Julius Hoffory

I learn with regret from the newspapers that my previous translator, Wilhelm Lange, has gone insane. This information did not, by the way, come as a surprise to me. Last month he did send me a couple of letters which seemed to suggest an abnormal state of mind. Still, I hope that his illness is only temporary. Besides, I do not intend, as far as it is up to me, to use him as a translator from now on. I could not wish for anyone better, more reliable and understanding than Baroness von Borch.[3]

9 February 1888 to Julius Hoffory

Yesterday I received from Berlin a proof-copy of the first act of *Emperor and Galilean*.

[…]

I have read the copy several times and I find the translation an unparalleled success; masterly in all respects. The original's tone of language is completely recreated; the ways of thinking as well, and with the finest understanding of the moods and the nuances.

26 February 1888 to Julius Hoffory

I have long feared the appearance of Brausewetter's translation [of *Emperor and Galilean*], as I have heard a rumour that such a one is under preparation; but hoped to the very last that the time of publication was not that close. Both he and Reclam have maintained total silence towards me.

It is doubly dear to me under these circumstances to learn that the Berlin edition [of your translation] will be speeded up as much as possible. I also feel extremely obliged to Mr Fischer for this, and hope that his competitor will not cause him as much damage if he immediately announces his own legitimate and authorised edition as imminent.

27 September 1888 to Julius Hoffory

I am truly sorry that Miss Klingenfeld could have let herself be carried away enough to write you such a letter as the one I hereby return to you. [...]

I suppose it is possible that my letter to her might have said that I would have been 'very happy to' entrust my new play to her [*The Lady from the Sea*], if the matter had not already been settled. But I think she ought to have understood that this was only to be taken as a general phrase of politeness. Had I really wanted her to translate this play, I would of course have approached her about it. But I would not dream of doing that, because I do not consider her qualified for the job. It is not all that long ago that she said to my wife that she did not understand the meaning of *The Wild Duck*. And I am quite certain the case would be the same with my new play.

17 December 1888 to Julius Hoffory

In answer to your friendly letter of the tenth of this month, I hereby inform you that I have written to Mr Reclam about a postponement according to your wishes, which are in total agreement with mine. To completely prohibit him from publishing a translation of the new play [*The Lady from the Sea*] would after all lead nowhere, as there is no judicial remedy to make the prohibition effective.

I have reason to believe that Mr Reclam will respect what I expressed in my letter to him, and organise his course of action accordingly. But as an additional measure, I still feel it would not be a bad idea if you as well as Mr Fischer would exert some influence on Mrs v. Borch, who, as I believe you know, has offered to hand the translation to the Reclam Universal Library Series. She wrote to me some time ago about this matter, and my answer was to request that she abandon this idea. However, it seems that my request has been to no avail.

And as far as the theatres are concerned, we may also fear competition. To secure our interests in this regard, it would undoubtedly be advisable to hand in *The Lady from the Sea* to Felix Bloch's agency without delay. The theatres in Berlin may of course be excluded. Such exclusions with regard to one particular place is not uncommon. But all circumstances considered, I believe the head start in time we have gained should be exploited to the utmost degree. This is because I have heard that Ernst Brausewetter in Stuttgart is working on a translation, which will most probably be offered to the theatres.

6 March 1890 to Samuel Fischer
(German publisher.)

Your valued communication has just reached me and I hasten to reply to it in order to bring to your attention the fact that *An Enemy of the People* has not been published by Ackermann. The only translation that exists is that organised by Wilhelm Lange, and authorised by me, with the Universal Library Series, Reclam, Leipizig. I should therefore like to suggest that you contact either Miss Emma Klingenfeld, at present in Berlin, or Mrs v. Borch, or perhaps Ernst Brausewetter in Stuttgart, with a view to obtaining an accurate and really fluent translation. I will, of course, not be able to formally authorise such a translation, but that seems to me relatively unimportant.[4]

19 November 1890 to Julius Elias

My new play [*Hedda Gabler*] is now finished, and I can therefore begin to think about the business side of everything.

First of all, may I ask if you would be so good as to inform Mr Fischer that I accept his offer of 300 marks as the honorarium for remitting the proof-sheets directly from Copenhagen, either to him or to the prospective translator.

The translation of this play presents a number of problems, and this necessitates my personal control. Therefore, I would like to ask that Mr Fischer is informed of my wish that he passes on this work to Miss Emma Klingenfeld, with whom he should start negotiations immediately.

Should the fulfilment of this wish of mine meet with practical difficulties, contrary to my expectation, I would also be able to accept Mrs M. v. Borch as the translator. However, only on the condition that her German proof-sheets are presented to me for revision.

Mr Fischer's choice must fall on one of these two. A third cannot be accepted by me. As well, I must be informed about his decision so I can give the necessary instructions in Copenhagen.

[...]

Last month Miss Klingenfeld instigated a written skirmish with me, caused by a misunderstanding on her part. I did not reply to her latest letter to me. Neither have I told her that I prefer her as the translator of my new work. Still, I cannot believe it is likely that she should refuse Mr Fischer's proposition, should she receive it.

17 December 1890 to Julius Elias

You will have learnt from my telegram tonight that I would never under any circumstance or any condition whatsoever allow my new play [*Hedda Gabler*] to be published act by act in a weekly journal.

The play shall be published in its entirety, as a book. And it must be published immediately. Without further delay. It is Mr Fischer's duty and obligation to see to it that this happens.

If Mr Fischer really believes that my work has the power to bring so much luck to the weekly journal, all he needs to do is print the book in a much larger edition and publicise in the papers that each new subscriber will be given a copy as a Christmas present.

For my part, I have already sacrificed more than enough to the advantage of Mr Fischer's pecuniary interests. I have, in fact, ensured Miss Klingenfeld half of the prospective theatre honoraria; thus he will come into possession of the translation without any expense to speak of. This method of payment, which is so comfortable for Mr Fischer, is one he himself recommended to Miss Klingenfeld and with which I complied. But it means that my pocket remains closed on this occasion.

Today the original edition of *Hedda Gabler* is published in the Nordic countries. Perhaps it has already been published yesterday. Thus, it is available from now on to any competing German translator.

On my table lies a whole pile of written enquiries from German theatre directors, among them from Berlin directors too, with a request to have the play sent to them for possible production.

My resolute demand is therefore that Mr Fischer immediately, without further delay, hand the remaining proofread sheets to Miss Klingenfeld, and with the same immediacy makes sure that the book reaches the bookstores at once.

18 December 1890 to Julius Elias

A strange and sudden transformation overcame Mr Fischer when he realised that his own interests, and not just mine, were threatened. A couple of days ago, he declared in his letter that it was impossible to have the book finished before the new year. Now he believes he can have it finished on Monday. A couple of days ago he assured me that I need not fear competition. Now it seems he is beside himself with the very thought of Mrs v. Borch. But let those matters lie!

4 January 1891 to August Larsen

You may send the copy of *Hedda Gabler* ordered by Philipp Reclam to Mrs v. Borch, as the book will not be published by him in the near future. And as long as his translator does not compete with me in regard to the theatres, I have nothing against his editions. This is because they cause my works to be widely distributed, especially in the circles to which they would not otherwise gain access. He himself expressed this quite recently in a letter in which he enclosed a particularly considerable voluntary honorarium.

11 January 1891 to Julius Elias

I did not reply to your letter of 3 January, as I had already once before informed Mr Fischer, through you, that in accordance with his wishes, I had approached Mr Reclam and did not fear any kind of surprise attack from him. I have repeatedly had proof that Mr Reclam is an honourable man. And even the rumour which Mr Fischer mentions in his letter to you, and which has disturbed him so much, furnishes such proof. For this rumour obviously stems from the fact that a certain notorious literary robber in Berlin had already approached Mr Reclam in December with an offer to deliver to him a translation of *Hedda Gabler* in the course of a few weeks, and as an honorarium, to be given a couple of hundred free copies. (Obviously, he would try to have these placed at the theatres.) However, Mr Reclam immediately and unconditionally rejected this offer. I have first-hand information about this. I have therefore found it unnecessary, as well as somewhat improper, to enter into new enquiries and representations with Mr Reclam. Besides, I cannot understand Mr Fischer's mortal fear of the possibility that he should be left with the greater part of his 3,000 copies. The two first editions of his version are already sold out, and I believe he can safely give in to the hope that a third edition will soon go the same way—if not before, then at least when the theatre productions begin to happen around and about. That aside, give my warm and most friendly regards to Mr Fischer. He is after all 'a good fellow'; it is just his exaggerated and unnecessary anxiety that I cannot become comfortable with.

1 November 1892 to Julius Elias

The manuscript of my most recent play [*The Master Builder*] has just been submitted to Gyldendal, and I can therefore now reply to your friendly letter of 19 September, for which I thank you most sincerely.

The German translation of the play will be written here [Kristiania] under my own supervision, and be sent in turn to Mr Fischer, provided he agrees to pay an honorarium of 600 marks, which will be sent to me as soon as the book is ready to be printed.

The performance rights will be *mine* exclusively; and Mr Fischer must submit twenty-five copies of the book to Felix Bloch Erben, Berlin [Ibsen's theatrical agent], as soon as it is published, and without remuneration. Likewise, I demand twenty copies for myself, to be delivered to me here.

In addition, Mr Fischer must consent to my authorised translation also being published by Philipp Reclam in Leipzig in his Universal Library Series.

For various strong reasons, I do not want to get involved with Mrs v. Borch and her mother as translators. Mrs Zinck has written to me that she intends to translate my 'Poems' for Mr Fischer. I ask him herewith in all friendliness to abandon this undertaking, as it totally goes against my own intentions.

[...]

I often receive sad testimonies from Hoffory about his condition. He regularly sends me old hotel bills he has paid, private letters and things like that without indicating what I should do with them.

1 November 1896 to Julius Elias

Unfortunately, I am not rich enough to continue using Mr Fischer as my publisher, which would more or less mean the same as letting him have my books for free. You see, with Mr Fischer, I have had to pay most of the translation costs myself, as I have had to hand over half of all of the theatre honoraria to the translators, while Mr Fischer himself has only paid a mere 'bagatelle' for the translation work. The last time my own honorarium was 1,000 Deutsche marks; and in a letter, which I received at the same time as your telegram, he very generously offers to pay all of 200 marks more! Now, that work is protected by the Berne Convention! Your telegram offers 3,000 marks; however, this is described as the largest sacrifice, and I do not want to impose that on Mr Fischer. —As a comparison, I would like to inform you how Mr Albert Langen in Munich sees himself capable of paying for my new book without it occurring to him to talk of any sacrifice. My author-honorarium from Mr

Langen is 5,000 marks, and all theatre honoraria go wholly to myself, as the translation costs are covered by Mr Langen. — After this, I hope you will find it reasonable that I can no longer impose on myself the pecuniary sacrifice of keeping Fischer as my publisher. —For further comparison with Mr Fischer's offer, I can inform you that my English publisher, Mr W. Heinemann, London, has paid the same honorarium for my two previous plays as Mr Langen now offers, and will pay even more this time, as I am now protected by the Convention.

As far as the new edition planned by Mr Fischer is concerned, this must be thoroughly revised in advance, and with my own contribution. Several of the translations are highly unfortunate as they fail to convey the original's complete and full meaning on many points. The translation of *Love's Comedy* is in this sense totally useless and must be replaced by a new one.

20 June 1897 to Julius Elias

I was extremely pleased to receive and make myself familiar with your and Dr Schlenther's plan to publish a new complete edition of my literary works [in German]. I can subscribe to the plan on the whole; I will only allow myself a few brief remarks: The Table of Contents of Volume One comprises Poems and Prose writings. Of the latter, I have not written anything suitable for German translation, and I would suggest that the poems are put in the last volume, as they have been written across my long career; besides, satisfactory translations could hardly be provided in the time left before the publication of the first volume.

Lady Inger and *The Vikings at Helgeland* are solely *my* property, as Miss Klingenfeld is paid by me for her work; thus, there will be no problem in allowing these plays to be given to Mr Fischer's publishing house.

The Burial Mound was published many years ago as a serial in a Norwegian journal, and I hope to get you a copy of it.

I have never wanted to publish the two other plays I wrote in my youth, and I do not want them to be translated.

19 September 1897 to Julius Elias

For the last time, I must categorically declare that I neither want nor *can* allow the play *St. John's Night* to be included in the collection of *my* works. [...] I think the translations of the other two works of my youth will be in the best of hands with Miss Klingenfeld.

24 April 1898 to Julius Elias

As I return the enclosed signed declaration, I shall merely note that at the time I paid Miss Klingenfeld the sum she herself demanded for her work, and that I am therefore not at all willing to pay her any extra honorarium for the, I believe, highly necessary corrections, alterations, changes and improvements which now turn out to be needful before her translation can be published again. In all circumstances, this has to be Mr Fischer's own business, all the more so when he considers the spot price for which he got it from me. —I am extremely busy at the moment and can see no prospect of engaging in any extensive letter-writing re the unwarranted Klingenfeld pretensions.

26 July 1898 to Fredrik Gjertsen
(Norwegian philologist, civil servant, and educator.)

My German poetic translator, Dr Morgenstern, has for months now been staying out at Nordstrand, busily working on *Love's Comedy*, *Brand* and *Peer Gynt*. For which reason, a book full of questions hovers threateningly above my head each day.

1 May 1899 to Julius Elias

I have the strongest desire that Mr Christian Morgenstern shall translate my new play [*When We Dead Awaken*] into German. He is a highly talented, genuine writer. [...] What is more, he is fully familiar with the Norwegian language, an advantage I have not always been lucky enough to find with many of my previous German translators.

2 January 1900 to Christian Morgenstern
(German author, poet and translator of nine plays by Ibsen.)

For some time now I really ought to have written to you to thank you for your masterly, sensitive translation into German of my new play [*When We Dead Awaken*]. Forgive me for the fact that this is happening only today. I have read through the translation carefully and cannot understand how you could manage to complete it in such a short time. And you have found such perfect equivalents for every turn of phrase! I am grateful to you from the bottom of my heart! Be assured that I understand very well what a share you have in the positive reception the book has received in Germany.[5]

3 January 1900 to Julius Elias

In the cast list [of *When We Dead Awaken*] I wrote 'A travelling lady'; in the German edition, this has been 'improved' to 'Irene'. It is impossible that my excellent, sensitive and understanding translator can be guilty of that. It must be the printer or one of his people. I hope that a watchful eye will be kept on him in the future. The defective 1,000 copies of the ninth volume will hopefully be discarded.

It is lucky for those involved that the hysterical paroxysms in the Fischer circle are now over and done with. Thus, there is hope for me to be spared any further telegram filled with such utter sophistry as the one Mr Fischer's lawyer and others found it suitable to send me.

It should be superfluous to add that I have never considered concluding any contract with Mr Albert Langen about my new play. Hence, I did not answer their threatening letters.

6 July 1900 to Julius Elias

I am ill. Cannot be burdened with business letters.
For help, approach Chr. Morgenstern. He understands it best.

1. Today there are a total of 1,223 translators listed in IbsenStage.
2. Translated from the German.
3. The exact circumstances of Ibsen's break with Lange is unknown, but a growing hostility towards him can be detected in several letters written by Ibsen between 1887 and 1894.
4. Translated from the German.
5. Translated from the German.

7
Ibsen and the Christiania Theater

While Ibsen was living in Germany and Italy from 1870 to 1890, he maintained a detailed correspondence with the Christiania Theater in Kristiania.[1] These letters form the core of this chapter.[2] The Christiania Theater premiered many of Ibsen's early plays: *The Burial Mound* (1850), *The Pretenders* (1864), *The League of Youth* (1869), *Love's Comedy* (1873) and *Peer Gynt* (1876). Of his later works only *An Enemy of the People* (1883) and *The Lady from the Sea* (1889) were premiered on the Christiania stage; but after the company was reconstituted as Nationaltheatret (the Norwegian National Theatre) in 1899, it became increasingly tied to the Ibsen repertoire. Today it is the home of the biennial International Ibsen Festival.

Although language barriers prevented Ibsen from communicating directly with many European theatres, his letters are surprisingly knowledgeable about the performances of his plays, even at theatres where he had no copyright protection. He corresponded in German with major theatre managements particularly in Munich and Vienna, and with Duke Georg II at the Saxe-Meiningen Theatre. His knowledge of productions in English and French language theatres came from his translators, particularly William Archer and Moritz Prozor, and he wrote brief letters in French to the avant-garde Parisian directors André Antoine and Aurélien Marie Lugné-Poë. Yet it is from Ibsen's correspondence with Scandinavian theatres that we gain the greatest insights into his thoughts on casting, rehearsals, staging, acting, and the business of theatre.

Scandinavian theatres in the late nineteenth century were divided into three basic tiers. At the top were the major State companies that paid the biggest royalties: these included Det Kongelige Teater in Copenhagen;[3] Kungliga Dramatiska Teatern in Stockholm;[4] and the Christiania Theater in Kristiania. Regional theatres formed the second tier, the venues most relevant to Ibsen being Gothenburg and Bergen. Finally, there were the touring companies: they paid writers less well, but served large populations in both rural and urban areas. The Chr. W. Foght and Olaus Olsen companies toured Ibsen's plays to Norway's provincial towns,[5] while August Lindberg toured his plays across the whole of Scandinavia and Finland. Ibsen's dealings with all three tiers showed considerable business acumen. He stimulated demand by notifying managements of the negotiations he was conducting with their competitors, offered alternative plays to managements if the rights they requested were already sold, and wrote threatening letters to managements in breach of contract. He defined the geographical limitations of touring circuits and even, on occasion, stipulated which venues should be used for performances. He negotiated fees and followed up late payments. In some instances, he insisted that reviews were sent to him together with details of audience reception. The following letter to August Lindberg is a perfect illustration of Ibsen's attention to detail in these negotiations.

19 August 1883 to August Lindberg

You wish to produce *Ghosts* also in Kristiania.

Permission for this may be given under certain conditions.

First and foremost I must demand that Mrs Winter-Hjelm will be playing Mrs Alving there as well. I take this as a given.

Then I must demand the full right to refuse performing the play in Møllergadens Theater. This venue is so narrow and encumbered, the distance between the audience and the actors so small, that a full effect cannot be achieved.

If the [Ch]ristiania Theater could be handed over, I would see this as the best solution. If not, I have no particular objection to the Tivoli Theater. This theatre has been dignified by earlier performances by Mrs W-H and by a couple of other excellent artists.

Then I must reserve the right to demand that the play shall not be performed in Kristiania before it has been staged in Stockholm and Copenhagen. I shall not enter into the reasons for this.

In connection with the above I must maintain that *Ghosts*, although only in three acts, still fills a whole evening in the theatre. Of course, nothing else must be performed either before or after the play.

I would prefer that this work of mine is played everywhere without the use of an orchestra, either before the performance or between the acts.

As honorarium for the performance rights in Kristiania I shall confine myself to asking 500 crowns, a sum which must be paid to Nils Lund Bookshop in Kristiania before the first performance can take place.

Ibsen's correspondence with Lindberg lasted seventeen years and the tone of his letters changed from strident demands to warm friendship. He kept abreast of Lindberg's itinerary and could give exact tallies of his performances: '*Ghosts* for the fiftieth time in Sweden […], twenty-one times in Denmark and Norway, seventy-one times altogether in a little over four months' (to Frederik Hegel, 17 January 1884).

Although there are many fascinating aspects to the Lindberg correspondence, we have chosen to focus this chapter on Ibsen's relationship with the Christiania Theater, which lasted for over fifty years. The Christiania Theater had been established in 1827 by the Swedish actor and director, Johan P. Strömberg. For nearly forty years, the company employed foreign managers and actors, principally from Denmark performing in Danish. This made the theatre a site of ideological struggle for all those publicly demanding an authentic Norwegian theatre, with Norwegian actors speaking Norwegian. Ibsen had his one-act drama *The Burial Mound* performed there in 1850, before the public debate about the foreign domination of the theatre became acrimonious. A public controversy known as the Viking Feud broke out when *The Vikings at Helgeland* was accepted by the Christiania Theater but the performance was delayed for lack of funds. Ibsen and his supporters argued that the production had been cancelled because of the Board's reluctance to produce Norwegian plays. Extracts from the newspaper articles Ibsen wrote during the feud are reproduced at the beginning of this chapter. It would be another three years before the Christiania Theater performed *The Vikings at Helgeland*. By this time, the struggle for Norwegian control over the theatre was almost won, and shortly afterwards financial necessity forced the company to amalgamate with its under-resourced rival, the Kristiania Norske Theater. The latter was the only genuinely Norwegian acting company in the city and Ibsen was its artistic director from 1857 to 1862. With the amalgamation, many of the artists associated with the nationalist theatre movement were absorbed into the Christiania Theater: Ibsen joined the company briefly before leaving Norway to begin a new life as a writer in voluntary exile.

For twenty years, Ibsen negotiated with the Christiania Theater over the production of his plays. The tone of his language shifts from his initial attacks on the management in newspaper articles, to a more conciliatory manner, and finally to authoritative instructions. He had strong views about the leadership of the company: Ibsen considered the Swede Ludvig Josephson to be excellent, even though the theatre was back in his foreign hands between 1873 and 1877. He considered Josephson's replacement, Johan Vibe, to be incompetent and was delighted when he left the position after two years. Ibsen's relationship with Vibe's successor, Hans Schrøder, began badly when the Christiania Theater rejected *Ghosts* in 1881, but as Schrøder controlled the theatre for twenty years through his position on the Board and his subsequent appointment as director, Ibsen developed a working relationship with him over time.

Ibsen uses different titles when describing the leadership of the Christiania Theater reflecting the ways in which artistic responsibility was divided under successive regimes. These titles are translated using four terms: 'director' denotes individuals with overall managerial responsibility of the theatre including the repertoire; when this leadership role is combined with participation as an actor, stage director, or playwright, then the term 'artistic director' is used; 'stage director' refers to company members assigned the task of directing specific productions; and 'literary manager' for consultants employed to advise on repertoire and conduct negotiations with playwrights.

On three occasions, Ibsen was asked if he would be interested in taking the position of artistic director at the Christiania Theater. The first offer came in 1864, when Ibsen was living in Rome. He declined the invitation and Bjørnstjerne Bjørnson, his fellow playwright, assumed the position from 1865 until 1867. Although the friendship between Ibsen and Bjørnson was stormy, they shared many views on the artistic leadership of the Christiania Theater. When Ibsen was approached for the second time in 1870, he suggested that the Board re-engage Bjørnson; and when the question was raised again in 1884, he wrote to Bjørnson expressing his ambivalent feelings about working within Christiania Theater and querying whether accepting the artistic directorship would undermine the position of Bjørnson's son Bjørn, who was a stage director with the company from 1884 to 1893.

The other personalities populating Ibsen's letters in this chapter are the Christiania Theater's resident actors. Ibsen was corresponding with the theatre management from Germany or Italy, but the actors he writes about were the first generation of Norwegian actors and his peers. Four of them had been directed by Ibsen at Det norske Theater in Bergen and appeared in the plays he wrote for this company. When Ibsen was sent on a three-month European study tour by Det norske Theater in 1852, he travelled to Copenhagen with two of these actors, Johannes and Louise Brun. He does not appear to have been in direct correspondence with them, but a third actor, Andreas Isachsen, received letters from Ibsen offering career advice and instructions for rehearsals. This friendship came undone when Isachsen planned a series of public readings of *Emperor and Galilean* without seeking Ibsen's permission. He warned Isachsen that unless the readings were cancelled: 'I intend, through the press, to revive, if not yours then the Kristiania public's sense of decency, at least to the degree that they stop supporting an occupation which elsewhere would be considered a stain on the morals of society' (to Andreas Isachsen, 2 November 1873). Lucie Wolf, the last member of this quartet, was also the target of Ibsen's ire when she refused the role of Berte in *Hedda Gabler*. Ibsen failed to persuade Wolf to play the role, but this was unusual: successive theatre managements followed his casting suggestions assiduously.

When Ibsen returned to Kristiania in 1891 his long correspondence with the Christiania Theater ceased, except for a few brief notes requesting tickets for performances. The chapter ends with eye-witness accounts of the opening of the Nationaltheatret in 1899. Bjørnson's son was appointed the first artistic director of the new theatre and statues of his father and Ibsen adorned its entrance; these two elderly dramatists, who had contributed so much to the creation of Norwegian culture, sat side by side as honoured guests at the theatre's gala opening.

10 March 1858 from 'A Feature of the Christiania Danish Theater's Management', Aftenbladet

After I had finished a new play last autumn, entitled *The Vikings at Helgeland*, I handed in the manuscript to the Board of the Christiania Theater, enquiring whether the play could be performed there.

[…] I called upon the director, and learnt from him that the play had been accepted and was scheduled for performance in the month of March this year. I later approached the esteemed director to make an arrangement to meet about the cast, etc; however, as it turned out that he did not—at least on that day— have as clear a perspective of the play's subject matter and characters as one would wish, we agreed to postpone our meeting for the time being. As this depended on the director re-reading the play, I found it advisable to wait a couple of months, after which I once more approached him with the above-mentioned intention, only to learn that the theatre's management, God knows when, had made the following decision: 'as the theatre's economic status and the prospects of its profits in the near future in relation to already fixed and inevitable expenses do not allow the theatre's coffers in the current season to defray honoraria for original works, it will not be able to stage Mr Ibsen's delivered drama, *The Vikings at Helgeland*, in the current season'.

[…]

Therefore, the management of the Christiania Theater has in clear and straightforward words proclaimed its programme; it has testified to how it understands its own purpose and mission. Now the public must judge. […] What is important here is the theatre's own declaration that in 'the near future', it will be unable to support, advance, yes, to have any kind of engagement at all with Norwegian dramatic literature.

[…]

However, it is good that this statement has finally been made; the peace in our dramatic world must and shall now be broken, the general public must take sides *for* or *against*; for the present in-between state is unacceptable. We must *either* have a Norwegian theatre which understands and has the power to work for the interest of the national arts, *or* we must, all of us, join the so-called main stage; i.e. we must in the future, all of us, flock there when, three times a week, it serves up translations thrown together from every corner of the world. No national sympathies anymore! No struggle, no consideration for nurturing our own seeds which carry a possibility and a future within them!

31 March 1858 'Yet Another Contribution to the Theatre Issue', Aftenbladet

My objection to the theatre's foreign tendencies and its elitist activities has never been directed at its staff, but only at its Board; […] It is not a matter of the actors' birth certificates, nor their proofs of being born in Denmark or Norway, which make a stage Danish or Norwegian; for that, more is demanded; it requires both a management and a staff who understand the significance of 'nationality'.

31 March 1861 from 'The Two Theatres in Christiania Part III',
Morgenbladet

[…] The Christiania Theater's history may be said to go
twenty-five to thirty years back in time. So the foundation of
the theatre is in a period when Norway did not in any spiritual
sense manage to provide sustenance for itself, but had to order
even the daily necessities from the brethren on the other side
of Kattegat [in Denmark]. The Norwegian language was
taught in schools through Danish grammar textbooks, excerpts
from Danish authors were set up as ideals and norms for a
Norwegian way of expression; we were supposed even to keep
up with the process of Germanisation which Denmark kept
going through after the separation, and nowhere did the
thought break through that the spirits of the brother-languages
are just as different as both countries' natures, histories and
other conditions based on languages.

[…]

When the norms of language and pronunciation were to be
taken from Denmark, then it is natural that we also took our
dramatic art from there. We still did not feel like a nation, in
any other sense than the political; despite the separation, the
whole spiritual communication remained unchanged. A very
large part of the reigning generation had received their education in Copenhagen or at least under conditions which had
their immediate roots in Danishness. Especially the Danish art
of acting had acquired a hegemonic position around the country through touring companies, and almost none of its own
children had yet tried to set foot on the dramatic path. Norwegian dramatic authors were as good as non-existent;
Oehlenschläger and Heiberg [both Danish playwrights] had
gained entrance everywhere, and no one was closer to interpreting these masters than their own countrymen.

Thus it was highly natural that a Danish theatre was
founded in Christiania. This theatre was fully justified at that
time, as it was fully compatible with the contemporary national
viewpoint, and did not bar the way for a more home-grown

institution, for which the time was not yet ripe. I shall there-fore willingly admit that this theatre has done much good in this country, as it has to a certain degree kept us in line with trends in the dramatic arts and literature in other places, and thereby contributed to bringing about the conditions for an independent theatre life in Norway.

[...]

It has often enough been said, in oral as well as written criti-cism, that the Norwegian theatrical language is raw and offensive; it has been described as an Oslo plebeian dialect, and thus ineligible for all artistic presentation. There have been sharp complaints against the repertoire; the theatre has been described as a 'Vaudeville-theatre', an appellation which was supposed to be an insult. The frequent presentation of plays belonging to the so-called lower dramatic art forms has met with strong vituperation, not to mention the reproaches for having accepted plays which have essentially been built around dance or stage spectacle. The larger works have been seen to be beyond the forces of the theatre. Finally, every now and then the performances have been described as flat and much too closely related to reality, and a great portion of the personnel has been charged with lacking the necessary culture and education.

[...]

This whole list of the Norwegian dramatic death-sins is besides, as everyone will recognise, totally useless for its pur-pose, as long as there is no proof that our so-called Danish theatre is not infested with the same weaknesses as those with which the Norwegian theatre is blamed.

16 May 1869 to Andreas Isachsen
(Norwegian actor. Isachsen performed in ten plays by Ibsen at the Christiania Theater between 1866 and 1891.)

You can rest assured that during my long journey abroad, I have followed theatre matters at home with interest, as well as everything connected with them. I subscribe to Norwegian and Danish newspapers, so I have been able to keep up with what is happening. But one thing surprises me, namely that you actors do nothing to get out to see the world. I speak from experience; I know the kind of development that travelling brings about. I find it especially heartrending that you, with your talent, have not been able to get out. You must and you shall do something about that. Listen to my advice! You must try to come here to Dresden this summer; the theatre performs throughout summer and there are excellent artists here.

10 February 1870 to Jens Peter Andresen
(Chair of the Christiania Theater Board from 1866 to 1871.)

The unrest [concerning *The League of Youth*] is nevertheless still present and most probably will not calm down for a while yet. But that is the exact reason for my grave doubts whether it would actually benefit the theatre should I now agree to your proposal of taking on any kind of position there, however flattering your offer is to me. I am now regarded by a certain vociferous party as something I am least of all, and what I least of all want to be—a party man; and I am hardly mistaken when I predict that my appointment at the theatre will be regarded as throwing down the gauntlet, which will surely not be left lying on the ground. An arts institution needs peace to function, and especially under our constricted conditions it does need the whole public on its side. A division can be stimulating for a while; however, it is not productive in the long run. […] Dare I ask you a question? Do you regard Bjørnson to be impossible as artistic director; and is a reconciliation between him and the current Board inconceivable?

24 October 1872 to Hartvig Lassen
(Literary manager at the Christiania Theater from 1872 to1878. He continued to give occasional advice on repertoire until 1899.)

From the first time I had the satisfaction of knowing that the literary management of the Christiania Theater is in your hands, I have been waiting down here with a silent hope to receive a suggestion that you consider presenting *Love's Comedy* to the Norwegian audience.

[...]

The reservations I entertained at one stage about the play being performed have long since disappeared. Many indications have convinced me that the public has now opened its eyes to the truth that the core of this work rests on an unconditional moral foundation, and as far as the play's artistic structure is concerned, I am now more than ever of the opinion that this is immaculate; at least, it is not surpassed by any of my other dramatic works. Altogether, I consider *Love's Comedy* among the best of my creations.

That I therefore wish to see the play staged at home is a matter of course, and I do not believe the audience would be dissatisfied should this happen. And yes, I do believe my position in Scandinavian literature to a certain extent entitles me to present this friendly request, a request which for an author in a similar position in other countries would be unnecessary.

From what I can imagine, this season will hardly be particularly rich in original pieces, and they are the ones that give a theatre season both lustre and character, at the same time as they strongly contribute to a revival of interest in the theatre, if in no other way, at least by an animated discussion for and against.

The play can easily be cast in Kristiania. I attach a suggestion for a cast, but obviously leave it to you to make the changes which you might find desirable for artistic reasons. It would set my mind at rest in certain ways if Mr Johannes Brun could, without damage to the whole, be kept out of it.

It is my firm conviction that this play, well cast and in every way thoroughly rehearsed, i.e. with the characters being naturally represented and the points in the dialogue being finely observed, will capture a permanent place in the repertoire. Its design does not demand much, and the season is not so far advanced that, as long as the production is tackled with strength and interest from every quarter, it could still be put up with ease in the most favourable part of the season.

14 November 1872 to Hartvig Lassen

[…] Thank you most sincerely for accepting so readily my suggestion that you produce *Love's Comedy*.

[…]

It is a shame that *Mr Wolf cannot be counted on to play Gulstad's role*; however, this cannot be helped. To *give the role to Mr J. Brun alarms me* for many reasons. What the play requires first of all is a flawless memorisation. But is Mr Brun capable of learning a role fully by heart these days? Or may he be prevailed upon to submit to this necessary inconvenience? Even if there is nothing to fear in that regard, I doubt that he will be able to give the role the right colour. Should he apply his comic talent to it, then Svanhild's decision, the most dangerous point in the play, could easily appear in much too harsh a light; should he play it with dignity, without comedy, he would find himself in unfamiliar territory. But would it not be possible *to try Mr Reimers*? Mr R is an intelligent man, and if he can play the role at all, I think he will play it in such a way that the leap from Falk to the businessman will not seem too incredible, and therefore much would be gained.

16 December 1872 to Andreas Isachsen

I think you will agree with me when I claim that you have seen less of the European theatres than required for the position you occupy at the moment, and especially the position you perhaps will occupy one day at the Christiania Theater. You must see with your own eyes the contemporary scenic facilities they are employing, you must study arrangements and design, administration, and artistic as well as technical management. In a word, you must travel. If you do not, you will not be able to assert the necessary authority in the long run, and most importantly, you will not even be able to achieve the necessary self-confidence and assurance.

The new Albert Theater here in Dresden opens at Easter. The Royal actors will give performances at this theatre until the large Opera House is finished. They will play there all year round; therefore, in summer as well. This is exactly a place where you will have something to learn. I would do my best to get you introduced everywhere. You shall and must come down here!

1 December 1874 to the Board of the Christiania Theater

While thanking you [for the extra honorarium received for the production of my plays] I also have the honour to hand in to the theatre my play *Lady Inger*, enquiring if the Board would be willing to accept it for inclusion in the present season.

The play has not been produced at the Christiania Theater. It is now available in a reworked form, especially where the dialogue is concerned. The previously declamatory style has been removed, and replaced with a more realistic and natural mode of expression. I believe the play is well suited to the theatre's ensemble; Mrs Gundersen has already expressed a strong wish to play the title role, which I believe she would do with considerable effect. New set designs or costumes are unnecessary.

Should *Lady Inger* be accepted for performance this year, I suppose it will be a matter of course that *Peer Gynt* will be postponed to the next season; this might well be expedient for everyone concerned, as the latter play needs lots of preparation […].

7 February 1875 to Ludvig Josephson

(Artistic director of the Christiania Theater from 1873 to 1877.)

[…] I would find it highly regrettable should you, in all seriousness, consider leaving the Christiania Theater. After all the things you have achieved there, and not least after you organised the opera, I think you should be able to make any demand you wish of the business management; should the Board restrict you with its inexpert intervention, you must demand its abolition, for as far as the public is concerned you and no one else are considered to be responsible. You should also consider that the theatre is now entering a better time; there is no doubt about that. In a few years, they will inevitably have to think about a new and larger theatre building, and with that will come larger and more comfortable conditions in every respect.

16 August 1875 to Hartvig Lassen

That *Peer Gynt* can only be brought to the stage in a shortened form goes without saying. When I first wrote to Grieg about the music, I described to him how I had imagined that Act Four should be replaced by a tone-painting, which was to suggest the content be accompanied by a couple of live pictures or tableaux vivants representing the most suitable situations in the omitted act; for instance, Peer Gynt and the Arab Girls, Solveig waiting at her cottage at home, etc. I informed Mr Josephson about this plan, but he did not agree with me; instead he presented me with a suggestion for cuts in the dialogue, which I found to be made with great discernment and to which I gave my consent.

From a distance, I dare not decide which of the two methods is preferable. I would rather that you and Mr Josephson discuss and decide the matter. He has assured me that if his intention is complied with, the play will be a popular favourite and a box-office success. However, I would rather keep out of this whole thing, and will be satisfied when the performance is cut down to a suitable length; if not, all will be ruined. Therefore, I am asking the theatre's authorities to act to the best of their judgement. There are advantages with both alternatives; to decide conclusively between them, one has to be on the spot, be familiar with the planned cast, know the theatre's resources in terms of designs and decorations, what the technical department has as its disposal, etc.

I have only one special wish, that the play will be presented on stage before Christmas, and indeed, as early in the season as possible. Plays which are postponed until spring cannot expect to attract proper interest from audiences, and a play's reception in its first year is always conclusive in terms of its future life in the repertoire.

22 January 1876 to Hartvig Lassen

[…] P.S. Just as I am about to send this letter, I see in the Norwegian newspapers that Bjørnson will be handed the profit of the twentieth performance of *A Bankruptcy*. How am I to understand this? Does Bjørnson get paid on more favourable terms than I do? If that is the case, I will have to request equal terms. If not I shall never again deliver a new play to the Christiania Theater. I would like to know how many times *The Vikings at Helgeland*, *The Pretenders*, *The League of Youth* and *Love's Comedy* have been performed at home. True, I have previously heard that Bjørnson is paid much better than I am; however, I have never wanted to believe it. But now I do not know what to believe, and ask you for clear and straightforward information.

5 March 1876 to Ludvig Josephson

Thank you for *Peer Gynt*! Your kind telegram was the start of a series of gratifying messages which I have received from home in the week that has passed. This outcome of the theatre's daring enterprise has exceeded all my expectations, although I did not actually entertain any fears. I knew the case was in your hands, and that no man in our two countries would be able to drive it through like you would. It also pleased me greatly to learn that this is the common and unanimous opinion at home.

Allow me also to request that you, on my behalf, thank the personnel involved, not just those who had the big, paid parts, but also all those who through participation and cooperation have supported my work here; this play depends utterly on everyone who takes part doing their very best [...].

[...] The state and the municipality cannot in the long run abstain from supporting the Christiania Theater, nor can a large and modern house be far away.

24 June 1877 to the Board of the Christiania Theater

I learn from Norwegian newspapers that two of your theatre's actresses have arranged private evening entertainments—one in the theatre's premises, the other in Klingenberg—during which they have, among other things, performed the fourth act of *Brand*.

I presume the Board is not unaware that the theatre has failed to obtain the performance rights to this play. Likewise, the Board will surely know that, according to the 'Law of protection of the so-called administrative right of intellectual property' of 8 June 1876, §32, you are unauthorised to transfer the performance rights of *any* of my dramatic works to a third party and that, as a result thereof, my plays may not be performed at the actors' benefits, as long as my consent has not been obtained.

Before I take legal action concerning this violation of my rights as an author, however, I would ask what the Board can inform me about the matter.

I would like to add that it is not merely the financial question that is at stake. I am, you see, very familiar with the form of recklessness with which such benefit performances are rehearsed, and from the programme for the two mentioned above, one can see the imprudence with which the performances are put together; *Brand*'s fourth act appears between two farces. I would not under any circumstance have given my consent to the performance at Klingenberg. These are all matters I want to have control over, and that is why I am warning you against future property encroachments, just as I will prosecute those that have already taken place.

23 August 1877 to Frederik Hegel

I enclose covering letters to Det Kongelige Theater [in Copenhagen] and the theatre in Gothenburg. I will personally negotiate with the theatres in Stockholm. […] I will not deliver a copy [*Pillars of Society*] to the Christiania Theater for the time being. The new director [Johan Vibe] is a totally incompetent man, and as soon as my play is in the shops, I intend to declare in a Norwegian newspaper that I cut off all connections with this theatre during this man's leadership. I have reason to believe that Bjørnson will do the same. Knowing the circumstances up there, I can assure you that this approach, far from damaging the book, will contribute to the play being bought and read to a much larger degree. Similarly, I take it for granted that if Bjørnson and I stand shoulder to shoulder on this, it will contribute to the new director having to resign very soon.

2 November 1878 to Harald Holst
(Norwegian senior public servant. Member and Chair of the
Board of the Christiania Theater from 1878 to August 1880.)

Certainly, one essential reason for my decision not to hand *Pillars
of Society* to the Christiania Theater at the time was my opinion
of the character of the present director. During his visit to
Munich, I had the opportunity to convince myself of his total lack
of knowledge of, and insight into, the enterprise he had been
called upon to undertake, just as I was given reason to doubt that
he would ever in any way be able to satisfactorily fill the place as
successor of a man [Ludwig Josephson] with such an excellent
practical capability that hardly any other theatre in Europe would
have let him go voluntarily. The Chamberlain is surely familiar
with the present director's previous critical activity, and I hardly
lay myself open to any contradiction when I describe his behaviour towards me and other up and coming Norwegian authors as
unheard of and without precedence. Quite apart from his lack of
insight in the field of theatre, I could not even count on his goodwill. Under such circumstances, to entrust a quite new, not yet
printed, and not yet performed, dramatic work to the Christiania
Theater seemed irresponsible towards myself and the play. The
majority of our audiences are unable to judge a new play independently from the staging it is given.

But on top of that I could hardly expect either the theatre
board or the literary manager to be any more well-disposed
towards me. The Head of the Board had shortly beforehand
given me a brief and negative answer to my complaint that a
couple of the theatre's actresses had, without authorisation,
performed plays by me at their benefits, partly at Klingenberg,
partly in the theatre itself, claiming that it was not in the
Board's power to prevent such things; an answer testifying as
much to the incompetence as it did to the contrariness of the
person in question. As far as the literary manager is concerned,
he does not seem to have a particularly good eye for our newer
dramatic literature, or for what is new in general. In any case,
I am hardly wrong when it seems to me as if neither he nor the
Board of the time have been able quite to forgive that *Peer Gynt*
was forced on the theatre by Mr Josephson, and, predictably,

disappeared when he resigned. During his last year in Kristiania, he informed me about his many future plans. He intended to stage *Brand* as well as *Emperor and Galilean* in edited form; at least the first part of the latter to start with. After his resignation, there has of course, been no mention of such plans. But as long as the theatre is not interested in producing older dramatic works of mine that are available, it would not occur to me to offer it anything new. And as the Chamberlain has himself remarked, nor has the theatre ever expressed any desire to receive my latest play, which I, with the repertoire of the literary manager and director in mind, find quite explicable.

However, as I now learn from the Chamberlain's honoured letter, that such a wish exists within the theatre's new Board, and as *Pillars of Society* has now been available in book form for quite some time, as well as having proven itself on so many different stages, so that the risk of an unsuccessful production in Kristiania would not be mine but the theatre's, I shall not be unwilling to allow the theatre to produce the play on certain conditions. But it is a matter of course that the Board secures a satisfactory stage director. In my opinion, for such a difficult play, this role cannot in any way be entrusted to the present director.

No doubt, the best thing would be to persuade Mr Josephson to come to Kristiania for this occasion and leave the whole rehearsal in his capable hands. But for one thing, he is on a trip abroad, as far as I know, and for another, I presume the theatre's Board would have reservations against such a step; therefore, I will not insist further thereon. On the other hand, I must demand, as an absolute condition, that the Board—not the director—presents to me for approval suggestions regarding the casting, and that no actor or actress will be promised this or that role until the final decision has been made.

21 November 1878 to Harald Holst

Upon receiving your esteemed letter yesterday, I had the pleasure of seeing that the board's opinion about the cast of my new play [*Pillars of Society*] conforms with my own on most points. But there are a few discrepancies, as you will see from the following list [...].

It would be too time-consuming to give reasons for each of these discrepancies in writing; I will therefore confine myself to remarking that it is especially important to me that Aune is played by Johannes Brun, while on the other hand, I doubt he would be suitable for Hilmar Tønnesens's role. In many ways, Mr Isachsen would, especially on account of his appearance, be more suited for the role of Bernick than Mr Gundersen; but I fear he would give this character an air of affectedness, and therefore seem repulsive. Besides, from afar, it is impossible for me to offer a decisive opinion about the details of all the casting; therefore, I ask the Board to use their own judgement. That Johannes Brun is the stage director of the play is probably the best solution at this time. I must especially ask that Mr Brun is told to make absolutely sure that the roles are learnt properly from the beginning, without which an ensemble is impossible. Moreover, I allow myself to request that the tempo at which the lines are delivered, especially in the strongly emotional scenes, must obviously be somewhat faster and livelier than is usual at the Christiania Theater. I hope proper attention will be paid to groupings and positions. Actors being lined up in the foreground must be avoided, the individual positions should change as often as is natural; overall, each scene and each image should, as much as possible, be a reflection of reality. Thoughtless actors may easily want to caricature certain of the characters in the play. It is my hope that such a thing does not happen; a smooth naturalness on all points is what I would prefer.

31 December 1882 to Hans Schrøder
(Director of the Christiania Theater from 1879 to 1898.)

Unfortunately, I find it necessary to bother you again with a few lines.

From your honoured letter, which I received yesterday, I learn of your plan to let both the boys in my play be performed by two actresses. This has made me somewhat uneasy, as I believe it can be seen as a testimony to the fact that proper attention has not been paid to the spirit in which this play is written, and the way it requires to be performed.

To let boys' roles be played by women may at a pinch work in an operetta, in vaudeville, or in the so-called romantic drama, for they do not demand unconditional illusion before anything else; every audience member is fully aware that he is merely sitting in a theatre watching the performance of a play.

But it is different when *An Enemy of the People* is staged. The spectator must feel as if he is invisibly present in Dr Stockmann's living room; everything must be real; both boys as well. Hence they cannot possibly be played by two disguised actresses with curly wigs and laced-up waists; the female forms cannot be hidden by a coat, vest and trousers, and they would never make the audience believe that they are watching two real schoolboys from one of the smaller towns. Besides, how can an adult woman come to look like a ten-year old child?

Both roles must therefore be played by children, in the utmost emergency by a couple of young girls, whose forms have not yet been developed; and then, away with the corsets and let them wear large, thick boys' boots on their feet. They must obviously also be taught the way boys behave.

The play stipulates that Dr Stockmann wears black clothes at the people's meeting; but the suit must be neither new nor elegant, and his white necktie may well sit a little lopsidedly. But Reimers will think of such things himself.

I am pleased that Mr Johannes Brun will be the stage director. This task will cause him a good deal of work and effort, but I am certain he will do his best in every respect and that he will reap recognition for it. Incidentally, I cannot imagine that the play will be ready to be performed as early as the middle of January.

25 May 1883 to Lucie Wolf
(Norwegian actor with the Christiania Theater from 1853; she moved with the company to Nationaltheatret in 1899. During her career, she performed in eleven plays by Ibsen.)

At the beginning of this month we had the unexpected pleasure of receiving a letter from you. Although the letter was addressed to my wife, I take the liberty to answer it myself since it mainly concerns me.

You want me to write a prologue for the gala performance to be given at the Christiania Theater on the occasion of your thirtieth anniversary as an artist there.

I do wish I could accommodate your request. Nothing would be dearer to me. But I cannot; I cannot do it for the sake of my conviction and my artistic principles. Prologues, epilogues and all such things should without question be banished from the stage. The stage is for dramatic art; and declamation is not dramatic art.

The prologue would have to be in verse, of course, for that is the etiquette. But I cannot be part of keeping this etiquette alive. Verse has inflicted much injury on the dramatic art. An actress whose repertoire is contemporary plays should not willingly let a line of verse pass her lips. Verse drama will hardly be used in any form of theatre worth mentioning in the future, for the intentions of future writings will no doubt be incompatible with it. Therefore it is doomed. Forms of art become extinct just like the preposterous prehistoric animal species did when their time was up. A tragedy in iambic pentameter is just as rare these days as the dodo bird, whereof there are only a few specimens on some African island.

I myself have hardly written a single verse line in the last seven to eight years, having exclusively cultivated the far more difficult art of writing in a plain, realistic everyday language. This is the language which has made you the excellent artist you now are. Smooth verse has never helped you to win anyone's approval.

But added to this is what I believe is the main argument. A prologue tells the audience all sorts of pleasant things. They are thanked for their indulgence and their instructive criticism; the artist has to make himself as minute and small as possible in the nooks and crannies of the verse. But is there truth in that? You yourself know, as well as I do, that there is not. Truth is the opposite. You are not indebted to your audience; the audience is in deep debt to you for your thirty years of faithful work.

This is the point of view I believe a significant artist, out of consideration to the self and the profession, has a duty to maintain.

9 January 1884 to Bjørnstjerne Bjørnson
(Artistic Director of the Christiania Theater from 1865 to 1867.)

I neither can nor want to take any leading position at the Christiania Theater. My theatre experiences and memories from home do not make me feel a trace of desire to revive them in practice. I could certainly feel a responsibility and an obligation in this matter if I thought that by doing so I, as an artistic director, could achieve something to benefit our art of theatre. However, I have grave doubts about that. Our theatre personnel are demoralised, refusing to accept discipline and unconditional obedience; moreover, we have a press which is always ready to take the side of the recalcitrants against the leader. This is the main reason we cannot cultivate a proper ensemble, like most other countries, where the anarchic tendencies are less developed. I do not think I would succeed in replacing these conditions with something better; they are too closely connected with our whole national view of life for that to happen. Moreover, my inclination towards the practical side of theatre is too small. Therefore, I cannot under any circumstances occupy myself with those things.

But my dear Bjørnson, the main point is this: it is not *me* the Board wants. It is you and no one else. I cannot judge whether the reservations you entertain in accepting the offer are totally insurmountable; however, it would please me greatly if they were not. In any case, I take it for granted that you have rejected the offer only after the most careful deliberation.

But whatever your decision is, the proper authorities must ensure that your son is attached to our theatre—assuming that he is still willing to be so. I exchanged a couple of letters with him this past autumn about other affairs, and I had my conviction confirmed that we will get in him exactly the stage director that we most of all need. Schrøder could then remain at a pinch; that is, should you find that you absolutely cannot accept the Board's offer.

Besides, I must say that I am not quite sure whether Kristiania's public really do have the need for a good theatre at the moment. The influx of people that the operettas and equestrian performances at the Tivoli almost always enjoy, and the interest which the dilettante pieces by students and the business clerks excite there, seem to me to suggest a level of cultural refinement still incapable of appreciating dramatic art. So I do regret that the opera at the Christiania Theater was closed down. Opera demands a less cultured audience than drama does. Therefore it flourishes in the large garrison cities, in the mercantile towns, and where an aristocracy is gathered in plentiful numbers. But can an opera audience gradually be raised to the level of a drama audience? And the opera has a disciplinary influence over the theatre's personnel; the individual must adapt to the beat of the baton.

29 September 1884 to Bjørnstjerne Bjørnson

When one has had to do with the management of the theatre for as long as I have, and when one has been as exclusively occupied with writing for the theatre as I have, one cannot help wanting to lend a hand to the practical part of theatre now and then. The theatre has something peculiarly attractive about it, and the two times you have now thrown the thought at me, a certain feeling of restlessness and yearning has come over me. Besides, I cannot deny that I sometimes feel the need for a settled and responsible occupation. Therefore, there could be plenty of motivation for me to go home and take charge of the theatre, if such a thing were practicable.

However, the misfortune is that this is not possible at the moment. The faction that is now in power at the theatre is certainly no more in favour of me than of you. My wife just wrote to me from Norway: 'I would never have believed that we were in such total disfavour with the Conservatives as the numerous signs show to be the case.' I do not doubt for a minute that her observation is correct. To offer me the artistic directorship of the theatre would therefore be equivalent to placing the management and the theatre in a hostile relationship to a great number of well-to-do families and people whose support the institution cannot manage without. Therefore, it will not happen. I will absolutely not become the artistic director of the theatre as long as the current Board is in power.

Perhaps you will argue that I could come home anyway, and try in the meantime to act as a private reformer, helping to accelerate the construction of the new theatre building, and thereby possibly contribute to the creation of such conditions that the choice of myself as the artistic director might become conceivable. All this might have been feasible if I had sufficient means to live from in the meantime. But I do not. As of now, I have not been able to put aside nearly enough to support me and my family should I give up my literary activity. And I would have to give it up if I came to live in Kristiania. It is not only the distressing theatre matters I am mostly thinking of. No, the point is that I would not be able to write freely and unrestrainedly and wholeheartedly up there. And that means that I would not write at all. When I sailed up the fjord ten years ago after ten years' absence, I literally felt my chest constricting in anxiety and debilitation. I felt the same during the whole sojourn up there; I was no longer myself before all these cold and uncomprehending Norwegian eyes at the windows and in the streets.

[…]

But there is one more consideration. Do you think Bjørn would like me to come up there? I doubt it. I think he would feel free and uninhibited in his position as stage director under Schrøder's leadership. And what substantial use could I be of as long as they perform in that old, awful, narrow box? The current building is useless when it comes to the kind of artistic reforms I would want to introduce. Bjørn will soon come to acknowledge this, if he does not already. He will have to reduce his artistic intentions as to staging and production to such a degree that he will soon agree with me that if our theatrical art is not to perish, we must have a state-of-the-art playhouse.

18 December 1886 to Hans Schrøder

As an answer to your very kind letter of fourteenth of this month, I allow myself to inform you that I agree to your suggestion of setting the honorarium for *Rosmersholm* at 10 per cent of the gross profit.

30 December 1886 to Hans Schrøder

I have been so busy with other things since I wrote to you last that I have not found the time to think about the production of *Rosmersholm* in Kristiania.

[…]

But under any circumstances I must insist that the dreadful Isachsen is kept out of it. I know from a reliable source that he, with his raving mad interpretation and desperate representation of Dr Relling in *The Wild Duck*, ruined the total impression of this play. It should have been the director's unconditional duty to take the role away from him as soon as the rehearsals showed that he could not play it. The indifference shown at the time to a new play by me has given me much to think about, and I touch upon this old story because I want to state my expectation that a serious eye is kept on rehearsals of *Rosmersholm*.

2 January 1887 to Hans Schrøder

I received your letter concerning the casting for *Rosmersholm* the day after my own letter concerning the same topic was sent from here.

I will not hide from you that your statements in this matter have made me even more worried about my play's fate at the Christiania Theater than I already was. The book has obviously been read through extremely superficially and, furthermore, read without any plasticity of imagination; nothing else is possible. If you had seen the characters alive in front of your eyes in their mutual relationships with each other, a proposal like yours could not be set forth.

25 May 1890 to Bjørn Bjørnson

I was very pleased to hear that the Christiania Theater is considering reviving *Peer Gynt* and that you will take over the title role. I have a strong impression that this task will be extremely well suited to you, while Klausen is hardly suitable any longer for the role in the first three acts.

To divide the performance over two evenings is a worrying matter, however. But should you wish to perform it unedited, such a division would be necessary.

27 December 1890 to Hans Schrøder

I have had the honour to receive your friendly message that the Christiania Theater wants to perform my new play *Hedda Gabler*, and bring you herewith my obliging gratitude for your enquiry in that regard. I hope my preliminary answer via telegram has reached you.

It was a special satisfaction for me to learn from your comprehensive presentation that your interpretation of the play's characters fully coincides with what I have wanted and aspired to.

As a result, I also agree with your opinion on every point concerning those who, among the presently available forces at the theatre, must be considered the most suitable casting.

Hedda must without doubt be played by Miss [Constance] Bruun, who hopefully will strive to find expression for the daemonic substrata of the character. I saw Mrs Heiberg five years ago in the theatre in Bergen and I then received a very strong impression of her natural talent. But both for the sake of my play and for her sake, I do wish that she is not assigned a task that she will hardly be able to acquit fully in several important respects at this time.

As for the rest of the casting, surely there can be no doubt. I agree with everything you have suggested in this regard in your letter. Naturally Miss Parelius and not Mrs Gundersen must play the role of Miss Tesman.

Reminiscence from William Archer

On 1 September 1899, Ibsen and Björnson sat side by side in the place of honour at the opening of the Norwegian National Theatre. That night crowned the life-work of the two men. They had created a national drama which had gone forth over all the world; and here at least it had found a fitting home in their own country which they had so loved—and chastened. A few days later, I parted from Ibsen for the last time, at his house in Arbins Gade. Punctilious as ever in his courtesy, he accompanied me to the outer door and we shook hands on the threshold. [...] What I said I do not remember, but doubtless it was not the right thing. The right thing to have said was very plain. Thinking of all that I owed to the poet and the man, I should have used the simplest and most comprehensive of the formulas of gratitude in which Norwegian abounds, and said to him, 'Tak for alt,' or 'Thanks for all.' (1906, 19.)

1. This spelling of the 'Christiania Theater' conforms to the venue record in IbsenStage. The city of Christiania was renamed Kristiania in 1877 in accordance with Norwegian spelling reforms; Ibsen uses both spellings for the place and the theatre in his correspondence.
2. The complete production record of Ibsen performances at the Christiania Theater can be found in IbsenStage: ibsenstage.hf.uio.no/pages/venue/11704
3. ibsenstage.hf.uio.no/pages/venue/11738
4. ibsenstage.hf.uio.no/pages/venue/12360
5. ibsenstage.hf.uio.no/pages/organisation/33093
    ibsenstage.hf.uio.no/pages/organisation/33101

Appendix 1
Early Writings on Theatre

Ibsen concentrated his creative energies on theatre from the beginning of his career as a writer. Whereas many of his contemporaries had ambitions to become public intellectuals, Ibsen focused principally on the building of a Norwegian national theatre and the development of his skills as a theatre practitioner. In addition to his plays and poems, he published a total of seventy-six articles between 1850 and 1864, of which forty-four are devoted to theatre. The remaining articles concern politics or literature and frequently take the form of reviews of novels or short stories.

The impression we glean of Ibsen from these early writings is of an ironically modulated intellectual with strong leanings towards satire and humour who occasionally veers off into wild critiques. During his first year in Oslo he became co-editor of the journal *Manden* (*Andhrimner*) and the student journal *Samfundsbladet.* In the latter, Ibsen excelled in a playful, almost anarchic use of irony and logic ad absurdum, whereas the former was a more serious (if largely satirical) journal that gave Ibsen an arena in which to show glimpses of himself as a studious apprentice of theatre, particularly while arguing the need for a national stage. There are few references to the grand ideals and strong concepts of the German philosophical tradition that was influential in Norwegian academic culture through the writings of Hegel, and the Danes, Kierkegaard and Heiberg. Instead Ibsen acknowledges the practical limitations of producing theatre within a relatively poor country, and is alert to the difficulties of building and maintaining audiences. He stresses the necessity of speaking Norwegian rather than

Danish on the stage and suggests the production of popular theatre genres including comedies and vaudevilles.

The first extract in this chapter comes from Ibsen's review of *Braid and Sword* (*Haarpidsk og Kaarde*) by the German dramatist, Karl Gutzkow. Central to this review is Ibsen's analysis of the difference between the respective dramaturgical techniques of French and German playwrights and the reception of their work by Norwegian audiences. The core of his argument is that French drama is 'connected to life through the mediation of an actor's body; only then does it come into being', whereas German drama can violate 'the borders of drama' because it is written primarily for a reading public. He criticises French dramatists for creating dramatic worlds populated by 'angels and devils' and praises German dramatists for depicting 'human beings', pointing out that 'the ordinary person's character, from an artistic viewpoint, is not at all trivial'. Having framed his review with this comparative analysis, he gives a generous account of the acting in *Braid and Sword*, while reserving his criticism for the vulgar taste of the bourgeois audience who attended the performance. This combination of generosity towards actors, harsh critiques of foreign repertoire and ruthless social satire is typical of Ibsen's early reviews and newspaper articles.

The next three extracts come from a heated exchange between Ibsen and Paul Stub, a leading theatre critic in Bergen. Ibsen had arrived in the city on 21 October 1851, aged 23, to take up his position at Det norske Theater. During his first day in the city, he read a newspaper review of the production that was playing at his new theatre (Dingstad 2009, 12). The following night he saw the actual performance and the next day wrote an anonymous critique of Stub's review in a rival newspaper, declaring that the critic was incompetent and inept. A few days later, Ibsen published under his own name a much longer critique of Stub's practice as a theatre reviewer. He attacks Stub for being the worst kind of critic, who combines 'purely subjective opinion' with 'abstract theorising' disconnected from the specifics of the art form. He satirises Stub's writings, but warns his readers against underestimating the damage that he has done by undermining artists and misleading audiences with false judgements. Stub has misunderstood the nature of theatre as an art form, the relationship between performers and audience, and the quality of dramatic texts. He does not know how to judge actors. When Stub tried to counter these attacks, Ibsen relentlessly demolished his rival's professional reputation. Eventually, Stub was dismissed from his position as a theatre critic, and Ibsen celebrated his victory by publishing a malicious little play-text entitled 'The manner in which magister Stub was kicked out of a Bergen Newspaper. Tragi-comical play with one tableau.' Perhaps Ibsen's animosity was fuelled by the belief that Stub was the examiner responsible for the mediocre grades he had been given for his university entrance exams. Certainly, the resolution of the conflict demonstrates the powerful connections Ibsen had in Bergen from the day of his arrival. He could not have defeated Stub without the backing of local people with both economic and cultural capital in the theatre and newspaper worlds. This story contradicts the conventional view of Ibsen as an isolated and vulnerable young man living as an outsider in a strange city.

While he could be vicious towards an incompetent critic, Ibsen was generous and positive towards Norwegian writers and theatre artists, many of whom were as mediocre as Stub. As his review of Ø.H. Blom's now forgotten drama *Thorden-skiold* shows, Ibsen gave qualified support to some hopeless attempts at creating the new Norwegian drama. Here he stresses the necessity of giving new plays a chance and not dis-couraging writers with overly harsh criticism.

Ibsen wanted to build a strong national theatre that would make a difference in the country. He was never much of a nationalist, sceptical as he was by nature, but the sentiments expressed in his reviews were more than heightened rhetoric. He genuinely wished for a theatre with social relevance and was generous to other writers such as Blom, who shared his aspirations. His thoughts on the use of traditional culture, particularly folk ballads and Norse sagas, as the basis of this theatre, and his openness to learn from the expertise of Danish writers and actors, are the subject of the next set of extracts from his newspaper articles.

The Christiania Theater dominates the final group of writings, beginning with a review of Andreas Munch's *Lord William Russell*. This was probably provoked by another critic, whom Ibsen accuses in his review of having 'driven his nauseating pampering of the Christiania Theater to a pitch which might really harm the organisation'. He asks for a more modest and restrained mode of theatre criticism. While never attacking actors, his articles and reviews pay meticulous attention to their craft, and his experiences as a director make him particularly sensitive to the strengths and weaknesses of their physical and vocal technique. The final extracts return to the problems of building a national theatre in Norway, the dominance of foreign drama, the building of a new repertoire, and the expectations and responses of audiences.

The Ibsen we meet when reading his early writings is above all a man of the theatre. The art form is everywhere in his activities: even when writing about Parliamentary debates he represents them as theatre and performance. It is not the romantic idealist but an ironic satirist who leaps off the page. He is a pragmatist and craftsman trying to improve the local conditions of cultural production: as he says, 'in a theatre one learns to be practical'.

13 April 1851 from 'Braid and Sword, Play in Five Acts By K. Gutzkow', Manden (Andhrimner)

After our theatre repertoire has been recruited exclusively from France and Copenhagen for such a long time, a drama from the newest German school is at last appearing on our stage.

The audience did not seem to find this change in their daily fare particularly tasty; however, far be it from my intention to try to find the reason for this in the audience's fussiness. This would be highly improper; as God only knows, our audiences are anything but fussy! And the true reason is not difficult to find: when one has, like our theatre audiences, become used to Scribe and Company's dramatic confectioneries year in and year out, safely spiced with an adequate quantity of diverse poetic surrogacies, then it is only natural that the more solid German fare must eventually appear somewhat indigestible, even to our theatre audience's strong stomachs.[1]

There are essential differences between the modern French and German drama. The French drama (naturally, we use the word drama here in its true meaning as plays in general) must be connected to life through the mediation of an actor's body; only then does it come into being. The drama, as it comes from the French author's hand, is still unfulfilled, and is only fully realised when it is connected to reality through the dramatic *presentation*. To the Frenchman, the newer drama has no legitimacy as written literature, just as our mountain farmers fail to recognise the stanzas of the old ballads when they do not appear as living antiphony. The German writer, on the other hand, writes his play without specifically having an eye for the dramatic presentation. If it can be presented at the theatre in the form in which it emanates from his hand, then fine; if not, it may be read, and with this he considers that the demands one makes of a drama have been satisfied, because in Germany the drama's legitimacy to be read as literature is on equal footing with dramatic performance.

[…]

However, this is not to say that the French drama has any advantage over the German, because it depends on whether it succeeds in fulfilling the demands it has put upon itself. Reality in its immediacy is certainly unjustified in the world of art; however, the work of art that does not carry reality *within itself* is equally unjustified, and the latter is the exact weakness of French drama. Here the characters appear most often as pure abstractions; in order to bring out the greatest possible contrast, which is the French drama's hobby horse, the characters must appear either as angels or devils, but rarely as humans. On the other hand, when the German wants to deal with reality, which is generally beyond his domain, he does it with a vengeance— he paints human beings the way we see and hear them every day as ordinary people concerned with trivial things; but the ordinary person's character, from an artistic viewpoint, is not at all trivial: when reproduced in art he is just as interesting as any other person.

As far as this play is concerned, it is genuinely German in its mistakes as well as in its successes. It mainly belongs to the situation drama, for it is the situation which develops, not the characters. As a result, they are somewhat loosely drawn, with the exception of the King, who stands forth in almost plastic clarity.

[…]

Mr Jørgensen's portrayal of the main role is truly masterly, and although he always stands forth as an excellent artist, here he seems to have surpassed himself: the illusion is complete, nowhere are we reminded that we are in the presence of a dramatic reproduction, for the old soldier king stands in front of us in person.[2] Madam Rasmussen performs her role with the delicacy which this actress never fails to deliver. Miss Klingenberg gives us all the amiability which her role offers, and is on the whole successful. The play's other characters appear merely by suggestion, and all in all it feels as if the author has counted far too much on people's historical knowledge. It is only natural that this first performance of the play left much to be desired.

But now a little about our theatre audience's relationship to the play! Had it not been so fashionable today to stand in opposition to the theatre management and the 'Danish' actors, then this would have been an appropriate opportunity to express gratitude both to the management and the actors without offending any aesthetic conscience. But no—the audience took care not to do that! The play was given hardly any applause, with the exception of the places where the author tips the play a little towards the burlesque, as when the Dragoons march in with the soup tureens and the woollen stockings, and when the King appears without dress coat and trousers. And in what did our naïve audience rejoice in the latter case? Not that the King of Prussia received the Prince of Bayreuth in his underpants,

although this situation is comic enough; but at seeing Mr Jørgensen in this costume on stage, for this was so incredibly
funny!!!

Thus, the theatre management's choice of this play has not
satisfied the public's taste, or rather its lack of taste: for this we
should be doubly grateful to the management. And to think
that this audience demands a national stage! The truth is,
should this and the public's other present demands for theatre
be satisfied, then 'Goodnight, Muses!'

The Stub Controversy

23 October 1851 from 'Bergen 22nd October', Bergens Stiftstidende

Bergenske Blade [the newspaper that employed Paul Stub as its
critic] has finally found the man they were after. Mr Candida-
tus Magisterii P. J. Stub has appeared as criticus of the theatre.
Mr Stub is not unknown in our small literary world. He has
written a good deal under his own name in our Christiania
papers, in a genre that is peculiar to him. Undoubtedly *Bergenske
Blade* has reason to be happy that a man who declares himself
to be 'so totally nonpartisan' appears as an extremist of their
own persuasion, were it not for the fact that Mr Stub's genre,
which is the *ridiculous*, necessarily reflects a little on a journal
that 'indulgere' it. Another couple of reviews like the last one,
and Mr Stub himself will be suitable material for the *farce*.

*30 November and 4 December 1851 from 'A Few Comments Caused
By P.J. Stub's Theatre Articles',* Bergens Stiftstidende

It is a natural and commonly recognised principle that everywhere that an artistic struggle comes to light, a critical activity
must likewise be presupposed, the task of which is to compare
the product with the aesthetic idea. If artistic development is
left to itself, it will either very slowly move in the direction
which natural instinct indicates as the true one, or be in danger
of getting lost in intricate detours whose final destination,
sooner or later, is art's own negation. So, this is why criticism

is necessary; for it contains, as an absolute prerequisite, something which the artistic activity in and of itself lacks: namely a conscious cognition of the principles whereon the artistic activity is based. However, it is not enough that the critic has clarified to himself the abstract concept of art—he must also be conscious of the demands governing the specific art form he has in front of him. Only from such a vantage point does it become possible for the critic of art to fulfil his role and work positively to gain for art its true and justified development. If this is not the case, criticism degenerates into a useless and empty demonstration, a round of everyday phrases, which might well have validity as general abstractions, but which no one can be bothered to take to heart, for they reveal their inner emptiness and lack of substance when applied to a concrete instance.

[…]

After having offered different interpretations of the scene's Motto, 'which gave him something to speculate upon before the curtain went up', the author begins his own real criticism of *Fjeldeventyret* ['The Mountain Fairy Tale'].[3] Naturally one would expect that in a few swift strokes he would give us a coherent overview of the play, as the writer wishes it to be perceived, and then compare this with the performance; but instead we get to hear only that 'Marie… presented herself as a young lady quite without spiritual liveliness, and her movements are without grace'; that 'Ragnhild lacked all freshness and naivety'; that the 'middle of the play crossed the stage like the beginning, and the end like the middle'. The author continues in this manner. So, this is criticism! For whom is he writing? It cannot be for the audience, for they either agree with him, and so he does not need to tell them what they already know, or they are of the opposite opinion, in which case they will say no to the critic's assertions and hold on to their own beliefs. Neither can his criticism be aimed at the actors; for what could they possibly gather from a judgement which is purely negative. What can Mr Bruun [Brun] benefit, for example, from being made aware that in the role of the district sheriff he 'looked like a quick and slender middle-aged Captain, who has spent a few years in the provinces' (moreover, the writer says of this '*quick and slender* Captain' that 'his acting was *sluggish and drowsy*'!!)? Perhaps Mr Bruun [Brun] will hit the right note when he acts the Captain next time. If the critic is to lecture the actor, he must make it understandable *how* the role is to be played, and keep silent about how *not* to act it; because all he achieves is to make the actor uncertain instead of fortifying him. Nevertheless, the author continues incessantly in the same manner: 'the scene between the students was miserable'. Is there anything in this to guide the actors how *not* to make the scene 'miserable' next time?

18 and 21 December 1851 from 'Paul Stub As Dramatic Critic', Bergens Stiftstidende

In his critique of *Love's Dreams*,[4] the author solves an important problem concerning dramatic plasticity. After having presented several objections against Madam Bruun's [Brun] arm movements, he poses the following question: 'How shall a lady arrange her arms when she stands for a long time motionless on the stage?' Naturally we now prick up our ears; because this matter has been treated by the dramaturgs with lengthy arduousness, without finding any satisfactory solutions to the problem. But for my critical friend things like these are a mere trifle, he answers the assignment with true laconic shortness in this way: '*Her arms should never appear to be nailed fast.*' True: if our actresses have not been given sufficient instruction on this point, I do not see what more they require. As long as they make sure that their arms do not hang as if they were nailed fast, the acting must inevitably be quite excellent. Would my honourable friend still wish to contend that his criticism is not negative? Would he still wish to assert that he has told the actors *how* they should act, and never how they should *not* act? I could easily come up with more evidence, of which there is certainly no shortage; my friend would be wise not to deliver more denials […].

Further Reviews and Articles

18 January 1852 from 'H.Ø. Blom—Tordenskjold',[5] Theatervennen

[...] 'The theatre,' says Holberg, 'shall be a mirror where the people see their vices and defects.' With us, it should rather be called a mirror of the kind we put up outside the window to reflect the passers-by. While such a mirror has already allowed us to look into each corner of the other regions of Europe, our own country and our own conditions have still not received any lasting attention. [...] [I]t comes as no surprise that we prefer the foreign, which always shows itself to us in its poetic Sunday clothes, with made-up faces and powdered hair, to our own country's common everyday life, which always turns its customary, petit-bourgeois side to us. Our ears have still not heard the deep fundamental keynotes which here at home stream from nature's rich well, when a singer first discovers how to strike the national strings. Our eyes have not seen the allure of our nationhood, nor our people's life, because art has not endowed these things with the magic enchantment that draws our attention to them. But that time will come.

22 July 1855 from '[Shakespeare's Hamlet]*',* Bergensposten

In today's *Adresseavisen* we see that Mr Mantzius, a royal actor from Copenhagen, intends to give a reading of Shakespeare's *Hamlet* on Monday. It may not be superfluous to recommend this recital here, as we can assume that only a small number of the cultured public has any thorough understanding of the paramount importance that Shakespeare has for the entire Scandinavian arts: even more so as his works have thus far been excluded from our repertoire.

It is extremely desirable that an appreciation of this unsurpassed poet should be awakened, and a better opportunity than the one we now have can hardly be expected for a long time.

10 May 1857 from 'On the Ballad and its Significance for Artistic Poetry', Illustreret Nyhedsblad

Concerning the art of the past, the Ballads, with all their variations are almost the only monuments that have continued throughout the times to be freshly and powerfully alive in the people's consciousness. For centuries, the Ballads have passed by oral transmission from generation to generation; probably somewhat distorted as time has gone by, as one can imagine under such conditions, but still with their basic tone preserved.

[…]

A beginning has already been made with the Saga; Oehlenschläger's genius felt the necessity of a national foundation for a national poetry, and this was the principle on which his whole activity was built. That Oehlenschläger turned passionately to the Saga and not to the Ballad was a natural consequence of the conditions that prevailed during his early period.

[…]

The Saga is […] completely and utterly epic. In the Ballad, however, the lyrical is present; clearly in a different proportion than in the drama, but present it is, and the dramatic poet who collects his material from the Ballads need not let that material undergo such a transformation as the poet who gets his from the Saga. This circumstance is an essential advantage, which enables the poet to incorporate the mirror image of the time and the events he is dealing with more closely and in a more heartfelt way in his work. Thus, he can (if he manages it) present his heroes in a manner already familiar to the viewer from national folklore. On top of that comes the fact that the Ballads' flexible metre allows many liberties, which is of great importance for the dramatic dialogue, and therefore, without a doubt, this poetic source will be industriously utilised, in a near or more distant future, by poets who will continue to build on the foundation laid by Oehlenschläger. […] The national poetry in the Nordic countries began with the Saga, now the turn has come for the Ballads […]

13 December 1857 from 'Anton Wilhelm Wiehe', Illustreret Nyhedsblad[6]

The actor Anton Wilhelm Wiehe, whose artistic significance and career we record here with a few brief remarks, was born in Copenhagen on 8 July 1826, and already seemed destined for the theatre from the cradle through the great traditions linked to his family—he is the grandson of the Norwegian Michael Rossing, one of the most masterful and richly talented actors among the many names of the Danish stage whose inspiring influence on contemporary writers was of such intensity as to accelerate the development of Denmark's dramatic literature, thereby helping to elevate it to its current level. […] In 1843, when hardly seventeen years old, he was accepted as a student at Det Kongelige Teater [The Royal Theatre]. […] It is clear that Wiehe raised great expectations from the very beginning, but even so, in a large theatre it is not easy for an up and coming artist to develop fully during those important early years; the bigger roles are in the older artists' hands […] He took employment here in Christiania in 1851, where, on 11 September, he made his debut as 'Oluf' in Oehlenschläger's *Queen Margaretha.* Over the past six years, he has performed at Christiania Theater more than 560 times, and in more than 100 roles of very different types. To recount them here would be too extensive. […]

Wiehe came up here to us at the beginning of a period rife with internal conflicts and struggle; the idea of a national stage was emerging, but no written demonstration, no logical arguments addressing the benefit and necessity of such an institution, are as capable of ripening the matter so quickly and easily as an inspiring example—and therefore Wiehe has exerted an indisputable influence on the progress of our national stage. He brought with him something new into the theatre and to the consciousness of the audience: all of the poetry of youth lay with strength and warmth over his acting— a soulful purity revealed itself in his performances, a deep feeling of the sacredness and meaning of art, an inspired striving, not after crass reality, but after truth, after the higher symbolic representation of life, the only thing which in the world of art truly deserves to be fought for, and which is recognised by so very few. It must be obvious to everyone, that such an artist, who is at the same time equipped with all the outer necessities, is of incalculable benefit during a period of fumbling development; a period when a germinating art seeks its ideals, and where it would seek recourse to the representatives of tradition if the men of progress are not to be found. It is a common complaint that the time of the great theatre artists has passed, le théâtre Français has had its brilliant period, the Danish theatre looks back to its past, and the German no longer owns any Eckhoff, no Iffland or Schröder. To a certain degree this is true, but the fault lies with the authors and the new dramatic direction in France; these technically perfect works of art which emanate annually from the Parisian authors' workshops and which so grievously contribute to the promotion of virtuosity at the expense of art—these laceworks, which are constructed solely with the intended effect of 'witty lines', can only pull art down to the level of the effect itself. Is it strange, then, that our time has so few true actors—what was it that made those past artists so great? It was that they built their performance on the totality and not the particular; that they described the universal and not that which an accidental fashion or a depraved society has created in this or that way just for the moment. But the actors of our time—what can they do? Look at their repertoire; does not nine-tenths of it consist of those Frenchnesses, which moreover are totally in conflict with our nationality? Thus, those artists who understand how to steer forward in these narrow waters without running aground deserve great acknowledgement, and Wiehe belongs to these; there are two ways to go, either to descend into virtuosity or lift the artifice upwards and create a work of art from it. The latter is the only way worthy of a true artist, and that is what Wiehe has done. Look at his 'Georges Bernard' in *A Bride by Conquest*—this powdered representative of materialism, what does he not become in the hands of the artist? Does not the poetry of the performance make us forget that the author has really only delivered a treatise on social conditions to us in dramatic form? All true artistic presentation is necessarily poetic,

but this poesy in Wiehe is of a highly national Nordic character. If we examine our folklore poetry, the Ballads, our Sagas,
etc., then we will rediscover the same fundamental conditions
for that effect: an unconscious symbolism, a spiritual elevation
and calmness, an understanding of the importance of atmosphere, which in larger or lesser degree inspires all the
life-warm figures Wiehe knows how to create from his roles.

However, Wiehe must therefore remember one thing: his
sojourn with us is more than an engagement; it is a mission,
and he must not let it fail.

20 December 1857 from 'Lord William Russell and its Performance at
Christiania Theater', Illustreret Nyhedsblad

We do not have any real right to demand the facts of history
from a genuine historical tragedy, but rather its possibilities;
not the verifiable historical persons and characters, but the
period's spirit and way of thinking. Thus, *Götz von Berlichingen*
[by Goethe] would still have been a historical tragedy, even if
its fable was wholly invented by the author himself, Schiller's
Wilhelm Tell, Wallenstein, Maria Stuart, etc., are unhistorical, just
as is Shakespeare's *Macbeth*, among others. Even if these works
do present historical facts, the presentations rest on a total sus-
pension of the particularities of the period of history in
question, or for that matter, of any other. That the historical or
non-historical in a drama does not affect its poetic value must
be obvious, and perhaps the author is right in *not* fulfilling
these norms and requirements of historic writing; the work
thereby must become a closed book, since one could never
count upon the public having the necessary qualifications for
an appropriate understanding. The true approval, the writer's
real victory, must come from the people's unmediated inter-
nalization of his work, and not as an effect of an atmosphere
excited by historical memories.

[...]

Any extraordinary personality is symbolic in life; symbolic in
his actions and in his relationship to historical events. But the

mediocre writers who have misunderstood the requirement that life's significant phenomena should be magnified in art, lift this symbolism within the personality into the consciousness of depicted figures, and thus disturb the natural relationship through a procedure just as deluded as that of a chemist, who lets a mineral enter into a higher connection with one of its basic components, believing thereby that he can extract a nobler material, while in reality, he simply achieves a different one. However, it is not only the symbolic meaning that lies within the personality which is thus dislocated from its natural relationship; the same is also true of the overall symbolism of the dramatic idea. Instead of its winding hidden through the work like the silver vein in a mountain, it is constantly thrust into the light of day. Any trait, any utterance or action points to it, as if saying: 'Look here, this is the meaning—this is the significance of what you see in front of you!' Why is this so? The reason lies in an unjustified distrust of the public's poetic ability to internalise the work, as if a poetic aptitude for the beautiful and meaningful were not the common property of both the producer and the recipient. Were this not the case, it would hardly be worth the trouble of putting two rhyming lines on a page. The author can satisfy his own creative need regardless, and he is not writing for the public to receive its applause, but to clarify the people's fermenting thoughts; the creative, the formative talent is his alone, but the capacity for poetic understanding and enjoyment of what is already created belongs to the whole people.

[…]

Here I must sound a general warning against a particular thing, and that is the thoughtlessness with which so many theatres treat exposition scenes. It may be that one will often find in these scenes a great many things that conform only with difficulty to the general characterization of the dramatis personae, and are plaited, as it were, into the play in order to clarify the situation. But if that is the case, the actor should then exert himself even more to unify the character with what is necessary for the play. It also often happens that the actor, because of his not unfounded distrust of exposition, fails to investigate a deeper meaning within it, even though one might be found with little effort.

12 April 1861 from 'The Two Theatres in Christiania Part IV', Morgenbladet

Of all the hallmarks within the domains of literature or art, the one which most often betrays a semi-cultivated public is a certain fussy taste, which especially taints that which is enjoyed with more than usual appetite. This fussiness has its quite natural explanation. Many people are conscious in their own minds, or at least they have a dim sensation of how falteringly the foothold is that supports their judgement; and when there is greater risk of making a fool of oneself by approving rather than by condemning, it is quite reasonable to select the latter; because if one does thereby commit an injustice it can be attributed to refined taste, and one's reputation is saved.

[...]

In that respect, we find a strange example in Scribe's history at Christiania Theater. There was a time when this author was unassailable all over Europe; at least, rumours that there should be differing opinions about his works had not yet reached us here. Thus, audiences could be in no doubt as to the correct response. But then a new dramatic direction emerged in France; the character play grew little by little out of the Scribean situation drama. Of course, the Parisians had artistic discretion enough to assign both types a place side by side; but the Germans, who for all their philosophy still find it difficult in so many cases to grasp that truth has more than one side, immediately began to construct a critical theory, according to which Scribe is designated as outdated, vacuous and lacking in poetry. It immediately became obvious that one had committed a terrible mistake in admiring and being amused by these empty trifles for so long a time. [...] It was laughable to see our theatre audience at the time; on the one hand, there was habit and inclination, and on the other, foreign opinion! Well, Scribe continued to be as entertaining as before, of course, but condemnation came with the curtain call in the last act. And for no other reason than those stated: the Scribean repertoire at Christiania Theater has been just as good since the turning point as it had been before: nor can it be denied that his most important female role has of late been, or at least could have been, in better hands than before.

It is easy to imagine what kind of criticism is written by and for such a public. This criticism only has two categories, a 'good' or 'bad' repertoire; and it rarely manages to lift itself to a concept higher than 'the lovely'. All authors who have a good name in literary history, or in public opinion abroad, are ascribed to the 'good' repertoire. Popular comedy and farce always belong to the 'bad' if the stage happens to be set within a city. If, however, the play is staged in a rural district beyond the city's borders, it is usually described as village historic: seen as deprived of dramatic action but granted a respectable poetic value, and thus assigned to the good repertoire. The abstract poetic is always set above the dramatic (N.B. but only afterwards, when the performance is over); although after all, it ought first be decided whether an un-dramatic play can ever be said to be poetic.

Moreover, it is required of the 'good' repertoire that it be extremely varied; it must alternate between Mallefille, Oehlenschlæger, Birch-Pfeif[f]er, Shakespeare, Iffland, Molière, Barrière, and to some extent Holberg. Now, one knows that the better theatres abroad, for example the Parisian, keep within the borders of the art forms represented by the aforementioned authors; but as Paris has at least five or six public theatres, and Christiania at the most two, we might feel entitled to demand a little of each of these art forms, whereas each of the five or six in Paris has its specialised repertoire.

[...] Even so, one may still ask what constitutes a 'good' repertoire. This can be answered in a few words. A good repertoire is one in which the chosen plays are suitable; that is, they lie neither beyond nor above the abilities of the theatre which performs them. It is thus an entirely conditional concept, as one and the same repertoire may be good in one of our two theatres and bad in the other, or good or bad in both. But there are some among us who neither can, nor wish, to acknowledge this simple truth, and it is this group which always has the negative ready at hand concerning the greater part of what our Norwegian Theatre offers, while it will acknowledge without further ado everything that Christiania Theater stages.

26 October 1862 from 'Christiania's Theater's Repertoire', Morgenbladet

The Painter, the Poet, the Sculptor or the Musician can be performed effectively on the stage, but not the Actor. Decorative scenery can depict a castle, a church or any kind of locality, but it cannot depict the *stage* itself. If this is done, the illusion is broken, and without illusion, all artistic effect is gone. Even worse, when, as in this play [*I Am My Brother* by Karl Wilhelm Salice-Contessa], there is communication between the actors on the one hand and the prompter and orchestra on the other. If the artist moves outside the stage lights, then he literally crosses the border of his art. Neither is it beneficial that the theatre's audience is initiated into the mysteries of the space between the wings; the world behind the stage ought to be a closed world. If the spectators at a play like this become too knowledgeable, they will subsequently be deprived of the full enjoyment of not knowing: they will still know and will not be able to free themselves from the knowledge. If despite all this, one wishes to bring such a play to the stage, it ought to be localised. The plots and the intrigues would have to be adjusted according to our corresponding reality: if the illusion has once been broken, then let it be done all the way. Given the way the play is now presented, the satire has no effect because it does not strike home; the frailties and faults that are exposed are more usually known to us from novels and stories from elsewhere.

[…]

Mr Jørgensen's thoroughly prepared performance is a true masterpiece [in *The Gentlemen of Bois-Doré* a dramatic version of the novel by George Sand]; he knows how to utilise the pauses, the rise and fall of his voice, the variations of tempo to create a unity of effect which we otherwise only receive at the best theatres. Most of our younger actors could learn from him what a pause is; at the moment, there are not many who know this; most seem to believe that a pause is the same as keeping silent. Besides, what we must admire almost more than the excellent performance is the love of the art which is revealed in such a detailed study. This devotion to art is certainly not worth it for the sake of the reward it receives here: if an actor builds his performance on a refined attention to nuance, he will find it difficult to escape the impression that he is playing to virtually empty seats, even when the house is sold out.

9 November 1862 from 'Christiania Theater', Morgenbladet

[...] Norwegians are a people of the future, that is, a people who for two reasons can sleep confidently in the present, and will be able to sleep just as confidently through every future moment. Firstly we share an historic certainty that our ancestors have done a considerable day's work; and secondly because we are so deeply convinced that our descendants will one day awaken to a great mission of the future. But if we are such a people of the future, then there is nothing wrong with skipping a few formalities in the development of our dramatic art. After all, we are not, strictly speaking, responsible for what we do in our sleep. Besides, the Norwegianising standpoint is only a transitional passage; it presupposes a Scandinavian movement that will take over from it; and after that comes Pan-Germanism. Thus, if we wake up one fine afternoon and find a German opera on the ruins of the Norwegian and the Danish-Norwegian theatre, no real damage will have been done.

1. Although rarely performed today, Eugène Scribe was an extraordinarily successful nineteenth-century French playwright. The demand for his work in Europe was so great that he employed collaborating writers in his 'factory'. He wrote, alone or in collaboration with these employees, five hundred plays between 1815 and his death in 1861. Ibsen worked as a stage director on twenty-one Scribe productions during his years at Det norske Theater in Bergen, one of which, *Bataille de Dames* (Scribe and Legouvé, 1851), resembles the plot of his *The Feast of Solhaug* (1856).

2. Christian Jørgensen directed and played Bernhard in *A Burial Mound* at the Christiania Theater in 1850.

3. A romantic play by Henrik Anker Bjerregaard with music by Marcus Thrane, first performed in 1825.

4. *La somnambule*, a vaudeville in two acts, by Eugéne Scribe and Casimir Delavigne, translated into Danish by L. Heiberg, and performed at Det norske Theater in Bergen on 5 November 1851.

5. The Norwegian writer, Hans Ørn Blom, was twenty-two years old when his first play was performed at the Christiania Theater, *Den hjemkomne søn eller en nutidens Jean de France* ('The Returned Son or a Contemporary Jean de France'). His vaudeville, *Tordenskjold*, followed in 1844.

6. Wiehe had played Gudmund Alfson in *The Feast of Solhaug* at the Christiania Theater in 1856.

Appendix 2
Biographical Notes

The following biographical notes are designed to throw light on the relationships between Ibsen and the recipients of the letters and the authors of the recollections that appear in this collection. Wherever possible the entries are linked to contributor and venue records in IbsenStage; these records list all relevant associations with productions of Ibsen's plays.

[Karin] Sophie Adlersparre, b. Leijonhufvud, 1823–1895

Author and leading figure in the Swedish women's rights movement and co-founder and editor of the first Scandinavian women's magazine, *Home Review* (1859–85). The lecture by Adlersparre that is mentioned in Ibsen's letter became the basis for her publication: *Ibsen's 'Ghosts' from an Ethical Viewpoint* (1882).

Hildur Andersen, 1864–1956

Concert pianist, musicologist, and translator of Wagner's operas into Norwegian. Ibsen knew her family from his years in Bergen; he became close to her after his return to Kristiania in 1891, and they corresponded extensively during her stays abroad. Andersen destroyed much of their correspondence before she died.

Theodor [Vilhelm Jacob] Andersen, 1835–1909

ibsenstage.hf.uio.no/pages/contributor/441948

Danish actor and director based in Copenhagen. Andersen was the artistic director of Casinoteatret (1869–84), and of Dagmarteatret (1884–87) where he produced *Peer Gynt* and *The Feast at Solhaug* in 1886.

Jens Peter Andresen, 1818–1871

Norwegian lawyer and Chair of the Christiania Theater Board from 1866 to 1871; responsible for offering Ibsen the position of Artistic Director in 1870.

William Archer, 1856–1924

ibsenstage.hf.uio.no/pages/contributor/427434

Scottish theatre critic, writer and translator. A major advocate of Ibsen's dramas in Britain. His translations of Ibsen's plays have been used in English-speaking theatres worldwide (184 IbsenStage records); they have also been source texts for relay translations into other languages. Archer met Ibsen for the first time in Rome during the winter of 1881–2, and saw him for the last time in 1899. He recorded his impressions of these meetings in articles, and in letters to his brother Charles, who also translated Ibsen for theatres in the United States of America. For production records of Charles Archer see: ibsenstage.hf.uio.no/pages/contributor/449694

Elise [Sofie] Aubert, b. Aars, 1837–1909

Norwegian author of novels and short stories who wrote newspaper articles on women's education and training. She reviewed the Christiania Theater productions of *Pillars of Society* and *A Doll's House* for the major Kristiania newspapers.

Ole Andreas Bachke, 1830–1890

Norwegian lawyer and politician who belonged to a group of young writers and intellectuals in Kristiania known as the Holland Circle. Ibsen was a member of this group from 1859 to 1864.

Herman [Joachim] Bang, 1857–1912

ibsenstage.hf.uio.no/pages/contributor/427854

Major Danish novelist, known for his impressionist style, depicting 'quiet existences', particularly of lonely and unsatisfied women. Amongst his best known works are *Fædra* (1883) and *Tine* (1889). Bang tried to build a career as an actor as a young man, but failed; he described his Bergen performance of Osvald in *Ghosts* as a fiasco. He collaborated on the productions of Ibsen's plays in France, Denmark and Norway: most notably with the Théâtre de l'Oeuvre and the Théâtre du Vaudeville in Paris. He wrote articles and reviews on Ibsen productions in major newspapers in Norway, Denmark and Germany.

Emilie Bardach, 1862–1955

Ibsen met Bardach, the daughter of an Austrian merchant, while on holiday in Gossensass in 1889. She was the first of three young women that Ibsen referred as his 'princesses', the other two being Hildur Andersen and Helene Raff. These women are believed to have inspired elements within his late plays. Ibsen gave Bardach a photograph of himself inscribed 'To the May sun of a September life'. His letters to her were published by Georg Brandes in 1906. In 1923, Bardach collaborated on two articles for *The Century Magazine* (October/November) that described her relationship with Ibsen.

Victor Barrucand, 1864–1934

French author and journalist. Barrucand worked as a musician in Paris as a young man and became involved in theatre and anarchist politics; he wrote about several of Ibsen's plays. In 1899, he was elected delegate to the Socialist Congress in Paris; later sent to Algeria by the League of Human Rights where he advocated for colonial reform.

Kaarlo [Johan] (Juhani) Bergbom, 1843–1906

ibsenstage.hf.uio.no/pages/venue/11657

Co-founder with his sister, Emilie Bergbom, of the Suomalainen Teatteri (the Finnish Theatre). During their joint directorship of the company (1872–1905), produced twelve plays by Ibsen including *Nora* (1880), the first performance of an Ibsen play in Finnish; and in 1897, they shared the world premiere of *John Gabriel Borkman* with the production at Svenska Teatern, the Swedish theatre in Helsinki.

Vilhelm Bergsøe, 1835–1911

Danish author and zoologist with a background in entomology. In 1865, he published a book (known to Ibsen) on the Tarantula spider, the Tarantella dances of Southern Italy and their connection to the medieval history of Tarantism.

Hagbard Emanuel Berner, 1839–1920

Norwegian politician, serving as a member of parliament with the Liberal Party, and a senior public servant. He founded the newspaper *Dagbladet*, and The Norwegian Society, which promoted the use of Nynorsk as an alternative to the official use of the Dano-Norwegian language. Together with the feminist pioneer Gina Krog, he established the Norwegian Association for Women's Rights and served as its first Chair.

Michael Birkeland, 1830–1896

Norwegian national archivist, historian and politician. Like Ibsen, he was a member of the group of young writers and intellectuals in Kristiania known as the Holland Circle.

Bjørn Bjørnson, 1859–1942

ibsenstage.hf.uio.no/pages/contributor/439889

Norwegian actor, theatre manager, and playwright. The son of Bjørnstjerne and Karoline Bjørnson, he trained as an actor in Berlin and Vienna and began his career at the Saxe-Meiningen Theatre with Duke George II. From 1884 to1893, he was an actor and stage director at the Christiania Theater, and from 1899 to 1906, he became the first director of Norway's National-altheatret, a position he resumed from 1923 to 1927. He directed fourteen plays by Ibsen, acted in *Pillars of Society*, and played Peer Gynt in his own production.

Bjørnstjerne [Martinus] Bjørnson, 1832–1910

ibsenstage.hf.uio.no/pages/contributor/439205

Norwegian playwright, director, novelist and public intellectual. *A Bankruptcy* (1874) was his most successful play; *A Gauntlet* (1883) was his most controversial. He was considered by his Norwegian contemporaries to be as significant a playwright as Ibsen: he was the first Norwegian playwright to achieve success in the German theatre, and became the first Norwegian Nobel Laureate when he won the Nobel Prize for Literature in 1903. Bjørnson was four years younger than Ibsen and followed him as the director of Det norske Theater in Bergen; when Ibsen refused the directorship of the Christiania Theater, Bjørnson took the position and staged over sixty plays between 1865 and 1867. At the opening of Nationaltheatret in Oslo in 1899, he received equal honours with Ibsen, and statues of both men were placed outside the theatre entrance. The relationship between the two men was turbulent, as is evident from their considerable correspondence; their families were united by the marriage of Bjørnson's daughter, Bergliot, and Ibsen's son, Sigurd.

Peter [Michael] Blytt (Blydt), 1823–1897

Norwegian merchant and city governor. He was a member of the board at Det norske Theater in Bergen while Ibsen was working with the company. His account of the early history of the theatre, *Minder fra den første norske Scene i Bergen i 1850-årene* ('Memories from the first Norwegian stage in Bergen in the 1850s'), was published in 1894; it is the main source of information on Ibsen's activities in Bergen.

Erik [Nicolai] Bøgh, 1822–1899

Danish theatre director, editor, and author of light comedies. Bøgh was the artistic director of Casinoteatret in Copenhagen from 1855 to 1860. Ibsen directed some of his plays in Bergen. Bøgh also wrote newspaper reviews and articles about Ibsen's plays for over twenty years.

Marie von Borch, 1843–1895

ibsenstage.hf.uio.no/pages/contributor/434932

German translator. Von Borch translated at least thirty works by Scandinavian authors, of which ten were by Ibsen. Supposedly, it was the character of Mrs Alving that attracted her to his plays. IbsenStage hold records of 210 production events over 123 years that used her translations.

Otto [Frederik Christian William] Borchsenius, 1844–1925

Danish author and editor. Borchsenius wrote newspaper and magazine articles about *The Feast at Solhaug*, *The League of Youth*, *Ghosts*, *An Enemy of the People*, *When We Dead Awaken* and *Hedda Gabler*.

Georg [Morris Cohen] Brandes, 1842–1927

Danish critic and author. Brandes was a significant intellectual influence on Ibsen and more broadly on European literature. His lectures on aesthetics drew large audiences and were published in the first volume of his major work, *Hovedstrømninger i det 19de Aarhundredes Litteratur* ('Main Currents in the Literature of the Nineteenth Century'). Reading these lectures had a profound influence on Ibsen; he wrote to Brandes:

> A more dangerous book could not have fallen into a fertile writer's hands. It's one of those books that creates a yawning abyss between yesterday and today. […] It reminds me of California's goldfields when they were first discovered; they could make you a millionaire, or crush you in misery. Is our spiritual constitution robust enough at home? I don't know; however, that's not what counts. Whatever cannot support the ideas of the time, must fall. (4 April 1872.)

Brandes is associated with the 'Modern Breakthrough' that replaced romanticism with naturalism and realism in Scandinavian literature. In December 1883, he published *Det moderne Gjennembruds Mænd* ('The Men of the Breakthrough') about Ibsen, Bjørnson and a group of Danish writers.

Ernst Brausewetter, 1863–1904

ibsenstage.hf.uio.no/pages/contributor/441709

German author and translator of three plays by Ibsen. Ibsen-Stage holds records of twenty-eight production events over seventy-eight years that used his translations.

Francis Bull (1887–1974)

Prominent Norwegian professor of literature, the son of Edvard Bull, Ibsen's doctor in his last years.

[Carl] Theodor Caspari, 1853–1948

Norwegian author. His early poetry, written in the 1880s, was directed against the 'Modern Breakthrough' in Scandinavian literature; it was particularly critical of Ibsen and Bjørnson, and more generally, the realist genre. He wrote newspaper articles and reviews of several Ibsen plays, and in 1895 published a short comparative study of the dramaturgy of Shakespeare and the late plays of Ibsen.

[Jacobine] Camilla Collett, b. Wergeland, 1813–1895

Norwegian author and pioneer of Norwegian feminism. She described her major novel *Amtmandens Døttre* ('The District Governor's Daughter') as 'my life's long-suppressed scream'. It dealt with the social repression of women and the need for female autonomy. She was a friend of Suzannah Ibsen and wrote literary criticism of both *Ghosts* and *Peer Gynt*.

Jonas [Sigismund] Collin, 1840–1905

Danish zoologist. Collin donated a large manuscript and letter collection, which included works by Ibsen, to the Danish Royal Library.

Ludvig Ludvigsen Daae, 1834–1910

Norwegian historian and classical philologist. Daae belonged to a group of young writers and intellectuals in Kristiania known as the Holland Circle. Ibsen was a member of this group from 1859 to 1864.

Rodolphe Darzens, 1865–1938

ibsenstage.hf.uio.no/pages/contributor/440773

French author and secretary of André Antoine's Théâtre Libre from 1887. He translated *Ghosts* (with the assistance of a Norwegian speaker) for the Théâtre Libre; the production opened in Paris in 1890, toured to Switzerland, Italy, Germany and the Netherlands, and was last performed in 1905.

Lorentz [Henrik Segelcke] Dietrichson, 1834–1917

Norwegian poet, academic, and historian of art and literature. Dietrichson met Ibsen in 1857; they spent time together in Rome during the summer of 1864. He wrote critiques of *Brand* and *Peer Gynt* for *Ny illustrerad Tidning* ('New Illustrated Periodical') and provided a short biography of Ibsen first published in the same journal, and later used as part of the introduction of Ibsen into Germany. His memoirs, originally serialised in *Morgenbladet* (1892–1901) and dedicated to Suzannah Ibsen, have proved to be a major source of information for Ibsen's biographers.

Erik [Wilhelm] Af Edholm, 1817–1897

ibsenstage.hf.uio.no/pages/venue/12360

Theatre manager and Swedish Officer of the Crown who belonged to the inner circle of the court of Karl XV. Towards the end of the 1860s, he introduced plays by Ibsen and Bjørnson into the repertoire of Kungliga Dramatiska Teatern (the Royal Dramatic Theatres in Stockholm), which hitherto had been dominated by opera, French comedies and Shakespeare.

Julius Elias, 1861–1927

ibsenstage.hf.uio.no/pages/contributor/429024

German translator and historian of art and literature. A major advocate of Ibsen and Bjørnson in Germany, Elias first met Ibsen in Munich. He was responsible for the first edition of Ibsen's *Sämtliche Werke* (Collected Works), which he published with Paul Schlenther and Georg Brandes (S. Fischer, 1898–1904). A collection of Ibsen's letters was published for the first time in Volume 4, with an introduction and commentary by Elias and Halvdan Koht.

[Morten] Edvard Fallesen, 1817–1894

ibsenstage.hf.uio.no/pages/venue/11738

Danish officer, politician and theatre manager who also wrote reviews and translated plays. He was the manager of Det Kongelige Teater (the Royal Theatre in Copenhagen) from 1876 until his death in 1894. During this time, Fallesen programmed six plays by Ibsen in the theatre's repertoire, including the world premiere of *A Doll's House*; he was also responsible for rejecting *Ghosts* and *Rosmersholm* for performance.

Samuel Fischer, 1859–1934

German publisher, born in Hungary. Fischer established his own publishing house in 1886. He published German translations of *Rosmersholm* and *The Wild Duck* in 1887; *Emperor and Galiean* and *The Lady from the Sea* in 1888; and *The Pretenders* and *Love's Comedy* in 1889. He was responsible for publishing the German first editions of Ibsen's plays from the 1890s, and several new translations of his older plays. Fischer's commitment to publishing Ibsen culminated in a ten-volume collected works (1898–1904); it was the first collection of Ibsen's writings to appear in any language.

[Laura Mathilda Edla] Rosa Fitinghoff, 1872–1949

Swedish author and daughter of prize-winning novelist Laura Fitinghoff. She met Ibsen near the end of his life, first in Stockholm 1898 and later in Kristiania in 1899. In 1928, she published her recollections of these meetings.

Georg II, Duke of Saxe-Meiningen, 1826–1914

ibsenstage.hf.uio.no/pages/venue/12441

A significant figure in the history of nineteenth-century European theatre, the theatrical innovations introduced by Georg II at the Herzogliches Hoftheater (the Saxe-Meiningen Court Theatre) influenced Henry Irving, André Antoine and

Constantin Stanislavsky. The theatre developed an ensemble style of acting and introduced theatrical mise-en-scène that privileged historical accuracy. The theatre's trial staging of *The Pretenders* (30 January 1876) was the first presentation of an Ibsen play in Germany; it was followed by a full production of the play, which Ibsen saw when the company toured to Berlin. Ten years later, Georg II invited Ibsen to Meiningen to see the company perform *Ghosts*. Ibsen was awarded two medals by Georg II: the Knight Cross, and Commander of the Saxon-Ernestine Order. The Herzogliches Hoftheater presented fourteen plays by Ibsen between 1876 and 1916.

Fredrik Gjertsen, 1831–1904

Norwegian philologist, civil servant, educator, and translator. He wrote poems, speeches, and songs, one of which was sung in the march organised by students to celebrate Ibsen's visit to Kristiania in 1874.

Edmund [William] Gosse, 1849–1928

ibsenstage.hf.uio.no/pages/contributor/440993

English poet, author, art and literature critic. Gosse read Ibsen's *Digte* (Poems) during a visit to Norway in 1871. He subsequently wrote a series of articles about Ibsen for English journals, the most important being 'Ibsen's Social Dramas' for *The Fortnightly Review* (1 January 1889). He translated *Hedda Gabler* (1891) and *The Master Builder* (1893) with William Archer; he also acted in the first London readings of *Little Eyolf* and *The Master Builder* that were organised by William Heinemann to secure Ibsen's copyright in England. In 1907, he published the biographical study, *Henrik Ibsen*. As well as promoting Ibsen, Gosse was an advocate for both W.B. Yeats and James Joyce.

Gerhard Gran, 1856–1925

Norwegian literary historian, editor, and essayist. He founded *Edda*, the *Scandinavian Journal of Literary Research* in 1914 and was the journal's chief editor until his death in 1925. He was a prolific biographer, publishing studies not only of Ibsen (1918) but also of Bjørnstjerne Bjørnson (1910), Jean-Jacques Rousseau (1910–11), Alexander Kielland (1922) and Charles Dickens (1925).

Edvard [Hagerup] Grieg, 1843–1907

ibsenstage.hf.uio.no/pages/contributor/427079

Norwegian composer and pianist. Grieg met Ibsen at the Scandinavian Club in Rome while they were both living in Italy during 1865–6. When the Christiania Theater programmed the premiere of *Peer Gynt* for 1876, Ibsen invited Grieg to write the music; it was the most expensive production ever staged in Norway. Ibsen was delighted with their collaboration and invited Grieg to visit him later that year in Gossensass.

Marcus [Fredrik Steen] Grønvold, 1845–1929

Norwegian artist. Ibsen owned several of his paintings, including a self-portrait from 1878. Grønvold wrote about Ibsen in his 1925 memoirs *Fra Ulrikken til Alperne* ('From Ulrikken to the Alps').

Peter [Hans Christian] Hansen, 1840–1905

ibsenstage.hf.uio.no/pages/venue/11738

Danish journalist, translator, literary and theatre historian. He published an anthology of nineteenth-century Scandinavian writers, *Nordiske Digtere i vort Aarhundrede* (1870, 'Nordic Poets in our own Century'), which featured five of Ibsen's poems together with an extract from *Brand*. Ibsen provided him with a short biographical account of his life as a playwright and poet for this collection. Hansen was the artistic director of Det

Kongelige Teater (the Royal Theatre in Copenhagen) from 1894 to 1899, during which time the company staged five plays by Ibsen, including the Danish premiere of *Little Eyolf*.

[*Niels*] *Frederik Vilhelm Hegel, 1817–1887*

Danish bookseller and publisher. In 1850, Hegel took over Gyldendal, the Danish publishing house, from his employer Jacob Deichmann. Under Hegel's leadership, the company was closely associated with the 'Modern Breakthrough' movement which replaced romanticism with naturalism in Scandinavian literature. In 1860, Bjørnson introduced Ibsen to Hegel: *Brand* was published by Gyldendal the following year, and the company became Ibsen's Scandinavian publisher. HIS holds 280 letters from Ibsen to Hegel. The correspondence deals not only with the delivery of manuscripts and print runs, but also a range of other services that Hegel provided for Ibsen: he managed advances, the investment of earnings, and collected theatre royalties. He supplied Ibsen with newspaper articles, reviews, and the books he needed as background research for his plays. Ibsen wrote to him at length about the necessity of managing the German distribution of his plays through translation, publication and performance: together, they managed to minimise the loss of earnings from unauthorised German translations. Ibsen and Hegel remained close until the latter's death in 1887.

Gunnar [*Edvard Rode*] *Heiberg, 1857–1929*

ibsenstage.hf.uio.no/pages/venue/11623

Norwegian journalist, playwright and theatre director. Heiberg met Ibsen during the winter of 1878–79. They were both members of the Scandinavian Club in Rome and Heiberg wrote an account of a meeting at which Ibsen put forward two proposals: that women should have full voting rights within the Club; and that the post of librarian should be open to women. Heiberg published several books that contained reminiscences of Ibsen and critiques of his plays, including *Ibsen og*

Bjørnson paa scenen (1918, 'Ibsen and Bjørnson on the Stage'). From 1884 to 1888, he was the artistic director of the Den Nationale Scene in Bergen; he included nine plays by Ibsen in the company's repertoire, including premieres of *The Wild Duck* (9 January 1885) and *Rosmersholm* (17 January 1887).

Peter [Arnold] Heise, 1830–1879

ibsenstage.hf.uio.no/pages/contributor/439321

Danish composer. Heise began composing for the theatre in the 1850s; Ibsen asked him to write the music for the Copenhagen production of *The Pretenders* in 1871. Ibsen suggested that they continue collaborating on a new work, 'Sigurd Jorsalfar', but the project was never completed. As a young man, Heise collected hundreds of folk tunes that influenced his compositions; he wrote settings for poems and songs by Shakespeare, Hans Christian Andersen, Bjørnson and Ibsen.

Julius [Johan Peter] Hoffory, 1855–1897

ibsenstage.hf.uio.no/pages/contributor/440504

Danish philologist and translator. Professor of Scandinavian Philology and Phonetics at the University of Berlin from 1887, Hoffory published on linguistics and the history of literature. He established the *Nordische Bibliothek* ('Scandinavian Library') with the German publisher, S. Fischer: the first volume in the series was his translation of Ibsen's *Die Frau vom Meere* (*The Lady from the Sea*). He wrote about 'Henrik Ibsen in Berlin' in the Danish journal *Tilskueren*. Hoffory had a mental collapse and died four years after being clinically diagnosed as insane in 1893.

Harald Holst, 1817–1882

ibsenstage.hf.uio.no/pages/venue/11704

Norwegian senior public servant. From September 1878 until August 1880, he was both a member and Chair of the Board of

the Christiania Theater. During this time, the company presented five plays by Ibsen.

Cornelis Honigh, 1845–1896

ibsenstage.hf.uio.no/pages/contributor/440887

Dutch author and translator. One of the Netherlands' foremost
experts in Nordic languages and literature, Honigh's publications included *Bjørnstjerne Bjørnson* (1887), and a translation of
Hedda Gabler (1891).

Sigurd Ibsen, 1859–1930

ibsenstage.hf.uio.no/pages/contributor/441359

Norwegian diplomat, politician, translator, and author. Sigurd
Ibsen was the only child of Henrik and Suzannah Ibsen. (His
half-brother, Hans Jacob Henriksen, was illegitimate; Ibsen
paid paternity costs for fourteen years but refused to acknowledge his elder son.) Sigurd was educated in Italy and Germany;
he joined the diplomatic service during the political union
between Sweden and Norway and worked as an attaché at the
Department of Foreign Affairs in Stockholm. He was given a
stipend to join the General Consulate in Washington, and lived
briefly in New York before being transferred to Vienna. He left
the diplomatic service to earn his living as a writer: he translated three of Ibsen's plays into German, wrote two plays of his
own, and published essays, articles, and a biographical study.
He served as the Prime Minister of Norway in Stockholm for
the two years that preceded the dissolution of the political
union between Norway and Sweden in 1905. Sigurd married
Bergliot Bjørnson, the daughter of Bjørnstjerne Bjørnson, thus
uniting the two most famous theatrical families in Norway.

Susanna/Suzannah Ibsen, b. Daae Thoresen, 1836–1914

In 1856, Ibsen met SuzannahThoresen at the Bergen house of
her stepmother, the playwright Magdalene Thoresen. They
married two years later and were living in Kristiania when their

only child, Sigurd, was born in 1859. Ibsen claimed that elements of Suzannah's personality were reflected in the characters of Hjørdis in *The Vikings at Helgeland* and Svanhild in *Love's Comedy*. She was an avid reader, particularly of contemporary Scandinavian and European literature, and her translation of *Graf Waldemar* (1847) by the German dramatist Gustav Freytag was performed in 1861. She admired the novels of George Sand and was a friend of Camilla Collett, the Norwegian author and pioneer feminist. In later life, she suffered from debilitating rheumatism and regularly travelled to health resorts in Southern Europe with her son Sigurd. She was too ill from rheumatism to attend Ibsen's funeral in 1906.

Andreas [Hornbeck] Isachsen, 1829–1903

ibsenstage.hf.uio.no/pages/contributor/430289

Norwegian actor born in Grimstad, where Ibsen first met him. In 1851, while students in Kristiania, Isachsen and Ibsen for a brief time co-edited the handwritten student newspaper, *Samfundsbladet*. He began his acting career with Ibsen at Det norske Theater in Bergen (1851–8), and moved with him to the Kristiania Norske Theater where he was employed until the theatre went bankrupt in 1862. After three years with the Trondheim norske Theater, he returned to the capital and joined the Christiania Theater. Ibsen was very supportive of Isachsen during the actor's early career, encouraging him to expand his knowledge of theatre by travelling abroad. In 1873, Ibsen learnt that Isachsen was giving public readings of *Emperor and Galilean* without his permission. The animosity created by this incident soured their relationship.

Henrik [Bernhard] Jæger, 1854–1895

Norwegian literary historian, man of letters. Jæger worked as an artistic consultant at the Christiania Theater (1879–83) and as a director with Den Nationale Scene in Bergen (1888–9). He wrote newspaper articles and critiques of twelve of Ibsen's plays; he gave a series of public lectures strongly criticising

Ghosts in the winter of 1881, but two years later he reversed his judgement. In 1888, he published a literary biography of Ibsen; it was translated and published in Germany, England, and the United States of America.

Emil [Jacob] Jonas, 1824–1912

ibsenstage.hf.uio.no/pages/contributor/43954

German editor and author. Jonas worked as journalist, author, and translator of Scandinavian literature including works by H.C. Andersen, Bjørnson and Viktor Rydberg. Ibsen was incensed by his translation of *Pillars of Society*: it made major cuts to the text, removed minor characters, and robbed him of theatre royalties. It is difficult to ascertain which translation was used in many early German productions of the play: Ibsen-Stage identifies thirteen productions that used the Jonas version, but it is highly likely there were more.

Ludvig [Oscar] Josephson, 1832–1899

ibsenstage.hf.uio.no/pages/venue/11704
ibsenstage.hf.uio.no/pages/venue/13829

Swedish actor and theatre manager. Josephson wrote newspaper articles and essays about theatre, translated numerous plays, and wrote two historical dramas. He worked extensively in Sweden before assuming the role as artistic director of the Christiania Theater (1873–7). He included five of Ibsen's plays in the theatre's repertoire, the most significant production being the world premiere of *Peer Gynt* (1876). Much to Ibsen's disappointment, his contract was not renewed by the Board of the Christiania Theater. Josephson returned to Sweden and became the head of Nya Teatern in Stockholm (1879–87) where his adventurous repertoire choices included Goethe's *Faust*, the prose version of Strindberg's *Master Olof*, and four plays by Ibsen, including the first production of the entire text of *Brand* (1885).

Laura [Anna Sophie Müller] Kieler, b. Petersen, 1849–1932

Norwegian/Danish author. Kieler met Ibsen after dedicating her novel to him: it had been inspired by *Brand* and was titled, *Brands døtre: et livsbillede af Lili* ('Brand's Daughters: A Life Portrait of Lili'). Her early married life had some parallels with the plotline of *A Doll's House* and in her eightieth year, she published an article in the Danish newspaper, *Nationaltidende*, entitled, 'Hvem var Modellen til *Et dukkehjem's* "Lærkefugl"?' (12 January 1929, 'Who Was the Model for *A Doll's House*'s "Skylark"?'). She represented Denmark at the International Congress of Women held in Chicago in 1893.

Emma Klingenfeld, 1846–1935

ibsenstage.hf.uio.no/pages/contributor/439422

German translator. Klingenfeld lived in Munich and translated from Scandinavian languages, English and French. Ibsen employed her to translate *Pillars of Society*, *Lady Inger* and *The Vikings at Helgeland* in order to minimise financial losses from unauthorised versions in the German publishing and theatre markets. She continued to collaborate with him, translating a further three plays, including *The Feast at Solhaug* for his sixtieth birthday. She contributed revised versions of her translations for the publication of the first German edition of his complete works (1898–1906). IbsenStage cites her as the translator of fifty-seven production events, the last of which was staged in 2007.

Bjørn Kristensen, 1869–1935

Norwegian editor. Kristensen was Bjørnstjerne Bjørnson's nephew. He became the editor, and later owner, of the local newspaper in Moss.

Wilhelm Lange, 1849–1907

ibsenstage.hf.uio.no/pages/contributor/430996

German scholar and translator specialising in literature from Scandinavian, Romance and Slavic languages. Lange published unauthorised translations of *Pillars of Society* and *The League of Youth* and sold them to German theatres. Subsequently, he entered into a business agreement with Ibsen: in exchange for privileged access to future manuscripts he agreed to share the profits from his German translations. This arrangement lasted until the late 1880s. Lange has proved to be Ibsen's most enduring German translator: in IbsenStage, he is cited in 325 production events tied to ten plays over a period of 129 years.

Albert Langen, 1869–1909

German publisher. He established Buch und Kunst-Verlag Albert Langen in 1893. His company concentrated on publishing modern Scandinavian and French authors including Bjørnson, Brandes, Drachmann, France, Hamsun, Lagerlöf, Lie, Maeterlinck, Maupassant, Prévost, Taine, Tolstoy, Chekhov, Strindberg, Wedekind and Zola. In 1896, he married Bjørnson's daughter, Dagny, but they divorced twelve years later. In 1896, he published a German translation of *John Gabriel Borkman* by Sigurd Ibsen.

August [Gottlieb] Larsen, 1843–1906

Danish publisher and bookseller. While Larsen worked at the Danish publishing company Gyldendal, he was responsible for proofreading Ibsen's manuscripts. When Hegel died in 1887 and his son Jacob took over the firm, Larsen became more directly involved with the Gyldendal authors and negotiated with theatres on their behalf.

Hartvig [Marcus] Lassen, 1824–1897

ibsenstage.hf.uio.no/pages/venue/11704

Norwegian editor and literary historian. Lassen was a literary manager at the Christiania Theater: he worked closely with Ludvig Josephson, the artistic director from 1873 to 1877, and occasionally with Hans Schrøder, the director from 1879 to 1899. He edited several periodicals, translated plays for the Christiania Theater, and edited the collected works of Norwegian Romantic poet Henrik Wergeland (1852–57, 9 vols).

Heinrich Laube, 1806–1884

ibsenstage.hf.uio.no/pages/venue/13591

German author, theatre director and critic. As a young man, Laube challenged the political regime in Germany through his political essays. He was placed under police surveillance, his books were confiscated, and he was twice sentenced to imprisonment. Ten years later, he spent a brief time as an elected member of the Frankfurt Parliament. From 1839, he established a career as a playwright and was the director of several theatres before being appointed in Vienna as the director of the new Stadttheater, where he presented Ibsen's *A Doll's House* (*Nora*) in 1881.

Jonas [Lauritz Idemil] Lie, 1833–1908

Norwegian lawyer and author. Lie met Ibsen while preparing for his matriculation exam at the Heltberg crammer school in Kristiania. He began his writing career in journalism and was responsible for publishing *Love's Comedy* (1862) in *Illustrert Nyhedsblad*, which he ran from 1861 to 1864. From 1870, his reputation as a novelist grew and he received an artist stipend from the Norwegian government. Like Ibsen, he chose to live abroad, only returning to Norway from Germany and France in 1893. His most critically acclaimed novel *Familjen paa Gilje: et interieur fra Firtiaarene* (1883, 'The Family at Gilje: A Domestic Story of the Forties') addresses the limitations placed on women in bourgeois society.

[Catharina] Fredrika Limnell, b. Forssberg, 1816–1892

Swedish philanthropist and pioneer feminist. Limnell campaigned for child care, married women's property rights, worker's protection, and evening courses for women. She created a salon for prestigious artists which was central to the cultural life of late nineteenth-century Stockholm. When Ibsen visited the city in 1869, Limnell invited him not only to her salon, but also to spend a few days at her country villa on Lake Malaren. In thanks for her hospitality, he wrote one of his best known long poems, *Ballonbrev til en svensk dame* (1870, 'Balloon Letter to a Swedish Lady').

[Johan] August Lindberg, 1846–1916

ibsenstage.hf.uio.no/pages/contributor/431148

Swedish actor manager. As a young man, Lindberg achieved critical acclaim for his performance as Hamlet. His first Ibsen performance was as Consul Bernick in a Swedish production of *Pillars of Society* staged in Finland in 1878. Over the next thirty-six years, he performed in another eleven Ibsen plays; IbsenStage holds 147 event records for these productions. His independent theatre company, August Lindbergs Sällskap, toured ten Ibsen plays, the most significant being its production of *Ghosts* in which he played Osvald (European premiere in Helsingborg 22 August 1883). Ibsen saw a restaging of this production eight years later. Lindberg negotiated directly with Ibsen for touring performance rights to his plays in the Nordic region; HIS holds a collection of thirty of Ibsen's letters from this extensive correspondence. In 1898, Lindberg was one of the speakers at Ibsen's seventieth birthday celebrations in Kristiania.

Aurélien [François] Marie Lugné-Poë, 1869–1940

ibsenstage.hf.uio.no/pages/contributor/434444

French actor and theatre manager. As a young man, Lugné-Poë worked as an actor at the Théâtre Libre and the Théâtre d'Art.

He founded the Théâtre de l'Oeuvre (1892–1929), an experimental company initially tied to the symbolist theatre movement. The company staged contemporary plays by August Strindberg, Alfred Jarry, Gerhart Hauptmann, Maurice Maeterlinck, Paul Claudel and Oscar Wilde. Lugné-Poë directed and performed twelve plays by Ibsen for the Théâtre de l'Oeuvre that were also toured throughout Europe. In 1895, the company was invited by the Independent Theatre to perform an Ibsen season in London. Lugné-Poë was married to Suzanne Desprès, who played Nora in a Théâtre de l'Oeuvre production that toured as far east as Turkey; in addition, she managed her own tour of the play to Brazil. Lugné-Poë published a book entitled *Ibsen* in 1936: it contains details of his productions and recollections of his meetings with Ibsen.

Christian Morgenstern, 1871–1914

ibsenstage.hf.uio.no/pages/contributor/427477

German author, poet and translator. Morgenstern was the last of the German translators who worked with Ibsen during his lifetime; he translated nine of his plays, six of which were included in the collected works published by S. Fischer (1898–1904). Ibsen was delighted with his translation of *When We Dead Awaken*. IbsenStage holds records of 370 production events between 1899 and 2014 that cite Morgenstern as a translator, the great majority of which are performances of *Peer Gynt*.

Ernst Motzfeldt, 1842–1915

Norwegian politician and Minister of Justice (1894–5). Motzfeldt published an article in *Aftenposten* (23 April 1911) that contained recollections from his visit to Ibsen's Kristiania home on New Year's Day, 1901.

Oscar II, 1829–1907

Crowned King of Sweden and Norway in 1872, Oscar II abdicated from the throne of Norway in 1905, when the union of the two countries was peacefully dissolved. He was an amateur musician, writer and theatre enthusiast.

Ludwig [Louis] Passarge, 1825–1912

ibsenstage.hf.uio.no/pages/contributor/442584

German civil servant, author and translator. Passarge published a series of books on Norwegian culture, literature and travel. In 1880, he approached Ibsen for permission to translate *Peer Gynt*; he also translated *Brand*. Passarge visited Ibsen in 1884, after publishing his monograph *Henrik Ibsen: ein Beitrag zur neuesten Geschichte der norwegischen Nationallitteratur* (1883, 'Henrik Ibsen: A Contribution to the Newest History of the Norwegian National Literature'). IbsenStage holds twenty production event records that cite Passarge. His version of *Peer Gynt* was last performed in 1989.

John [Olaf] Paulsen, 1851–1924

Norwegian author. As a young man, Paulsen travelled with Edvard Grieg to Copenhagen, Bayreuth and Gossensass, where Grieg introduced him to Ibsen in 1876. Over the next five years, Paulsen spent a considerable amount of time with Ibsen: he travelled with him, accompanied him to the theatre, and visited the family in Munich and Rome. Ibsen broke off all connections with Paulsen in 1882, when the latter published a novel, *Familien Pehrsen* (1882, 'The Family Pehrsen'), which contained a thinly disguised portrait not only of Ibsen but also of his wife and son. Paulsen continued to publish on the Ibsen family in two further books: *Samliv med Ibsen: Nye erindringer og skitser* (1906, 'Life with Ibsen: New Memoirs and Sketches') and *Samliv med Ibsen: Sommeren i Berchtesgaden* (1913, 'Life with Ibsen: The Summer in Berchtesgaden').

Moritz (Maurice) Prozor, 1849–1929

ibsenstage.hf.uio.no/pages/contributor/432448

Lithuanian-Polish-Russian diplomat and translator. In 1883, Prozor saw a performance of *Ghosts* in Stockholm which made such an impression on him that, with the help of his wife Märta Margareta Bonde, he translated *Ghosts* and *A Doll's House* into French. In 1890, he became Ibsen's authorised French translator; by 1908, he had published eleven of the plays. His advocacy of Ibsen within French-speaking theatre was acknowledged in several scholarly works published in 1928. IbsenStage holds ninety-eight production event records that cite Prozor; his most popular translation was of *A Doll's House*.

[Petra] Sophie [Alette Christine] Reimers, 1853–1932

ibsenstage.hf.uio.no/pages/contributor/432565

Norwegian actor. In 1879, Reimers made her debut as Svanhild in Ibsen's *Love's Comedy* at Den Nationale Scene in Bergen; this was also her first role in Kristiania two years later. While resident with the Christiania Theater and later as a member of Nationaltheatret, she performed in thirteen plays by Ibsen. She was a member of Johanne Dybwad's company when it toured four plays by Ibsen to Norway, Germany and Denmark in the autumn 1907. She published her memoir, *Taeterminder fra Kristiania Theater*, in 1919. Her brother, Anoldus Reimers, was also a well-known actor; he performed in thirteen plays by Ibsen.

Peter Andreas Rosenberg, 1858–1935

ibsenstage.hf.uio.no/pages/contributor/506477

Danish writer and theatre director.

Julie Ruhkopf (1799–1880)

German author of books for youth and children. Ruhkopf published a translation of *Brand* in 1874, and made a translation of *Emperor and Galilean* that was never published.

Sophus [Christian Frederik] Schandorph, 1836–1901

Danish novelist and poet. Schandorph was influenced by Georg Brandes; his work is associated with the 'Modern Breakthrough' in Scandinavian literature. He reviewed the production of *An Enemy of the People* at Det Kongelige Teater (the Royal Theatre in Copenhagen) in *Morgenbladet* (3 March 1883) and the publication of *The Master Builder* for *Illustrerte Tidende* (1 January 1893).

Hans [Fredrik Ludvig] Schrøder, 1836–1902

ibsenstage.hf.uio.no/pages/venue/11704

Norwegian educator and director. In 1878, Schrøder joined the Christiania Theater Board; he became artistic director of the theatre the following year. Initially, he was criticised by the literary and political left of Kristiania society for refusing to programme *Ghosts* and two plays by Bjørnson. But as he controlled the programming of the theatre for twenty years, his repertoire eventually included eighteen plays by Ibsen. Schrøder received thirty-five letters from Ibsen, many of which contained detailed production and casting suggestions.

P.F. [Peter Friedrich] Siebold, 1827–1911

German commercial traveller. Siebold contacted Ibsen and suggested that he undertake a German translation of *Brand*. Published in 1872, this was the first translation of an Ibsen play to appear in a non-Scandinavian language. There is no record of Siebold's translation being used as the basis of any performance.

Bolette Sontum, 1885–1944

Norwegian-American. Bolette was the eldest daughter of Dr Christian Sontum, Ibsen's friend, and his doctor when he returned to Kristiania in 1891. In 1913, she published an article entitled: 'Personal Recollections of Ibsen' (*The Bookman* 37: 247–56).

Kristine [Wilhelmine Petrea] Steen, 1840–1931

Norwegian teacher. Steen was employed at a private school in Kristiania.

[Adolph Heinrich] Adolf Strodtmann, 1829–1879

ibsenstage.hf.uio.no/pages/contributor/439409

German poet, literary historian and translator. Strodtmann fought and was injured in the 1848 conflict between Germany and Denmark; he was incarcerated on a prison ship in Copenhagen harbour. After his release, he attended the University in Bonn until he was suspended for political activism; he emigrated to America, where he worked in publishing and journalism. He returned to Germany, settled in Berlin, and devoted his energies to literary history and translation. He specialised in translations of English literature (Byron, Shelley, Tennyson) and a wide range of Scandinavian authors. He published German editions of Ibsen's poems, *The League of Youth* and *The Pretenders*. His translation of the latter was used in the first German performance of an Ibsen play (see above: Georg II, Duke of Saxe-Meiningen).

Johan Sverdrup, 1816–1892

Norwegian politician. Sverdrup was Prime Minister of Norway from 1884 to 1889. In November 1859, he helped Ibsen and Bjørnson form Det norske Selskab (The Norwegian Society) to promote national art and literature. He also contributed to a private fund set up by Bjørnson to augment Ibsen's stipend in 1865. He reacted negatively to *Peer Gynt* and was assumed to be one of the public figures satirised in *The League of Youth*.

Johan Herman Thoresen, 1832–1914

Norwegian senior civil servant and brother of Suzannah Ibsen. He held various positions within the Norwegian Parliament. Thoresen managed Ibsen's finances in Kristiania during the years that Ibsen lived abroad.

[Anna] Magdalene Thoresen, b. Kragh, 1819–1903

Danish-Norwegian poet, novelist, short-story writer and play-wright. Thoresen was Suzannah Ibsen's stepmother and Ibsen's mother-in-law. Her home was an important meeting place for Bergen artists. Four of her plays were produced anonymously at Det norske Theater in Bergen. Her most successful play, *Et rigt Parti* ('A Rich Party'), was performed anonymously at Det Kongelige Teater (the Royal Theatre in Copenhagen), and later under her name at the Christiania Theater, and at Kungliga Dramatiska Teatern (the Royal Dramatic Theatres in Stockholm).

Martin [Andreas] Udbye, 1820–1889

Norwegian composer and organist. Udbye composed the music to the first Norwegian opera, *Fredkulla*. He responded positively to Ibsen's request that he compose music for an opera-libretto called *Fjeldfuglen* ('The Mountain Bird') based on *Olaf Liljekrans*, but Ibsen never sent him a completed libretto.

Franz Wallner (1854-1940)

ibsenstage.hf.uio.no/pages/contributor/440296

German actor and author. As well as playing Osvald in *Ghosts* at the Berlin Residenz-Theater in 1887, he performed in *An Enemy of the People* at the Prague Neues Deutsches Theater in 1890.

Roman [Michael] Woerner, 1863–1945

ibsenstage.hf.uio.no/pages/contributor/445172

German literary historian. Woerner studied in Munich; he was appointed as a professor of German language and literature at Adelphi Academy in Brooklyn and as a lecturer at Harvard College and Brooklyn Institute (1888–92). He returned to Europe and held positions at various German universities.

Woerner published biographical studies of Ibsen and literary criticism of his plays, as well as translating *Emperor and Galilean*.

[*Karen*] *Lucie Wolf, b. Johannessen, 1833–1902*

ibsenstage.hf.uio.no/pages/contributor/434288

Norwegian actor. Wolf began her career at Det norske Theater in Bergen where she met Ibsen and played the Goblin in his production of *St. John's Night*. She joined the Christiania Theater (1853–99), later the Nationaltheatret (1899–1900), where her repertoire included roles from eleven of Ibsen's plays presented over a period of forty-five years. She declined to play Berte in *Hedda Gabler*, despite Ibsen's insistence on the importance of the role.

Select Bibliography

Online Resources

Henrik Ibsens skrifter (HIS). Available at www.ibsen.uio.no

IbsenStage. 2015. Available at ibsenstage.hf.uio.no

National Library of Norway. 2012. *The International Ibsen Bibliography*. Available at www.nb.no/baser/ibsen/english.html

National Library of Norway. 2015. *Repertoire Database*. Available at ibsen.nb.no/id/110728.0

The Centre for Ibsen Studies, University of Oslo. *Ibsen Studies* [Journal]. London: Taylor & Francis. Available at www.tandfonline.com/loi/sibs20

Background Material

Standard Editions of Ibsen's Plays in English

Ibsen, Henrik. 1960–1977. *The Oxford Ibsen*. Vol. 1–8. Translated by James MacFarlane et al. London: Oxford University Press.

Ibsen, Henrik. 2014. *The Master Builder and Other Plays*. Translated by Barbara J. Haveland and Anne-Marie Stanton-Ife, and edited by Tore Rem. London: Penguin Books (the New Penguin Ibsen Series).

Ibsen, Henrik. 2016. *A Doll's House and Other Plays*. Translated by Deborah Dawkin and Erik Skuggevik, and edited by Tore Rem. London: Penguin Books (the New Penguin Ibsen Series).

Ibsen, Henrik. 2016. *Peer Gynt and Brand*. Translated by Geoffrey Hill and edited by Tore Rem. London: Penguin Books (the New Penguin Ibsen series).

Speeches and Letters

Ibsen, Henrik. 1905. *Letters of Henrik Ibsen*. Translated by John Nilsen Laurvik and Mary Morison. New York: Fox, Duffield and company. Available at: babel.hathitrust.org/cgi/pt?id=mdp.39015005058386;view=1up;seq=5
Ibsen, Henrik. 1910. *Speeches and new Letters [of] Henrik Ibsen*. Translated by Arne Kildal. Introduction by Lee Milton Hollander. Boston: R. G. Badger. Available at: archive.org/details/cu31924102202581

Ibsen, Henrik. 1965. *Ibsen. Letters and Speeches*. Edited by Evert Sprinchorn. London: MacGibbon & Kee.

Biographies

Byatt, A.S. 2001. *The Biographer's Tale*. London: Vintage.

Ferguson, Robert. 1996. *Henrik Ibsen. A New Biography*. London: Richard Cohen Books.

Gosse, Edmund. 1907. *Ibsen*. London: Hodder and Stoughton (Literary Lives Series).

Heiberg, Hans. 1969. *Ibsen: a portrait of the artist*. Translated by Joan Tate. Coral Gables, Fla: University of Miami Press.

Jæger, Henrik. 1890. *The Life of Henrik Ibsen*. Translated by Clara Bell. London: William Heinemann.

Koht, Halvdan. 1971. *Life of Ibsen*. Translated and edited by E. Haugen and A.E. Santaniello. New York: B. Bloom.

Meyer, Michael. 1967. *Henrik Ibsen. Vol. 1: The Making of a Dramatist 1828–1864*. London: R. Hart-Davis.

Meyer, Michael. 1971. *Henrik Ibsen. Vol. 2: The Farewell to Poetry 1864–1882*. London: R. Hart-Davis.

Meyer, Michael. 1971. *Henrik Ibsen. Vol. 3: The Top of a Cold Mountain 1883–1906*. London: R. Hart-Davis.

Critical Writings

Budde, Antje, ed. 2011. 'Ibsen Intercultural: Nora's Door Slamming Around the Globe.' Special issue of *Canadian Review of Comparative Literature* 38(2).

D'Amico, Giuliano. 2011. 'Marketing Ibsen. A Study of the First Italian Reception, 1883–1891.' *Ibsen Studies* 11(2): 145–75.

D'Amico, Giuliano. 2013. *Domesticating Ibsen for Italy. Enrico and Icilio Polese's Ibsen Campaign*. Bari: Edizioni di Pagina.

D'Amico, Giuliano. 2014. 'Six Points for a Comparative Ibsen Reception History.' *Ibsen Studies* 14(1): 4–37.

Dingstad, Ståle. 2009. 'Om Ibsen anno 1851—og nytten av å lese aviser.' *Norsk Litteraturvitenskapelig Tidsskrift* 12 (1): 2–26.

Dingstad, Ståle. 2016. 'Ibsen and the Modern Breakthrough— The Earliest Productions of *The Pillars of Society, A Doll's House, and Ghosts*.' *Ibsen Studies* 16(2): 103–40.

Fischer-Lichte, Erica, Barbara Gronau and Christel Weiler, eds. 2011. *Global Ibsen: Performing Multiple Modernities*. New York: Routledge.

Fulsås, Narve, Aina Nøding, and Ståle Dingstad, eds. 2013. *Biografisk leksikon til Ibsens brev: med tidstavle*. Oslo: Centre for Ibsen Studies.

Fulsås, Narve and Tore Rem. 2017. *Ibsen, Scandinavia and the Making of a World Drama*. Cambridge: Cambridge University Press.

Gjervan, Ellen Karoline. 2010. 'Creating Theatrical Space: A Study of Henrik Ibsen's Production Books, Bergen 1852–1857.' Ph.D. University of Bergen.

Gjesdal, Kristin, ed. 2018. *Ibsen's Hedda Gabler: Philosophical Perspectives*. Oxford Studies in Philosophy and Literature. NY: Oxford University Press.

Hanssen, Jens-Morten. 2016. 'The Introduction of Bjørnson and Ibsen on the German Stage.' In *Perspectives on the Nordic*, edited by Jacob Lothe and Bente Larsen, 25–44. Oslo: Novus Press.

Helland, Frode. 2015. *Ibsen in Practice: Relational Readings of Performance, Cultural Encounters and Power*. London: Bloomsbury Methuen Drama.

Helland, Frode, and Julie Holledge, eds. 2016. *Ibsen Between Cultures*. Oslo: Novus forlag.

Holledge, Julie, Jonathan Bollen, Frode Helland, and Joanne Tompkins. 2016. *A Global Doll's House: Ibsen and Distant Visions*. London: Palgrave Macmillan.

Marker, Frederick J., and Lise-Lone Marker. 1989. *Ibsen's Lively Art: A Performance Study of the Major Plays*. Cambridge: Cambridge University Press.

Marker, Frederick J., and Lise-Lone Marker. 1996. *A History of Scandinavian Theatre*. Cambridge: Cambridge University Press.

Moi, Toril. 2006. *Henrik Ibsen and the Birth of Modernism: Art, Theater, Philosophy*. Oxford: Oxford University Press.

Postlewait, Thomas. 1986. *Prophet of the New Drama: William Archer and the Ibsen Campaign*. Westpoint, CT: Greenwood Press.

Sandberg, Mark B. 2015. *Ibsen's Houses: Architectural Metaphor and the Modern Uncanny*. Cambridge: Cambridge University Press.

Schmiesing, Ann. 2006. *Norway's Christiania Theater, 1827–1867: from Danish Showhouse to National Stage*. Madison, N.J.: Farleigh Dickinson University Press.

Shepherd-Barr, Kirsten. 2012. 'Ibsen in France from Breakthrough to Renewal.' *Ibsen Studies* 12(1): 56–81.

Shepherd-Barr, Kirsten. 2015. *Theatre and Evolution from Ibsen to Beckett*. New York: Columbia University.

Templeton, Joan. 1997. *Ibsen's Women*. Cambridge: Cambridge University Press.

Source Texts

All the original extracts from Ibsen's letters, articles, prefaces and speeches that have been translated for this volume can be found online at *Henrik Ibsens skrifter* (HIS), available at www.ibsen.uio.no or in the printed editions:

Ibsen, Henrik. 2005a. *Henrik Ibsens skrifter. Catilina, Kjæmpehøien, Norma, Sancthansnatten*. [*Henrik Ibsen's Writings. Catiline, The Burial Mound, Norma, St. John's Night*], Vol. 1. Edited by Vigdis Ystad. Oslo: University of Oslo / Aschehoug.

Ibsen, Henrik. 2005b. *Henrik Ibsens skrifter. Brev 1844–1871*. [*Henrik Ibsen's Writings. Letters 1844–1871*], Vol. 12. Edited by Vigdis Ystad. Oslo: University of Oslo / Aschehoug.

Ibsen, Henrik. 2008. *Henrik Ibsens skrifter. Brev 1871–1879*. [*Henrik Ibsen's Writings. Letters 1871–1879*], Vol. 13. Edited by Vigdis Ystad. Oslo: University of Oslo / Aschehoug.

Ibsen, Henrik. 2009. *Henrik Ibsens skrifter. Brev 1880–1889*. [*Henrik Ibsen's Writings. Letters 1880–1889*], Vol. 14. Edited by Vigdis Ystad. Oslo: University of Oslo / Aschehoug.

Ibsen, Henrik. 2010a. *Henrik Ibsens skrifter. Brev 1890–1905.* [*Henrik Ibsen's Writings. Letters 1890–1905*], Vol. 15. Edited by Vigdis Ystad. Oslo: University of Oslo / Aschehoug.

Ibsen, Henrik. 2010b. *Henrik Ibsens skrifter. Sakprosa.* [*Henrik Ibsen's Writings. Prose*], Vol. 16. Edited by Vigdis Ystad. Oslo: University of Oslo / Aschehoug.

Additional extracts from Ibsen's contemporaries:

Archer, William. 1906. 'Ibsen as I Knew Him.' *Monthly Review* 23(3): 1–19.

Archer, William. 1952. 'Samtale i Sæby. August 1887.' In *Hundreårsutgave. Henrik Ibsens Samlede Verker*, Vol. 19, edited by Francis Bull, Halvdan Koht and Didrik Arup Seip, 169–71. Oslo: Gyldendal.

Bang, Herman. 1906. 'Erinnerungen an Henrik Ibsen / von Herman Bang.' *Die Neue Rundschau* 17: 1497–99.

Bergsøe, Vilhelm. 1907. *Henrik Ibsen paa Ischia og 'Fra Piazza del Popolo'.* København: Gyldendal.

Blytt, Peter. 1907. 'Theatrets Instruktører Henr. Ibsen og Herman Laading.' In *Minder fraden første norske Scene i Bergen i 1850-Aarene: Et kulturhistorisk Forsøg*, 9–13. 2nd ed. Bergen: Fr. Nygaard.

Bull, Francis. 1932. 'Innledning.' In *Hundreårsutgave. Henrik Ibsens Samlede Verker*, Vol. 9, edited by Francis Bull, Halvdan Koht and Didrik Arup Seip, 9–48. Oslo: Gyldendal.

Bull, Francis, Halvdan Koht, and Didrik Arup Seip, eds. 1952a. 'Henrik Ibsens nye værk.' [interview from *Verdens Gang*]. In *Hundreårsutgave. Henrik Ibsens Samlede Verker*, Vol. 19, 225–6. Oslo: Gyldendal.

Bull, Francis, Halvdan Koht, and Didrik Arup Seip, eds. 1952b. 'Hos Dr. Henrik Ibsen. Om "Lille Eyolf". 18. desember 1894.'

[interview from *Dagbladet*]. In *Hundreårsutgave. Henrik Ibsens Samlede Verker*, Vol. 19, 203–4. Oslo: Gyldendal.

Bull, Francis, Halvdan Koht, and Didrik Arup Seip, eds. 1952c. 'Ibsen privat. Samtale med Arnt Dehli.' In *Hundreårsutgave. Henrik Ibsens Samlede Verker*, Vol. 19, 227–9. Oslo: Gyldendal.

Elias, Julius. 1940. 'Ibsen-minner av hans tyske oversetter.' *Samtiden* 51(26): 402–6.

Ferguson, Robert. 1996. [Letter from Camilla Collett to her son Alf 23 February 1872]. In *Henrik Ibsen: A New Biography*. London: Richard Cohen Books.

Fitinghoff, Rosa. 1928. 'Storverket som Ibsen drömde om blev aldrig fullbordat.' *Nya Dagligt Allehanda* 4(3): 5.

Gran, Gerhard. 1918. *Henrik Ibsen: liv og verker*. Kristiania: Aschehoug.

Ibsen, Henrik. 1952. *Hundreårsutgave. Henrik Ibsens Samlede Verker*, Vol. 19. Edited by Francis Bull, Halvdan Koht and Didrik Arup Seip. Oslo: Gyldendal.

Jæger, Henrik. 1888. *Henrik Ibsen 1828–1888: Et Literært Livsbillede*. Copenhagen: Gyldendal.

Jæger, Henrik. 1952. 'Referater og intervjuer. Samtaler i Frederikshavn, august eller september 1887.' In *Hundreårsutgave. Henrik Ibsens Samlede Verker*, Vol. 19, edited by Francis Bull, Halvdan Koht and Didrik Arup Seip, 172–3. Oslo: Gyldendal.

Lugné-Poë, Aurélien Marie. 1936. *Ibsen* (Vol. 21, Maitres des littératures). Paris: Les Éditions Rieder.

Meyer, Michael. 1992. *Ibsen*. London: Cardinal.

Midbøe, Hans. 1960. *Streiflys over Ibsen og andre studier*. Oslo: Gyldendal.

Motzfeldt, Ernst. 1911. 'Af samtaler med Henrik Ibsen.' *Aftenposten*, 23 April, p. 4.

Pall Mall Gazette. 1890. 'Ibsen on "Social Democracy".' [Interview with Ibsen.] 13 August, p. 6.

Paulsen, John. 1913. *Samliv med Ibsen: Anden Samling: Sommeren i Berchtesgaden*. Copenhagen: Gyldendal.

Rosenberg, P.A. 1952. 'Samtale i selskap i Kjøbenhavn. 3. april 1898.' In *Hundreårsutgave. Henrik Ibsens Samlede Verker*, Vol. 19, edited by Francis Bull, Halvdan Koht and Didrik Arup Seip, 215–21. Oslo: Gyldendal.

Rønning, Helge. 2006. *Den umulige friheten: Henrik Ibsen og moderniteten*. Oslo: Gyldendal.

Seip, Didrik Arup. 1936. 'Innledning.' [Reference to Ibsen interviewed in *Kjøbenhavns Aftenblad*, and quote from the Danish newspaper *Politiken* from 28 January 1897.] In *Hundreårsutgave. Henrik Ibsens Samlede Verker*, Vol. 13, edited by Francis Bull, Halvdan Koht and Didrik Arup Seip, 9–36. Oslo: Gyldendal.

Sontum, Bolette. 1913. 'Personal Recollections of Ibsen.' *The Bookman* 37: 247–56.

Thoresen, Magdalene. 1919. *Breve fra Magdalene Thoresen 1855– 1901*, edited by P.F. Rist and Julius Clausen. Copenhagen: Gyldendal.

Østvedt, Einar. 1976. *Et dukkehjem: Forspillet, Skuespillet, Etterspillet*. Skien: Rasmussen.

www.nickhernbooks.co.uk

facebook.com/nickhernbooks

twitter.com/nickhernbooks